# A SUCCESS STORY CONTINUES

The phenomenal success of *Star Trek* inspired two spectacular spin-offs, both of which have gone on to join the ranks of the most-watched television shows of all time.

This unauthorized guidebook, two complete volumes in one, examines both of these shows in fascinating detail—the characters and the creators, the episodes behind the episodes, the actors, the make-up artists, the special-effect geniuses, and the voyages that landed on the cutting room floor.

This complete guidebook to *The Next Generation* and *Deep Space Nine* is more than just a reference book. It is a behind-the-scenes look at how entertainment becomes legend.

Author James Van Hise, considered by many to be the world's leading *Star Tr*[illegible]rt, is also known for his work as edit[illegible]*ht Graffiti* magazine, where he br[illegible]tion such authors as Steph[illegible]

Look for

**TREK: THE UNAUTHORIZED A-Z**
by Hal Schuster and Wendy Rathbone

**SCI-FI TV: From The Twilight Zone to Deep Space Nine***
by James Van Hise

**STAR TREK MEMORIES**
by William Shatner with Chris Kreski

**STAR TREK MOVIE MEMORIES***
by William Shatner with Chris Kreski

Available from HarperPrism

*coming soon

# THE UNAUTHORIZED TREKKERS' GUIDE TO THE NEXT GENERATION AND DEEP SPACE NINE

BY JAMES VAN HISE

HarperPrism
*An Imprint of* HarperPaperbacks

HarperPaperbacks *A Division of* HarperCollins*Publishers*
10 East 53rd Street, New York, N.Y. 10022



Trade paperback editions of this material were published in 1992 and 1993 by Pioneer Books, Inc.

Cover photograph by Rob Atkins/The Image Bank

First HarperPaperbacks printing: April 1995

Printed in the United States of America

HarperPrism is an imprint of HarperPaperbacks. HarperPaperbacks, HarperPrism, and colophon are trademarks of HarperCollins*Publishers*

❖ 10 9 8 7 6 5 4 3 2 1

*Dedicated to*
*Gene Roddenberry,*
*who started it all*

# CONTENTS

# THE UNAUTHORIZED TREKKERS' GUIDE TO THE NEXT GENERATION AND DEEP SPACE NINE

PART

# INTRODUCTION

# THE ENDURANCE OF STAR TREK

"Like Spain's Francisco Franco, *Star Trek* has been fatally dead for a long time. Now and then the mortuary shoots an electric current through the corpse, and the resultant spasm releases yet another manual or quiz or convention or novel or book of fan fiction or whathaveyou, but after nearly a decade there's little life left in the old cadaver."

—Gil Lamont & James K. Burk
*DeLap's F & SF Review*
*(March/April 1978)*

This quote reflects the reception science fiction fandom gave *Star Trek* fans in the mid to late seventies. They looked down on *Star Trek*, and chose to dismiss it. These intemperate remarks ignored growing popular interests as fan interest attained a life greater than the TV image that inspired it.

This touched common chords in many individuals. Some went through life quietly enamored with the series, unaware they shared a common bond with countless strangers until they found a *Star Trek* fanzine or walked into a convention.

Before *Star Trek*'s fitful return to the screen in the 1979 *Star Trek: The Motion Picture*, a backlash of anti-*Star Trek* sentiment raged. It began with the attitude that "those people" were "invading" otherwise sedate science fiction and comic book conventions.

I wonder how many times those critics have watched the new incarnations of *Star Trek* in *The Next Generation* and *Deep Space Nine*. How quickly passion doth ebb and flow.

## EMBRACED BY THE MASSES

Critics to any new series were reacting to a TV show that had perished in 1969. They thought it should be buried. Many of these detractors read novels by dead authors or comic strips by dead artists. They pursued interests without practical purpose and with no hope of continuation by their talented creators. But *Star Trek*, they felt, was just a TV show in reruns.

Reruns (or reprints) can still be appreciated. H. P. Lovecraft, Robert E. Howard, E. E. "Doc" Smith, Edgar Allan Poe, Clark Ashton Smith, Rod Serling, Edgar Rice Burroughs, and many others, including H. G. Wells and Jules Verne, left books behind for fans to enjoy. Sir Arthur Conan Doyle died in 1930, yet Sherlock Holmes is appreciated by more people today than ever before. Every year, it seems, someone is inspired to take pen in hand and create an "untold" tale of London's famous sleuth.

"New" is not an easy word. Harlan Ellison is fond of pointing out that, "Any book you have not read is a new book."

I raised these points in a reply when the remarks

that opened this article first appeared. I had hoped for a reply befitting the stature of the magazine. Instead I witnessed the death of the publication. It ended in 1978 while the "corpse" of *Star Trek* looks amazingly healthy these days.

## SURVIVAL TRAITS

Why did *Star Trek* endure? Its whole proved to be greater than the sum of its parts. A special spirit struck a responsive chord in many people. It delivered something people searched for and wouldn't find again until *Star Wars* appeared in 1977, namely, optimism. They both offered a future in the stars, no matter what squalor lay at our feet.

When *Star Trek* premiered in 1966, the dream of reaching beyond the mortal confines of our world still seemed a dream. America was plunged deep into the quagmire of Southeast Asia. The future offered little when friends and relatives came home in bodybags.

Then *Star Trek* brought new hope. It proclaimed that not only would there be a future, but the future worked. The starship *Enterprise* astonished audiences with its futuristic design, giving us what appeared to be a window into a new, better world.

## INSIDE THE *ENTERPRISE*

Then the noble captain of the ship, Captain Kirk, appeared; fearless, yet touched by every death. McCoy, the ship's doctor and the captain's close friend, acted as his devil's advocate, offering the voice of traditional humanity. At the perimeter stood Spock, cool and austere, always logical. Spock was the enigma. He was second-in-command and possessor of an alien heritage.

The stories offered reality. People thought and bled; they made mistakes and expressed personal beliefs. Many episodes, including "The Naked Time," forced deeply rooted doubts of the day to the surface. No other cast of science fiction characters had ever tried this before.

*Space: 1999* arrived in 1975. Audiences waited for something good. It didn't have to be *Star Trek*; it just had to be enjoyable. The dreadful series triggered a violent backlash. One critic aptly dubbed it *Space: 1949.* It was so relentlessly awful that audiences felt betrayed.

Much the same expectations and resentment would also accompany the arrival of *Battlestar Galactica*.

*Star Trek* characters, on the other hand, took on lives of their own. Each script added bits of characterization. Viewers felt they recognized the humanity of the characters on screen.

## ALWAYS ETHICALLY CORRECT

Captain Kirk and his crew were idealizations. When push comes to shove, they do the right thing: Kirk, Spock, and McCoy don't possess normal human foibles. They might get angry, but then they meekly apologize. They always make the right ethical choice.

In Harlan Ellison's "The City on the Edge of Forever," Harlan wanted Kirk to try to save Edith despite knowing the disastrous consequences of her continued life. Kirk would have failed but he would have tried. This was Harlan's version for which he won the Writer's Guild Award. Gene Roddenberry thought Kirk would do the right thing when the time came, no matter how painful. Ellison insisted that bringing Edith to the future would bring the same result as letting her be run down in the street. Roddenberry (with an assist from Gene L. Coon) rewrote Ellison's screenplay. Captain Kirk deliberately prevented McCoy from saving Edith. Kirk experienced great anguish, but he did the right thing.

Although the characters in *Star Trek* are enduring, and certainly more believable than those on *Lost in Space, Space: 1999*, and others, they are still idealizations. *Trek* characters look like human beings only by comparison with other TV series from that period. They are noble and unblemished, but they agonize over decisions such as in the above example from "The City On the Edge of Forever."

## EARLY EVALUATIONS

After the cancellation of *Star Trek* in 1969, a revival wasn't dreamed. Fans were grateful for any mention of their favorite show, however tepid. One example is the brief dismissal given it by John Baxter in his 1970 book *Science Fiction in the Cinema*, where he devotes only three paragraphs to the series.

Baxter praises "The Menagerie" but drop-kicks stock sets with formula situations, discussing "Patterns of Force" (Nazi Germany) and "A Piece of the Action" (Chicago in the thirties) while ignoring such key episodes as "City on the Edge of Forever," "This Side of Paradise," "Mirror, Mirror" and others far more representative of *Star Trek*. He singled out "Charlie X" for praise, but never mentioned the obvious inspiration of *Stranger in a Strange Land*.

Baxter never mentions the series' characters, even though fifteen years before *Hill Street Blues*, and half a decade before *M*A*S*H*, *Star Trek* presented an ensemble cast representing wide interests and appeals.

## A SAFE PORT

Although both the original *Star Trek* and its offspring, *Star Trek: The Next Generation* and *Deep Space*

*Nine,* have been accused by some critics of science fiction of avoiding current social issues, the entire *Star Trek* family continues to express hope for the future, hope that mankind's possibilities are endless. And this, if nothing else, leads to a safe port in a troubled modern world.

PART

# THE NEXT GENERATION

CHAPTER

# ENTER THE NEXT GENERATION

"We grew beyond the original show. We love the original and those actors, but we see the world differently now and our show reflects that."

—Gene Roddenberry
*USA Today*
November 1, 1990

In 1987 something controversial was done. *Star Trek* was brought back to weekly television without any of the familiar faces who had graced the name since 1966. Gene Roddenberry was still at the helm, and the universe portrayed was not so different from what we had first been introduced to years before.

When Paramount announced that Gene Roddenberry was creating the first *Star Trek* spin-off series, and that it would be set seventy-five years beyond the *Trek* universe we were all familiar with, it was inevitable that this meant changes. How sweeping would those changes be? Clearly the technology would be updated, just as it had been for the motion pictures. Would the philosophy behind the show be retooled as well?

## NOT AGAIN . . .

"When Paramount originally approached me to do a new series, I turned them down. I did not want to devote the tremendous amount of time necessary to producing another show. In order to keep the original series going, I practically had to disown my daughters. I had no time for them when they were school age. I did not want to do that to my life again. There is only one way I know to write and produce and that is to throw my energy at the project all the time. So when they began to think about a second series, I said I would not do it. Then they said, 'Well, suppose we figure a way that it could be done so you would be in charge?' I thought they were kidding. The studio said that I could be in full control of the creative standard. I asked a few questions, and they said, 'Yeah, sure, you must know these things because you've been doing them anyway under network guidance.'

"I told the studio that if they went the syndication route I would go for it. Not only would I go for it, I would go for it full blast. I told them I would find ways of doing *Star Trek* that would give them extra elements. I think we have done that."

A *Star Trek* series would be launched with an all new cast, set (somewhat vaguely) seventy-five years after the original series, and featuring the *Enterprise* of that farther future, the fifth of its line, NCC 1701-D. Paramount was banking that a syndicated show would generate revenues. It seemed impossible, but . . . it happened. Gene Roddenberry worked hard to produce a new *Star Trek* that would be true to the ideals of the original but still have its own flavor.

Not having to deal with network or studio interference was a major load off him, and he made certain that no one broke that promise. Early in the new show's production, a group of junior executives walked into Gene's office and began going over a script demanding changes. He pointed out they had no right to do this under the terms of his contract and threw them out!

In discussing what the most difficult aspect was of creating *Star Trek: The Next Generation*, Gene quoted one of the original cast members who had commented on trying to create a new version of a classic. "The most difficult aspect?" Gene replied. "Leonard Nimoy said it. You can't catch lightning in a bottle twice. I was thinking, yes, he's probably right."

## RECAPTURING A DREAM

The thing that attracted Roddenberry to the new series was that he wouldn't have to deal with networks. "And then they said, maybe you shouldn't [try to do a new series] because it's impossible, and my ears perked up over that. The most difficult aspect was to go against all of that and put a show together and believe you could do it, and collect people that could do it, and collect a cast that in its own way has the qualities of the old cast. It was the impossibility of it that was the most difficult."

Roddenberry described what he hoped to accomplish with the new series when he stated, "What we want to do is to grapple now with the problems of the eighties and nineties and the turn of the century. I think we are going to surprise you on technology. You can only go so far in making things smaller and faster and more powerful. What other things should technology be worrying about? We're going to be getting into those areas. There's a reason to do another *Star Trek* now. We did the original *Star Trek* about the problems of the sixties. Many people forget that, in the mid-sixties, when we put on a multiracial crew, that was considered awful. People were shocked."

When asked what he kept from the old *Star Trek* to please audience expectations when creating *The Next Generation*, Gene explained, "While I listen to the audience, one of the secrets of whatever success

I've amounted to was that I never make shows for the audience. I listen to good advice, but the only person I make shows for is myself. I love any help you can give me, but I'll be damned if I'll make a show for you! I make it for myself and if you happen to like it I'm delighted that you do and great; we've got the best of both possible worlds. Writers and producers and directors and so on that create a show for specific audiences do schlock work. They should do selfish work; proudly selfish work, and that happens to be true about painters, and sculptors, too."

## THE NEW CREW

More worrisome at the time was resistance from old fans, although this turned out not to be the problem it could have been. Still, creating a new series when the original has grown to mythic proportions is a heavy proposition. As might be imagined, it took some doing. The characters took time to settle in. Once they did, they were believable.

First there was Captain Jean-Luc Picard. For this demanding role, Gene cast British actor Patrick Stewart, a noted Shakespearean with roles in films besides extensive stage work.

## CAPTAIN AND COMPANY

Gene said, "Patrick Stewart was my first choice after looking at him hard and long because here I'm faced with a bald-headed man for a captain and I'm used to him being jolly with hair, and Bill was rather athletic. The longer I looked at Patrick Stewart and saw the actor who was there, and the power that was there that was a different kind than Bill's, the more I became sure that he was the man. I'm so delighted to have him I cannot tell you! When you look at dailies, you always watch Picard even when he's not doing anything! Because he is doing something here [points to his head] constantly! England produces great actors and he's an example of that."

Roddenberry wanted no one character to emerge as the star. A whole ensemble of players was created for the new *Enterprise.* Since Captain Picard would never beam down to an uncharted, possibly hostile planet in this modern version, Gene in essence divided the command function in two, providing Picard with an executive officer, William Riker. There has been speculation that Picard and Riker are the two aspects of Captain Kirk, split in half. It is conjectured this was done both for dramatic reasons and to prevent any single actor from attempting to dominate a true ensemble program. In a nod to the old show's first pilot, as well as to nautical history, Riker is often referred to as "Number One." Riker, a canny poker player, is not afraid to take risks. He weighs them carefully, assuring the safety of his superior officer.

The notion of having "Away Teams" instead of sending the ship's executive officers on dangerous missions was suggested by David Gerrold.

## THE COUNSELOR AND THE ANDROID

Gene also created a new position for *The Next Generation*, that of Ship's Counselor, and a new alien race—the Betazoids. Although this position can be occupied by a member of any race, Picard is highly fortunate that his ship's counselor is a Betazoid. Betazoids are extremely empathic, if not telepathic, and can read minds to varying degrees. Picard's counselor, Deanna Troi, is a beautiful half-human woman, who can sense emotions with great acuity. Combined with extensive psychological training, this makes her a vital part of the captain's decision-making process. "Captain, I sense . . ." has become as familiar a line to *Next Generation* fans as "I'm a doctor, not a . . ." was for those of the original series.

Deanna once had a relationship with Riker, but it seems to have mellowed into an abiding friendship. Only in season six when a transporter-created double for William Riker was introduced did the old romance again resurface. Marina Sirtis enjoys the irony of being a British actress playing an alien on American television.

Most controversial at the show's inception was the android science officer, Data. Many saw him as a transparent Spock substitute. Indeed, there are many similarities between the two, but the differences have been developed more thoroughly. A much closer predecessor of Data is found in the android in *The Questor Tapes*. Gene cast Texas-born Brent Spiner as Data. He was very well prepared for his role by a strong belief in extraterrestrials.

## THE DOCTOR AND THE ENGINEER

An *Enterprise* without a ship's doctor would be unthinkable. Gene provided Chief Medical Officer Beverly Crusher. Dr. Crusher is the first regular role in a television series for actress Gates McFadden. The compassionate, dedicated doctor is the mother of a precocious youngster, Wesley Crusher. Not coincidentally, Gene's middle name was Wesley. Wesley Crusher was played by Wil Wheaton, who left the series in its fourth season to pursue school and a film career. Because he left on amicable terms, an opening was left for him to return to the show at any time, even if only in guest star roles. He came back for one in season seven's "Journey's End." Wheaton wanted to return to the status of being a regular on the final season, but what the actors called "studio politics" prevented that. Others connected with the show have stated that "Journey's

End" wrote a finish to the character of Wesley, who will apparently not be appearing in the *Next Generation* feature films.

McFadden was replaced by Diana Muldaur in the second season of *The Next Generation* and Roddenberry even issued a press release telling fans not to bother writing to him about the decision because his mind was made up—that is, until he changed it again and brought Gates McFadden back to the role in the third season.

Another new character, eventually to be promoted to the post of chief engineer, is Geordi La Forge. The role is named as tribute to the late *Star Trek* fan George LaForge, a cerebral palsy sufferer whose long survival was attributed to his strong identification with the show. Geordi contributes to the tradition of a multiethnic cast in *Star Trek*. He is blind, but due to the advanced technology of the twenty-fourth century, can see by means of an electronic visor linked with his nervous system. He can even see visual ranges inaccessible to most human beings. Geordi is a sincere, likable, confident man with slight insecurities. He always perseveres, communicating freely with others. The opposite of Picard, he affects an informal approach to life and is not hung up on protocol. Actor LeVar Burton, best known as the young Kunta Kinte in the classic miniseries *Roots*, plays the role. This character was reportedly created by David Gerrold.

## A KLINGON ON THE BRIDGE

The biggest shock in *The Next Generation*'s crew roster was Worf . . . a Klingon. Since Kirk's heyday, peace has finally been negotiated between the Federation and the Klingon Empire. Negotiations were underway at the time of the events of *Star Trek III: The Search for Spock*, a fact referred to by Commander Kruge in that film. This was further developed in *Star Trek VI:*

*The Undiscovered Country*. The two spheres of influence strive to get along and have established some mutual trust. There are no other Klingons in Starfleet.

Worf is unique. He was raised by humans after his family was killed in the massacre of their outpost during a surprise Klingon attack—an event that still haunts him. He is like Spock in that he is the product of two cultures, a warrior Klingon dedicated to his own culture but tempered by exposure to human ideals. Worf was added after the pilot for *The Next Generation* and does not appear in "Encounter at Farpoint." For a time, he would be little more than a grouchy guy standing in the background recommending aggressive action. He would be featured in more and more episodes, eventually opening up a window on the fascinating world of the Klingons. The six-foot-five Michael Dorn was cast as Worf. Dorn was born in Liling, Texas, but raised in Pasadena, California, just minutes away from Hollywood.

With the cast set, *The Next Generation* got under way. Creator Gene Roddenberry handed the executive producer's reins over to Paramount's Rick Berman.

## CREATIVE CONFLICTS

D. C. Fontana signed on as story editor, but soon left, unhappy with the treatment received by her script "Encounter at Farpoint." Sadly, the episode kicked off the new series with less than a bang. Fontana's initial story received a forced graft of Gene Roddenberry's "Q" subplot and the two concepts didn't cross over, much less merge. Instead of a genuine, two-hour movie, audiences received two separate stories. Like *Star Trek: The Motion Picture*, "Encounter at Farpoint" moved slowly, too enamored of its own special effects. It was no surprise that Gene Roddenberry's name was on the screenplay. Roddenberry said, "In the first *Star Trek* [series], I rewrote or heavily polished the first thirteen episodes so that Mr. Spock would be the Mr. Spock that I had in mind. This was enormous labor, and then this began to catch on and we got some good writers on this.

"In *Star Trek: The Next Generation* I rewrote thirteen episodes. I don't want to act out a big 'I did this, I did that,' but as far as the basic original writing, I had to do that again, with few exceptions. It is the way episodic television is. Now as the year's gone on," he said during the first season, "I've found some good people and I hope to find more. We got some good writing in the old series, and we've had some good writing in the new series. Most of the writing comes from very few, very good people who labor hard. Very often they are staff people."

Special effects for the first season were provided by Industrial Light and Magic, but they soon proved too expensive. Other effects teams were sought out. With a per episode budget of over a million dollars, *The Next Generation* was a major gamble for Paramount. They had to use the budget to the best of their ability.

## GROWING PAINS

The first season of *The Next Generation* was erratic. The actors had yet to settle into their roles, and the scripts, often rewritten by Gene, were uneven. Controversy ensued when both D. C. Fontana and David Gerrold felt they had contributed to the development of the series concept and neither received credit. Gene never acknowledged them. In fact, in regard to Gerrold, he went so far as to comment that ". . . Gerrold [had] been condemning the show, constantly. I had him on staff for many, many months, [and] he never wrote an episode we could shoot." He had, but Roddenberry refused to approve it. This contributed to their professional break.

Fontana is harder to dismiss. She worked on a total of four scripts for the first season of *The Next Generation*. She left following a particularly ugly encounter with Roddenberry when he supposedly asked her to write an entire script and attach his name as cowriter so that he could meet the studio's demand for his writing a certain number of scripts during the first season. When she refused because it would be a violation of Writer's Guild rules, Roddenberry claimed that he was the one who got her into the business (which wasn't true) and felt that she was ungrateful for not doing him this favor.

The dispute between Gene, Fontana, and Gerrold was settled behind the scenes for a monetary sum. No on-screen credit was given. Some regard this as more important than a lump sum payoff, because without screen credit there is no public acknowledgment of what a writer created. In spite of the settlement, Roddenberry may well have felt that he'd won.

The second season of *The Next Generation* showed marked improvement. Changes were evident. Jonathan Frakes now sported a beard. Some viewers, unimpressed by the first season, now use the sight of a clean-shaven Riker as their cue not to watch a rerun.

## TWO NEW SECOND-SEASON ADDITIONS

Doctor Pulaski, ably played by Diana Muldaur, a veteran guest star of the original *Star Trek*, joined the cast in the second season. Despite Muldaur's fine acting, this character didn't work. Perhaps the problem was that the crusty, no-nonsense Pulaski seemed to be a female "Bones" McCoy. The character provided much-needed friction on the bridge, but never really came to bear on the plots much.

Another new character also came onboard in the second season, although she may have been there all along for purposes of continuity. Guinan is a mysterious alien woman of great age who functions as bartender and freelance counselor in the *Enterprise*'s open lounge, Ten Forward. She serves synthehol, a marvelous brew whose mildly intoxicating effects can be shaken off at will. Guinan's background is intentionally shrouded in mystery. Although not featured on a weekly basis, she is a recurring presence.

## THE SHAPE OF THINGS

By this time, Gene had developed a stable of writers he could trust. His production team was learning to work the way Gene worked. On future plans for *The Next Generation*, Roddenberry stated, "We have a lot in store, and a lot of things we want to talk about. We can no longer claim we're brave because we have mixed races. Twenty-three years ago, that was very exciting. We had women in jobs other than secretaries. People were saying, 'My God, how far can they go!'

"Now we want to talk about hostage situations. I am amazed to see the hostage (takers) treated as bad guys always. Many of these people have legitimate complaints. The world is not as simple as we lay it out—good guys here, bad guys there. I am very concerned and want to find a way to get into the fact that most of the warfare and killing going on in the world is going on in the name of religion: organized religion. Not that I'm saying that there are not great plans and that we are not part of some great thing, but it is not the type of thing you see preached on television. I don't hold anyone up to ridicule. My mother is a good Baptist and she believes in many great things. I cannot sit still in a series of this type and not point out who's killing who in the world."

Roddenberry did do an episode questioning

religion, "Who Watches the Watchers?" in season three. On a primitive planet, an off-world survey team is accidentally discovered by the inhabitants, who come to regard the *Enterprise* crewmen and their miraculous feats (appearing and disappearing) as the actions of gods. "I've always thought that, if we did not have supernatural explanations for all the things we might not understand right away, this is the way we would be, like the people on that planet," Gene explained. "I was born into a supernatural world in which all my people—my family—usually said, 'That is because God willed it,' or gave other supernatural explanations for whatever happened. When you confront those statements on their own, they just don't make sense. They are clearly wrong. You need a certain amount of proof to accept anything, and that proof was not forthcoming to support those statements."

## HARD WORK BUT FEW REWARDS

The one thing that did disappoint Roddenberry about doing *The Next Generation* was the little recognition it first received. Even though it did achieve a Peabody Award for the first season episode "The Big Goodbye," it remained largely ignored thereafter, in spite of episodes like "Who Watches the Watchers?" and "Justice."

"It is a source of considerable amusement to me that we can do shows like this and get little or no public reaction. If these things were to be done on Broadway or in motion pictures, they would have stunned audiences. The audiences would have said, 'How wild, how forward, how advanced.' Because these subjects are done on a syndicated television show, in our time slot, no one really notices them.

"I thought several times that the world of drama would have stood up and cheered us, but no, only silence. There is one advantage. All of these episodes are brought back and rerun every year. What will happen with *Star Trek: The Next Generation* is almost identical to what happened to the original *Star Trek* as larger and larger audiences become acquainted with the program. The original *Star Trek* audience now says, 'Hurrah, what fine shows!' This has brought us considerable pleasure that they would notice it. *Star Trek: The Next Generation* is on that path now and more so. The time will come when the second series will attain its true stature. I just hope some of it happens while I am still alive. I'm not jealous that I don't have praise. This happens very broadly in contacts with humans. The world is not necessarily poorer because a painter or playwright is not recognized in his or her lifetime."

## NEW BUT FAMILIAR

Since Gene Roddenberry understood his audience, he did not stray far when he re-created *Star Trek*. Andrew Probert, who had contributed to the redesign of the *Enterprise* for *Star Trek: The Motion Picture*, was tapped for the job of redesigning the *Enterprise* for its new and far more advanced version. Although looking more sleek with a slightly squashed appearance, it was still quite recognizable. The biggest change was internal, such as the addition of the holodeck. The kinds of recreation areas on the original *Enterprise* were rarely referred to outside of the first movie. The only one that comes to mind is a reference to the "bowling alley" in "The Naked Time," and it has never been established whether or not this was a joke. After all, with the way the original *Enterprise* would periodically hurl its crew back and forth, the thought of bowling balls having similar violence done to them could only cause one to imagine large holes in the bulkheads on a fairly regular basis.

The other design alterations on *The Next Generation* extended to the expected: the uniforms, hand weapons and other items such as the tricorder. Just as they had been redesigned for the *Star Trek* movies, they were redesigned for the TV series. Again, the designs were superficial and seemed to have been done mostly for purposes of merchandising: more new *Star Trek* toys could now be licensed by Paramount.

Although set seventy-five years after the original series, the technical changes were not as major as they could have been. By making the changes so slight, Roddenberry insured that the old *Star Trek* fans would more willingly accept this new version in spite of the completely new cast.

## FINE-TUNING THE *STAR TREK* PHILOSOPHY

In describing the future life he envisioned for Earth in the twenty-fourth century, Roddenberry stated, "I do not perceive this as a universe that's divided between good and evil."

For *The Next Generation*, Gene Roddenberry chose to expand the *Trek* philosophy, and perhaps he went a little too far. Roddenberry decided that his crew of the *Enterprise*-D would, frankly, be perfect. He decreed that they would get along without complaint and never have the kind of personality clashes experienced by Kirk, Spock, and McCoy. The only time disagreements appeared on *TNG* was when someone who was not a part of this tightly knit inner circle came aboard, such as when Ensign Ro stepped aboard in the fifth season (about the time Gene Roddenberry died).

Otherwise the main crew members, consisting of Picard, Riker, Data, Dr. Crusher, Geordi, and Troi were always in harmony. Worf was the only wild card, but then he's allowed to be—he isn't human.

Tasha Yar seemed to have the makings of a character with spunk and personality, but she was quickly dispensed with.

Roddenberry remained the eternal optimist, in spite of all the failures, disappointments, and difficult times he had endured during the years between the cancellation of *Star Trek* in 1969 and its return to life in 1979. Roddenberry continued to promote his philosophy of life that consisted of bold optimism (there will be a future and it will be wonderful), a belief in social progress, the benefits of technological advancement (he did not equate progress with the diminishing of the quality of life), the pursuit of knowledge, life affirmation (he objected to Captain Kirk's casual killing of the Ceti Eel in *The Wrath of Khan*), the tolerance of other cultures, and secular humanism (the dominance of reason and experience over supernatural deities and mysticism).

## MAKING THE OLD WAYS BETTER

It is because Roddenberry's basic *Star Trek* philosophy had been reinterpreted and sometimes altered in the motion picture treatments that he made certain that all of his beliefs for the *Star Trek* universe were firmly in place for *The Next Generation*. With that as an underlying philosophy, the shows therefore exhibit a point of view and occasionally moralize.

There were some contradictions in the original philosophy, though, which Roddenberry himself sought to correct in *The Next Generation*. Instead of having the Klingons dismissed as being just the bad guys, he rewrote them as a proud warrior race with a culture as deep and diverse as anything seen on the other worlds in the Federation.

*The Next Generation* continued the use of the transporter with little alteration other than in visual effects and the sound. This is explained by the difference in technology. For instance, in *The Next Generation* episode "Relics," when a ship is found with the old-style transporter in it, the old-style sound effect is used when the transporter beam materializes. The transporter is perhaps the prime example of *Star Trek* magic. Created for the convenience of scriptwriters, it allows for the characters to move from the ship to a planet and back again instantaneously, thereby dispensing with scenes of ships landing and taking off again.

## REWRITING THE RULES OF REALITY

Which brings us to another device of magical technology: the holodeck. The holodeck that Roddenberry introduced on *The Next Generation* clearly alters our views of what is possible in reality in any number of ways. The computer can be programmed to create virtually anything in the holodeck, from the lush surface of a planet with jungles and a waterfall to London in the 1890s. The holodeck creates images of substance. In "The Big Goodbye" those images strike back with potentially deadly force. In that Peabody Award-winning episode, Captain Picard creates a realm in the holodeck based on his favorite detective stories. Set in the 1930s, Dixon Hill is clearly based on the hard-boiled detective thrillers of Raymond Chandler and Dashiell Hammett. Like Sherlock Holmes, they are archetypes that are very much a part of their era.

It's not unusual that a science fiction series should be so captivated by images from detective stories. Mystery fiction tends to be very popular among screenwriters and science fiction writers. Using this to create a film noir setting, *The Next Generation* created a *tech noir* in which the holodeck world became a reality. The people projected by the computer evidently are not just images that move according to a design but have a sense of self, which as time went on was enhanced, as shown in "Elementary, Dear Data." In "The Big Goodbye" the hologram people debated whether they were real and struggled to prove their individuality. One of them, who possessed memories of a wife and family, even questioned what would happen to all of them when the program was ended. This question would ultimately be addressed in the sixth-season episode "Moriarty."

## AIMING FOR THE STARS

Although Roddenberry was intensely involved with the creation and development of *The Next Generation,* the show had problems from the start.

In spite of a series bible that established who all the regular characters were, no detailed background had been worked out for them. Their personalities were largely being established during filming by the actors and their various directors, with a result that the characters were often inconsistent from one episode to the next, particularly Captain Picard. Worf was a late entry in the character roster because initially Roddenberry didn't want to bring the Klingons back. It was only when he decided to give the Klingons a real background and make them richer characters that he agreed to include them.

Although episode twelve of *The Next Generation,* "The Big Goodbye," won the coveted Peabody Award for television excellence, far too many of the first-year episodes suffered from a distinct lack of excellence. One of the other few exceptions is "Heart of Glory," the episode that established Worf as being more than just a fixture on the bridge.

The second year improved consistently, demonstrating that all involved had learned from their mistakes (and the mistakes of others) and were ready to finally get down to work.

Seasons three through seven continued the process of fine-tuning the characters and establishing them as individuals with distinctive personalities. Picard went from being an inconsistent leader to a seasoned starship captain worthy of the position as commander of the flagship of Starfleet. Episodes were done which spotlighted the many facets of Jean-Luc Picard while capitalizing on the fine acting abilities of actor Patrick Stewart.

Riker was the steadiest of the crew from the beginning, and subsequent seasons insured that he became even more firmly established as the finest first officer in Starfleet.

Data, who has no emotions, has been at the center of some of the most moving stories told in the series, including "Pen Pals" and "Hero Worship."

By year four, even the female characters, Deanna Troi and Dr. Crusher, were getting episodes that spotlighted them in powerful stories such as "Remember Me" and "Power Play."

## LOOKING FORWARD

While all too many series have run out of steam long before they complete seven seasons, and start repeating themselves endlessly, *The Next Generation* continued to search for ways to grow and strengthen itself. The series carries with it a proud legacy. It is not just a *Star Trek* spin-off: it was shepherded by the Great Bird of the Galaxy himself, Gene Roddenberry. The dream Roddenberry first brought to life in 1966 has been revised and expanded as Gene looked on like a proud parent.

The dream called *Star Trek* has lasted for more than twenty-eight years—*The Next Generation* gave it new life and exploration in new directions. It's evident Roddenberry's dream will never die.

# ABOARD THE NEW ENTERPRISE

The *Enterprise* NCC 1701-D is the fifth starship to bear that name. It is twice the length of Captain Kirk's ship and has nearly eight times the interior area to house the crew. The basic structure is the same, even though the vessel looks more sleek and cohesive.

While the first starships to bear the name *Enterprise* were designed to represent the Federation in political and military matters, the 1701-D was designed for exploration, de-emphasizing the importance of being a battle cruiser. This *Enterprise* serves as home to 1,012 people, which is two and a half times the ship's complement of the *Enterprise* 1701. This is the result of a century of technological evolution emphasizing human interaction with the hardware they use.

This new class of Starfleet vessel enables families to stay together. As the first captain on this bold new experiment in human exploration, Picard is uncomfortable with the idea of dealing with families. He's accustomed to a crew of professional, Starfleet-trained men and women who know their duty and understand their jobs thoroughly. The concept of children and other non-Starfleet personnel running around unnerves him even though he understands that it contributes to the morale.

The sophistication of the new *Enterprise* includes a variety of single and group family modules, various levels of schools, study facilities and other features designed so that children and spouses can live lives as normal as possible aboard what is practically a colony ship. Recreation has always been important on starships and now takes into account children.

## THE HOLODECK

There is a large selection of entertainment, sports, and other recreational forms, but the most elaborate is the holodeck. The holodeck, as seen in "Encounter at Farpoint," can simulate almost any landscape or sea world complete with winds, tides, rain or whatever is needed to make the illusion convincingly real. The special reality of the holodeck helps prevent the crew from feeling a sense of confinement from their prolonged voyage onboard the starship. The holodeck can also be used for purposes of exercise, as an opponent can be conjured up who is capable of responding to various modes of self-defense, as shown in the episode "Code of Honor."

The living and working areas of the *Enterprise* reflect an emphasis on the quality of life, being brighter and designed more for comfort than utilitarian compromise. Gone is the clutter and profusion of gauges, instruments, and control buttons. Instead the consoles feature black panels with touch-activated controls and voice-activated displays. This enables swifter activation of the necessary controls that could be crucial in emergency situations.

This new technology is especially important for the bridge. The new bridge is much larger and combines the features of ship control, briefing room, information retrieval area, and officers' ward room. Much the same kinds of things happen here as on the old bridge, but with less emphasis on the mechanics of steering the starship. It is a place where the starship officers can meet, check information, make plans or just catch up on what has been happening.

The control of the starship is handled by two bridge duty officers assigned to the tasks designated *command* and *control*. These are designated as CON (command and vessel control, including helm and navigation) and OPS (vessel operations, including some duties formerly performed in Engineering).

The center of the bridge consists of the Command Area, which is the focal point of all bridge activities. The captain, his Number One, and close advisors are located here. Just in front of this area are the previously described OPS and CON. Geordi La Forge and Data are in charge of these stations when not assigned to an Away Team. Their backups, who assume these duties when either Data or La Forge is unavailable, are simply referred to by the designations of their duties: OPS and CON.

At the rear of the bridge is a raised semicircular area separated from the Command Area by a railing, behind which is another set of console stations. This is the Tactical Control for weapons, defensive devices (such as the shields), and the internal security of the *Enterprise.*

## MORE CONSOLES

On the rear wall of the bridge are the Aft Consoles. These five stations are generally unsupervised functions unless specifically needed. Viewing them from left to right, they are as follows:

- **Emergency Manual Override:**
  In the event of main computer failure, many of the ship's primary functions can be operated from this station.
- **Environment:**
  This can adjust the life-support systems and related environmental engineering functions anywhere on the ship. A similar system was employed against the bridge crew in Kirk's time in "Space Seed" as well as against Khan's cronies during the same encounter. No doubt this is to prevent the vessel from being used as a weapon against its inhabitants.
- **Propulsion Systems:**
  This is a backup system to OPS and CON that ties in directly to Engineering and the control of the warp drive and impulse engines.
- **Sciences:**
  This is essentially a research station. It is used by the Science Officer and various mission specialists and can also be accessed by the Chief Medical Officer.
- **Sciences II:**
  This is a second console identical to the Science station next to it so that more than one researcher at a time can access information and interact.

The stage-left side of the bridge has two turbolifts and a door leading to the Captain's Office (also called the Captain's Ready Room). This has an auxiliary turbolift as well as the Captain's private head and washroom.

On the right side of the bridge is a door leading to

the bridge head and washroom, something they didn't seem to have on the original starship. A running joke at the time of Captain Kirk was that the Klingons didn't have a head anywhere on their ships, which is what made them so mean.

## WINDOW INTO SPACE

Continuing the overview of the bridge, the forward section contains a huge wall-sized holographic view screen. This viewer is almost always activated and dominates the bridge, giving the impression of a window into space. The view screen has magnifying capabilities and in some cases can lock into equipment on another vessel and send back an image of the other vessel's bridge.

Behind the bridge, but not immediately visible from inside the bridge proper, is a room filled with comfortable furnishings and lined with actual windows facing to the rear of the vessel. This affords an awesome view of the aft portion of the *Enterprise* saucer section as well as of the nacelles of the starship. This lounge is completely equipped as an observation deck and contains food units and often serves as a retreat from the pressures of duty by bridge officers. Access to it is a privilege.

The Transporter Room is more colorful than the plain battleship gray of the old *Enterprise*. Although people to be beamed out usually go to stand on the transporter pad, site-to-site transportation is also possible, and people can be beamed directly to the bridge or elsewhere in the ship. Communicators, now a part of the gold-plated chest insignia, can be locked in on by the Transporter when needed. The transporter beam has a range of 16,000 kilometers (roughly 10,000 miles). The transporter is also designed to filter out viruses, bacteria, and other alien matter that might be picked up on the surface of a planet. It can also be used to detect and, if necessary, deactivate weapons.

## QUICK ESCAPE

A special feature of the new *Enterprise* is the ability of the saucer section of the vessel to separate from the main hull in emergency situations. The only drawback to this escape procedure is that the warp engines are located in the main hull while the saucer section contains only impulse power from an engine located at the rear of the saucer.

There are also shuttlecraft aboard the *Enterprise* that are used when the transporter is malfunctioning or should the starship become disabled and evacuation in deep space become a necessity. This new *Enterprise* 1701-D is the most amazing in a proud heritage of ships bearing that title.

# SPECIAL EFFECTS

Special visual effects are those shots done separately from any live-action shooting. Some special effects shots, such as on-set explosions, are done by a different crew entirely. Optical effects are done after live-action shooting is completed.

In the 1960s, when the *Enterprise* was first given special-effects life, the process involved was difficult and time consuming. Thus new and extensive special effects didn't appear on the old series often, and shots of the *Enterprise* flying from left to right, orbiting a planet, or warping through outer space were reused over and over again. The audiences of the eighties and nineties, accustomed to the extravagant special effects of motion pictures in the post–*Star Wars* era of motion pictures, expect more.

In the fifteen years since *Star Wars* revolutionized special effects and the science-fiction film, television has found itself in the unenviable position of having to compete or look pathetic by comparison. While motion pictures can take days to get one shot right, television technical crews have only days to get upward of fifty shots done right. What has made this possible are the strides in video and digital technology.

When *Star Trek: The Next Generation* premiered in 1987, much was made of its tie-in to Lucasfilm's Industrial Light and Magic. But while ILM did contribute the dazzling special effects for "Encounter at Farpoint," they performed little for the series thereafter, because Lucasfilm was geared toward the more time-consuming schedules of motion pictures, not the rapid pace of television production.

Industrial Light and Magic produced some fifty special effects shots for "Encounter at Farpoint," but a new team of specialists was hired by the time the second episode was in production. In fact, two teams have worked on the series producing its special effects since 1987. One team consists of Robert Legato and coordinator Gary Hutzel, the other of Dan Curry and Ron Moore.

## TECHNOLOGICAL ADVANCES

They began with a weekly special effects budget of $75,000, only $25,000 more a week than the old *Star Trek* had for its FX shots twenty years before. But the modern technology surrounding both videotape and motion control gave them the advantages of speed unavailable to the old series.

For *The Next Generation*, special effects are shot on film and then transferred to videotape for both editing and composition purposes. This gives a sharper resolution to the image, which is why the new *Enterprise* never looks grainy or fuzzy the way the old TV *Enterprise* often did. While the special effects on the sixties series are still often impressive even twenty-five years later (particularly if you've seen one of the old shows projected on a large screen), the new generation of effects has opened the show up to more possibilities.

Originally the producers of *The Next Generation* had thought they could use the same approach that the sixties series did. They believed that from the shots ILM did for "Encounter at Farpoint" they'd be able to create a stockpile of special effects shots to use as needed.

*Battlestar Galactica* did this in the seventies, with the result that the show was already reusing effects shots even before it reached the conclusion of the pilot episode. It made for a less than satisfying effect overall. But upon cataloguing the special visual effects shots in "Encounter at Farpoint," it was discovered that most of them were so specific to the needs of that story that stock scenes for transitions and set-ups just weren't there. Few shots from that episode have been reused since.

## A DIFFICULT MODEL TO WORK WITH

The special-effects technicians brought in after ILM had done its work on the pilot had been led to believe that about ten new shots would be needed for each additional episode. This quickly escalated to an average of sixty to a high of one hundred new shots per show. Even in the first season the producers were hoping to find stock shots to match the demands of certain scripts. But there were no scenes available that could show the edge of the universe ("Where No One Has Gone Before") or the *Enterprise* being knocked end over end through space at warp speed ("When the Bough Breaks").

Complicating this was the fact that the new effects teams inherited the *Enterprise* model built by ILM. It was six feet long and was lacking in the kind of detail necessary for close-ups. Furthermore, at six feet in length it was too large to do a true long-shot, as the camera couldn't pull back far enough to make the *Enterprise* look very small. But since they also had a two-foot model available, they were able to make use of that one as well. A four-foot model was built for season three, which has been used for the new special-effects shots of the *Enterprise* ever since.

The lighting on the six-foot *Enterprise* was also difficult, as it involved wiring that had to be strung through the model. When the four-foot model was built, Gary Hutzel developed a neon transformer that enabled him to change the lighting scheme on the *Enterprise* model with the flick of a switch. By contrast, each lighting change on the old six-foot model took an hour.

Because only the six-foot ILM model of the *Enterprise* was built to have saucer separation capabilities, this model was brought out for Robert Legato's team to shoot in "The Best of Both Worlds," and the cumbersomeness of it made for a difficult time. It just reinforced all of their feelings about why a smaller model worked better for their specific needs.

## TIMING IS IMPORTANT

"The Best of Both Worlds" featured a higher than normal amount of optical effects, plus many that were more than normally complicated. In the scene where three Martian probes attack the Borg ship, that shot involved several elements—the starfield, the three probes blowing up, the planet Mars, and the Borg ship flying toward the camera and then away. Ten seconds of screen time for something that complex can take four to five days to shoot.

The head of whichever special-effects unit is working on an episode supervises the on-set effects filmed during the normal principal photography schedule of seven to eight days. The film editors then spend two weeks assembling the footage and deliver the final cut of the live-action part of the show to the special-effects team. The special-effects teams get the script for a show and plan out their shots, but are unable to do any real work on it until the live-action footage has been shot and edited.

From that they'll know how much time is allotted for the demands of the visual effects, and they generally then have from eight to ten days to deliver the needed special visual-effects shots. The special visual effects involve from five to nine days of shooting the *Enterprise* and other ships, with five or six days to composite all of the elements together into the finished shots. Specific instructions are then given on where to edit each scene into the episode.

Due to modern computer animation techniques, a phaser beam can be drawn right on the frame of film when it's being edited on videotape. Other previously used visual effects can be sometimes combined to create something new, such as a cloud image or a water pattern, which can be used to create an unusual-looking force field. Stock footage can be employed, such as using the orbiting space station first seen in *The Search for Spock,* wherein the new *Enterprise* is substituted for the old *Enterprise.* This has turned up in *The Next Generation* on an average of once a season since 1987.

## INGENUITY CAN GO A LONG WAY

Not all optical shots are time consuming or expensive. In the season-one episode "When the Bough Breaks," Robert Legato's team had to create a shot of the power station seen near the end of the episode. They built models and shot them against a black wall that was heavily backlit, and then matted that into a miniature, which created an effect of looking at a ledge that appeared to be a hundred feet off the floor. The shot cost only about $3,000 to do. Had they farmed it out, the shot would have cost $35,000 to accomplish. Ingenuity won out.

Some technical shots are more than ordinarily demanding. In the fifth-season episode "A Matter of Time," they had to show the *Enterprise* cleansing a planet's atmosphere of smoke and ash particles. This required shooting liquid nitrogen and dry ice in a tank in order to get the equivalent of cloud movements, which could then be manipulated in the context of the *Enterprise.*

While *The Next Generation* is filmed at Paramount Studios in Hollywood, the special-effects teams work across town in Santa Monica at Digital Magic. There the optical effects are shot on film and then sent out to a video transfer lab to be transferred to D-1 digital videotape, where the special-effects technicians can later combine various effects to create a single image.

For instance, the *Enterprise* is filmed separately from its lights as the use of motion-control cameras allows a separate pass to be made of the model with its lights glowing to be superimposed on the previous shot of the *Enterprise* now on videotape. The engine lights will be a brighter exposure with some diffusion while the cabin lights, filmed on yet another pass, will be dimmer. When composited in one shot, it's impossible to tell that it's multiple shots combined into a single image.

## SHORT ON TIME

Working on videotape allows color correcting and even light balancing to be done, which could not be as easily accomplished working with an effect on film. When effects are combined on film in an optical printer, the work goes down a generation in quality each time, thereby resulting in the grainy appearance of some special visual effects seen in past motion pictures.

After five years, some five hundred special visual effects have been created for *The Next Generation,* which allows the reusing of some shots and even compositing shots together. For instance, a scene of the *Enterprise* can be combined with a previously recorded image of a Romulan ship to create a completely new shot of the two ships in the same frame.

The now famous shot of the new *Enterprise* stretching as it enters warp speed (seen in the opening credits of each episode) was created using the slit-scan process pioneered in 1968 in *2001: A Space Odyssey.* ILM created three such shots for "Encounter at Farpoint," and Robert Legato's effects team later created two additional ones for an episode that Legato directed. Legato has directed two episodes, "Menage a Troi" and "The Nth Degree," the latter involving considerable effects work, which the director had to oversee after directing the live-action portions of the episode.

The special visual effects achieved on the series are often based on what can be achieved in the limited amount of time available. In an interview in *Cinefantastique* magazine, Robert Legato stated, "I get a big kick out of the fans who send letters and come up with reasons why things on the show look the way they do. You get letters from people telling you how brilliant this concept is because of the structural dynamics and design and air flow. In reality, you just thought it was a neat idea and it's the best you could come up with on the spur of the moment."

CHAPTER

# CHARACTERS AND CAST

# CAPTAIN JEAN-LUC PICARD

At the time of the voyages chronicled in *Star Trek: The Next Generation*, Captain Picard has recently completed a twenty-two-year mission as captain of the deep-space-charting starship *Stargazer* and is legendary in Starfleet. With only eleven percent of the galaxy charted, the *Stargazer* contributed important information to these chronicles. Tragedy was no stranger during those two decades of exploration, as it was near the end of the mission that Jack Crusher was killed saving the life of Picard. Jean-Luc accompanied the body when it was returned to the family, thereby meeting Jack's wife, Dr. Beverly Crusher, and the very young Wesley Crusher. Beverly requested posting with Picard on the *Enterprise*, even though she subliminally blamed him for her husband's death.

Picard feels some guilt himself, and in the episode "Justice" found himself having to weigh the Prime Directive against the life of Wesley Crusher when the boy violated the inflexible laws of a planet. Picard would have been troubled with any crew member thus endangered, but the dilemma took on added weight when the person in question was the son of the man who had saved his life. The inherent unfairness of the situation led Picard to confront the entities responsible, thus saving Wesley, whose progress since then has been watched by Picard with growing pride.

## PICARD'S ROOTS

Picard was born on Earth, in Paris, France, in the twenty-fourth century. His lack of ethnic accent is explained by advanced forms of language instruction. Picard betrays his Gallic background only in times of deep emotional stress. He uses French on rare occasions, as when he bade farewell to Dr. McCoy in "Encounter at Farpoint," or when he visited his ancestral home in "Family."

The young Picard was a far cry from the disciplined commander of the *Enterprise.* In "Samaritan Snare," he reveals to Wesley that he has an artificial heart since losing his original one in an ill-advised brawl. Still, his career has been an exemplary one; a young and awestruck Lieutenant Picard was in attendance at the wedding of the legendary Spock, an incident referred to in "Sarek" but not yet shown in any of the motion pictures.

Captain Picard can be very tough and pragmatic, but he is also a romantic who believes sincerely in honor and duty. He is a philosophical man with a keen interest in history and archaeology. He still accesses information in the old-fashioned way, from books, and is especially fond of Shakespeare and 1940s hard-boiled detective fiction. The past, to him, is as vast a storehouse of knowledge as the future, and must not be disregarded or forgotten. His gift to

Data, the complete plays of Shakespeare, is a fitting guide to the various aspects of humanity, and is much cherished by the android officer.

Although baldness had been cured generations before the twenty-fourth century, the men of this time find the natural look appealing, and Picard is content to remain so. He is not vain, and has no interest in cosmetic surgery or other artificial enhancements of his external appearance. With the advanced medicine and extended life spans of his time, Picard in his fifties is just entering his prime and would be comparable to a man of thirty in the twentieth century. Active-duty Starfleet males and females are in prime physical condition through their seventies.

While still relatively young by twenty-fourth-century standards, Picard remains content with a "starship love," a personality attribute accented by his twenty-two-year duty on the *Stargazer*. But on the *Enterprise* 1701-D, with its ship's complement of over a thousand crew and family members, Picard is facing new challenges to his skills, experience, and intellect, learning along the way that life is more complex than he ever imagined.

## PATRICK STEWART

Patrick Stewart reveals that he was "compelled" to become an actor "as a result of an argument."

At age fifteen, Stewart left school and landed a job on a local newspaper. He also happened to be an energetic amateur actor—the two vocations didn't mix.

"I was always faced with either covering an assignment or attending an important rehearsal or performance," he explains. "I used to get my colleagues to cover for me, but often I would just make up reports. Finally, I was found out. I had a terrific row with the editor, who said, 'Either you decide to be a journalist, in which case you give up all of this acting nonsense, or you get off my paper.' I left his office, packed up my typewriter, and walked out."

There followed two years of selling furniture. "I was better at selling furniture than I was at journalism," Stewart observes good-naturedly. He also enrolled in drama school at the Bristol Old Vic to bring his skills up to the level of his enthusiasm.

The actor used to see his roles as a way of exploring other personalities and characteristics, but nowadays it has become more of a means of self-expression. "When I was younger, I used to think in terms of how I could disguise myself in roles. Now I want my work to say something about me, contain more of my experience of the world."

## A FAMOUS BRIT

Patrick Stewart has become a highly regarded actor in Great Britain from his roles in such BBC productions as *I, Claudius*, *Smiley's People*, and *Tinker, Tailor, Soldier, Spy*, all of which have aired in America. His face is also known to American filmgoers from roles in a variety of motion pictures. In the David Lynch adaptation of *Dune*, he played Gurney Halek, one of the more prominent roles in the film. In *Excalibur*, he played Leondegrance.

More recently, he was seen in the strange science fiction film *Lifeforce* as the character Dr. Armstrong. On stage, he starred in London in a production of *Who's Afraid of Virginia Woolf?* which garnered him the prestigious London Fringe Best Actor Award. As an associate artist of the Royal Shakespeare Company, Stewart is considered one of the leading talents of the British stage. His impressive list of stage credits includes Shylock, Henry IV, Leontes, King John, Titus Andronicus, and many others. In 1986, he played the title role in Peter Shaffer's play

*Yonadab* at the National Theatre of Great Britain.

Patrick Stewart moved up to directing in *The Next Generation* in the fifth season, and his work includes the excellent episode "Hero Worship," as well as "In Theory."

After supervising producer Robert Justman saw Stewart onstage at UCLA, the actor was cast as Captain Picard. "A friend of mine, an English professor, was lecturing and I was part of the stage presentation," he recalls. A few days later he was called to audition for *Star Trek: The Next Generation*. Since then, he has become a well-known face, although occasionally fans get confused. One woman accosted him at a party and racked her brains until she recognized him. "You fly the *Endeavor*," she told him triumphantly, when her memory finally clicked, "and you play William Shatner!"

But Patrick Stewart got his biggest surprise when the July 18, 1992, issue of *TV Guide* revealed that in a poll of readers, he was voted the sexiest man on television with 54% of the votes, beating out Burt Reynolds, A. Martinez, John Corbett, and Luke Perry. He responded to the award by expressing, "Surprise . . . puzzlement . . . and pleasure." He said that it would have been nice had it happened when he was nineteen, which is when he lost all his hair and thought no woman would ever look at him again. Stewart had worn a series of wigs over the years and even wore one when he tested for the part of Captain Picard. The producers decided he looked fine without it. Apparently a lot of female viewers agree with them.

# COMMANDER WILLIAM RIKER

Not since the first starship *Enterprise* 1701 was under the command of Captain Christopher Pike has the executive officer been called "Number One." William Riker has been given this honor by his commander, Captain Picard, to whom he is responsible for vastly important duties. When a landing team, or Away Team, is assembled, Riker is generally in charge of the team. Although it is not strictly prohibited for the starship captain to head up the team, Riker correctly recognizes that too much depends on the captain remaining safe to guide and protect his vessel.

Sending the most experienced officer down into an unknown situation is deemed too dangerous by Number One until he checks out the status of the planet and its culture for himself. Picard isn't entirely happy being forced to remain behind, but he understands and respects his executive officer's viewpoint.

Riker is also in charge of overseeing the condition of the vessel and the crew. When a Federation propulsion expert came aboard in "Where No One Has Gone Before," Riker would not allow him to run tests on the system until they had been fully outlined to him and approved by the ship's chief engineer.

"Number One" is an expression whose meaning has not appreciably altered since Earth's seventeenth century, when the second-in-command of a sailing ship was generally known as a "first lieutenant" (hence "Number One" is used in the sense of "first"). The term also implies executive officer and captain-in-training.

## THE CAPTAIN IS NOT EXPENDABLE

In those bygone days, the executive officer was also generally in command of shore parties for the same reason Riker takes such tasks upon himself now—the life of a ship's captain is not considered to be expendable. But even though Number One is in charge of the Away Team on the ground, Captain Picard retains final authority over their actions.

William Riker joined the *Enterprise* crew when it picked him up at the Farpoint Station, which is where he also met some other crew members for the first time, including Beverly and Wesley Crusher, and Geordi La Forge.

Riker regards his captain with a mixture of awe and affection, but is also privy to Picard's self-doubts, such as his annoyance at having to deal with children and families in a starship setting. As time passes, Riker has seen the captain adjust to this new situation.

While Riker has a lively interest in women, he considers it a point of honor never to let it come between himself and his duty. He is intellectually committed to sexual equality and tries to live up to that. This was put to the test in "Justice," in which the people on Edo proved to be extremely affectionate and greeted the opposite sex with deep hugs and kisses instead of a bow or a handshake. The whole truth is that, at thirty, Riker is still young and hasn't learned yet how completely different the two sexes can be.

Number One was surprised to see Deanna Troi after beaming aboard the *Enterprise*. They had been in a previous relationship and had a strong attraction for one another. Riker is slightly uncomfortable thrown into a situation where he deals with Troi every day, but each treats the other with respect, and they seem to have put their past relationship behind them.

## ACCEPTING DATA

While Riker can accept Troi, and even the Klingon Worf, Lt. Commander Data posed some problems at first, but Riker has come to accept the android as an equal. He agonized when he was obliged to act as prosecutor in "The Measure of a Man," but carried out his duty, perhaps too well for his conscience. Data helped him cope with this by pointing out that if he had declined to fulfill that duty, the judge would have made a summary judgment against Data, but the full hearing gave Picard a chance to mount his most persuasive arguments.

While Riker is called Number One by the captain and crew alike, this distinction is reserved for starship personnel and not for people who are not a part of the ship's complement.

## JONATHAN FRAKES

"I knew this was a real part, a big one," says Jonathan Frakes regarding the six weeks of auditions he went through for the role, "and I had to get it."

The actor credits Gene Roddenberry with giving him the needed insight into the character that eventually became his.

"Gene was so very non-Hollywood and quite paternal. One of the things he said to me was, 'You have a Machiavellian glint in your eye. Life is a bowl of cherries.' I think Gene felt that way, which is why he wrote the way he did. He's very positive and Commander Riker will reflect that," states Frakes.

The actor sees Riker as, "strong, centered, honorable, and somewhat driven. His job is to provide Captain Picard with the most efficiently run ship and the best-prepared crew he can. Because of this he seems to maintain a more military bearing than the other characters in behavior, despite the fact that salutes and other military protocol no longer exist in the twenty-fourth century."

While Frakes cannot help but regard this role as "a real step up in my career," he's had recurring roles on other series such as *Falcon Crest*, *Paper Dolls*, and *Bare Essence*. For a year he was even a regular on the daytime drama *The Doctors*. Other television appearances include a role in the made-for-TV movie *The Nutcracker* and critically praised roles in the miniseries *Dream West* and both parts of the extended miniseries *North and South*. The actor has also appeared both on and off-Broadway and in regional theater productions.

## FRAKES'S ROOTS

Born and raised in Pennsylvania, Frakes did undergraduate work at Penn State before going to Harvard. He also spent several seasons with the Loeb Drama Center before moving to New York.

"I gave myself a five-year limit," he reveals. "If I wasn't making a living at acting in five years, I would find something else to do. After a year and a half of being the worst waiter in New York and screwing up my back as a furniture mover, I got a role in *Shenandoah* on Broadway and then landed a part in *The Doctors*."

Frakes spent the next five years in New York City and then moved to Los Angeles in 1979, at the suggestion of his agent. "I really have been very lucky. There's a cliché in this business that says the easy part of being an actor is doing the job. The hardest part is getting the job."

Jonathan Frakes resides in Los Angeles and is married to actress Genie Francis, who appears on *Days of Our Lives*. He's also started directing episodes of *The Next Generation*, including "The Offspring," "The Drumhead," "Reunion," and "Cause and Effect."

# LT. COMMANDER DATA

Data is an android so perfectly fabricated that he can pass for human. It was thought that he was the product of some advanced alien technology until the discovery of an earlier model, Lore, revealed him to be the work of Dr. Noonian Soong, a human cyberneticist believed to be dead.

Much of the information given by Lore may be false, as is learned in "Brothers," when a homing signal brings Data face-to-face with his creator, who in fact created both of his androids quite literally in his own image, with his own face.

The only clues to Data's true origin are his peculiar yellow eyes, pale skin, and encyclopedic memory comparable to that of a Vulcan, but actually more extensive. It takes a skilled biologist to detect that Data is composed of artificial tissues instead of real flesh and blood. Although he only uses it in extreme circumstances, Data also possesses superhuman strength.

Data was discovered by a Starfleet Away Team investigating the disappearance of an Earth colony. The colony was completely destroyed, but the android was near the site, deactivated, and programmed with all the knowledge and memories of the lost colonists—except for the memory of what eradicated them so utterly. All this was rediscovered later, when Lore was reassembled.

At the time of his discovery, Data had no memories of his own, and was impressed by the humans who rescued him. He chose to emulate them, hoping to become more human in the process. His remarkable abilities do not give him a superiority complex. In fact, he seems to feel a bit less than human, as he cannot feel emotions, but he seems somehow to overlook the truth that his loyalty and actions toward others would actually qualify him as an exemplary human being.

He excelled in the Starfleet Academy entry tests and has never received a mark against his performance. Data benefited from the Starfleet regulation that prevents the rejection of a candidate so long as it tests out to be a sentient life form. This was later put to the test by Commander Bruce Maddox, whose efforts to classify the android as a possession of Starfleet were thwarted by Jean-Luc Picard. Picard's spirited defense of his colleague also served to strengthen Data's rights and liberties.

## DATA CAN DO IT ALL

Data was created in the male gender, is fully functional (see "The Naked Now"!), and seems incapable of falsehood. While he speaks a more formal brand of English and does not use contractions, he tends to ramble on a bit because of his vast knowledge. He does learn and adapt, however, and discontinued calculating times to the exact second because he learned that this often annoyed humans.

He has difficulty understanding humor and idiomatic language, although he can learn vast glossaries of slang, such as that of the 1940s ("The Big Goodbye"), when he deems it relevant to the situation at hand. He also involves himself in amateur acting. Picard has shared his interest in Shakespeare with him, and Data's researches in theatrical history have led him to become an adherent of Stanislavsky's Method approach to acting, although his reasons are peculiar. The Method is rooted in drawing on deep emotions to bring characters to life; Data hopes to reach emotional depths through creating characters onstage, in essence reversing the original Method concept.

While Data appears to be an adult in his late twenties, he has probably existed a much shorter time than that. Because Data was never a child, he seems particularly interested in children such as Wesley Crusher, as they mark an aspect of existence he has never experienced and represent another example of his goal of being human.

In fact, his older "brother" Lore was given basic emotions, but Dr. Soong had overreached himself in this attempt and did not try to give emotions to Data after they went seriously awry in Lore. Years later, Soong developed circuitry to remedy this, but was fooled by the jealous Lore, who obtained the implant himself. Soong died soon afterward, leaving Data much the same as before. Data, despite his misgivings, continues to learn and grow as a sentient, and certainly very human, being.

## BRENT SPINER

"I'm one of those people who believes that mankind will find all the answers out in space," says Spiner, "but the first step is to get off this planet. The sun is going to burn out eventually and we better be somewhere else as a race of people by the time that happens. I think that's why everybody digs *Star Trek,* because they know it's a part of all of our futures and represents a vision of home."

"As the series opens, we don't know much about Data, only that he was constructed by beings on a planet which no longer exists. He's the only thing left. His creators programmed him with a world of knowledge—he's virtually an encyclopedia—but only in terms of information, not behavior. He's totally innocent. However, he does possess a sense of question and wonder that allows him to evolve. His objective is to be as human as possible."

Brent Spiner was born and raised in Houston, Texas, where he saw an average of three movies a day between the ages of eleven and fifteen. "At fifteen I was already a major film buff. I could quote lines from movies, tell you who was in it and in what year it was made. I always fantasized about being an actor. I was also lucky enough to have a brilliant teacher in high school named Cecil Pickett, who was capable of seeing potential, nurturing it, and making me aware of it."

## SPINER'S EARLY DAYS

Spiner did a lot of "gritty, ugly plays" off-Broadway after college. "The one that finally pushed me over into the serious-actor category was a Public Theater production of *The Seagull* for Joseph Papp." The actor went on to roles in the Broadway musical productions of *Sunday in the Park with George, The Three Musketeers,* and *Big River,* based on Mark Twain's *Huckleberry Finn.*

Since moving to Los Angeles in 1984, he's appeared in such plays as *Little Shop of Horrors* at the Westwood Playhouse. His feature-film credits include the Woody Allen film *Stardust Memories.* On television he has appeared on such series as *The Twilight Zone, Hill Street Blues, Cheers,* and *Night Court*.

One could say that he was very well prepared for his role as Data by his belief in extraterrestrials. "Obviously I'm from another planet." He laughs, but adds that he seriously does believe in beings from other planets and will continue to do so until such things are disproven.

# LIEUTENANT WORF

The prediction made by the Organians nearly a century before has come to pass. The Klingon Empire and the Federation are at peace. Even so, Worf is unique as the only Klingon officer on a Starfleet ship. When his family was destroyed in a treacherous Romulan attack on a Klingon outpost, Worf was rescued and raised by humans of Slavic extraction, who did their best to keep their adopted son in touch with his Klingon roots. He joined Starfleet and is treated with the same courtesy and respect shown any other bridge officer—possibly even more, since the Klingons still have a remarkable reputation for violence.

Although Worf is still very aggressive by nature, he is able to control his anger even when he feels he has been provoked. As a bridge officer, and the third in the line of command after Picard and Riker, Worf takes his duties very seriously. In combat situations, when the *Enterprise* or its crew is threatened, Worf instinctively wants to respond in kind and confront the menace head-on. The Klingon Empire does not stress cool deliberation as the preferred method for problem solving.

Worf rarely talks about himself and his culture, but in "Justice" Riker inadvertently gets Worf to talk about Klingon sexual attitudes. When Riker wonders why Worf is not enjoying the pleasures offered by the sybaritic Edo, Worf explains, quite casually, that only Klingon women could survive sex with a Klingon male. When Riker wonders if this is simply bragging, Worf is confused. He was merely stating a simple fact of Klingon life.

Eventually, Worf did renew a long-unconsummated relationship with the half-human K'Ehleyr, who came back into his life as a Federation emissary. Their encounter in "The Emissary" produced a son, but unfortunately K'Ehleyr was murdered in "Reunion," a crime that provoked Worf to a bloody and time-honored Klingon revenge. His son now lives with his Earth grandparents, since Worf's status in the Klingon Empire had at one point become a precarious one.

## UNFAIR BLAME

Years after Worf's rescue, the Klingons captured a Romulan ship whose records revealed the identity of the Klingon who betrayed the outpost. This Klingon was a member of a very powerful family, and his son was an important Klingon, so the Klingon High Council decided to avoid societal disruption by altering the records and blaming Worf's father for the crime.

They did not believe that Worf still kept the Klingon ways, or that he would even learn of this dishonor. They were unaware that he had a younger brother who had been secretly raised by another family. Worf's brother contacted Worf, drawing him into the Machiavellian intrigues of Klingon power politics. Ultimately, Worf underwent discommendation rather than let his brother be killed. This act corroborated his father's guilt to outside eyes, but also gave him time to set matters right. He had already scored one victory, for his enemy in this matter was also the killer of his mate. Worf's family honor was restored in "Redemption I & II" when he aided Gowron in a Klingon civil war.

It seems that Worf may turn out to be a key factor in Klingon–Federation relations. Klingons as a rule do not feel comfortable with humans, often holding them in contempt, and there may be a faction (see "The Drumhead") that favors improved relations with the Romulans. Even though Klingons have a deeply ingrained hatred of Romulans, they understand them better than humans, whose manners and motivations often must seem strange to the warrior Klingons. Worf occupies a unique position between these two cultures, and may provide the key to future developments between them.

## MICHAEL DORN

As a longtime *Star Trek* fan, Dorn says that this role "was a dream come true. First, because I'm a Trekkie, and second, I'm playing a Klingon, a character so totally different from the nice-guy roles I'd done in the past. Worf is the only Klingon aboard the *Enterprise*. That makes him an outsider, but that's okay by me because Worf knows he's superior to these weak humans. But he never lets the other crew members see that, because he's a soldier first and second."

The actor gives enthusiastic praise to series creator Gene Roddenberry for having the "genius and vision" to depict an optimistic future in which a peaceful alliance could be struck between Earth and the Klingon Empire. "Gene believed there is good in everybody—even Klingons!"

But the actor enjoys playing very different kinds of characters, and knows what it's like to appear in a series after playing a regular on *CHIPS* for three years. "I love doing cop roles, and as a highway patrolman I got to drive fast and never got hurt."

Dorn hails from Liling, Texas, but he was raised in Pasadena, California, just minutes away from Hollywood. He performed in a rock band during high school and college and in 1973 moved to San Francisco, where he worked at a variety of jobs. When he returned to L.A., he continued playing in rock bands until a friend's father, an assistant director of *The Mary Tyler Moore Show*, suggested the young man try his hand at acting. Dorn can be seen in the background, as a newswriter, in episodes from that classic comedy's last two seasons.

"I had done a little modeling by this time and had studied drama and TV producing in college. Once I started, I caught the bug."

## THE HUMBLE START

His first acting role was a guest spot on the series *WEB*, a show based on the satirical film *Network*. Dorn was introduced to an agent by the producer of the show and began studying with Charles Conrad. Six months later Dorn was cast in *CHIPS*. Following that series, Dorn resumed acting classes. "I worked very hard; the jobs started coming and the roles got meatier."

Dorn has made guest appearances on nearly every major series, most notably *Hotel*, *Knots Landing*, and *Falcon Crest*. He has also had recurring roles on *Days of Our Lives* and *Capitol*. His feature film credits include *Demon Seed*, *Rocky*, and *The Jagged Edge*.

Dorn hopes eventually to direct, but for now, "I want to take one step at a time and do the best work I can do." He's still interested in rock music, plays in a band, does studio work as a bass player, and writes music in his spare time.

# DOCTOR BEVERLY CRUSHER

Beverly Crusher worked long and hard to secure her posting aboard the *Enterprise*, where she is stationed along with her brilliant son, Wesley. Beverly's husband, Jack Crusher, was killed while serving under Captain Picard aboard the USS *Stargazer*. Jack Crusher died saving Picard's life, and to show his respect for the man, Picard accompanied the body back to Earth when it was returned for the funeral.

While Beverly knows that it is not logical to blame Picard, she associated him with her loss and was not, at first, certain how she would react to working with Picard. When Picard offered to have her transferred if she so desired, she declined, since she wouldn't have been there if she hadn't requested the position. Any initial misgivings have given way to mutual respect and understanding.

Dr. Crusher chose to sign aboard the starship commanded by Picard because she had an enviable

Starfleet record that had earned her this prestigious assignment. As demonstrated by the position held by Dr. McCoy on the *Enterprise* commanded by James T. Kirk, a starship's chief medical officer is in no way regarded as a rank inferior to that of Captain. In fact, outside of a court martial, the CMO is the only force capable of removing a starship captain from his or her post.

Beverly is an intelligent and strong-willed diagnostician. She has a profound sense of medicine, the kind of skill that takes years to develop. Often she uses her diagnostic skills to confirm what she has already seen and sensed about a patient's condition. First and foremost she is a brilliant ship's doctor.

## THE TRUTH REVEALED

In "The Naked Now" there were many truths revealed about various crew members. In Crusher's case it was revealed that she is interested in Picard, and certainly no longer harbors the suspicion and resentment she feared might affect her job performance. Being in her late thirties to early forties, the attractive Dr. Crusher has not escaped the notice of Captain Picard, but it is doubtful that this could develop into anything, as any good officer knows that complications arise when key personnel become involved.

Dr. Crusher's most difficult moments on the *Enterprise* generally involve Wesley, as in "Justice," when Wesley was sentenced to death for an inadvertent crime, only to be saved by Picard's intervention. She has also been trapped in a false reality inside a static warp field, which she narrowly escaped from, and recently found romance only to have it shattered by the bizarre secrets of the alien humanoid she'd fallen for in "The Host."

Her most difficult time with Wesley occurred in "The First Duty," when Wesley narrowly escaped death in a training exercise off Saturn, in which another cadet did die. Her son admitted to participating in a coverup of the accident. While Wesley Crusher did the right thing at the end, he was humiliated in front of all of his Starfleet Academy peers and was forced to repeat his final year at the Academy.

## GATES MCFADDEN

Dr. Crusher is the first regular role in a television series for actress Gates McFadden. Her character is presented with more background than most of the others, as she is the mother of Wesley Crusher, and the widow of the man who died while saving Picard's life on an earlier mission.

Gates trained to be a dancer when quite young, while growing up in Cuyahoga Falls, Ohio. "I had extraordinary teachers: one was primarily a ballerina and the other had been in a circus. I grew up thinking most ballerinas knew how to ride the unicycle, tap dance, and do handsprings. Consequently, I was an oddball to other dancers."

Her interest in acting was sparked by community theater and a touring Shakespeare company. "When I was ten, my brother and I attended back-to-back Shakespeare for eight days in a musty, nearly empty theater. There were twelve actors who played all the parts. I couldn't get over it—the same people in costumes every day, but playing new characters. It was like visiting somewhere but never wanting to leave."

She earned her Bachelor of Arts in Theater from Brandeis University while continuing to study acting, dance, and mime. Just prior to graduation she met Jack LeCoq and credits the experience with changing her life.

"I attended his first workshop in the United States. His theatrical vision and the breadth of its scope were astonishing. I left for Paris as soon as possible to continue to study acting with LeCoq at his school. We worked constantly in juxtapositions. One explored immobility in order to better understand movement. One explored silence in order to better understand sound and language. It was theatrical research involving many mediums. Just living in a foreign country where you have to speak and think in another language cracks your head open. It was both terrifying and freeing. Suddenly I was taking more risks in my acting."

## A WOMAN OF MANY TALENTS

McFadden lives in New York City, where she has been involved in film and theater both as an actress and director-choreographer. Her acting credits include leads in the New York productions of Michael Brady's *To Gillian on Her 37th Birthday*, Mary Gallagher's *How to Say Goodbye*, Caryl Churchill's *Cloud 9*, and, in California, in the La Jolla Playhouse production of *The Matchmaker* with Linda Hunt.

Gates was the director of choreography and puppet movement for the late Jim Henson's *Labyrinth* and assisted Gavin Miller in the staging of the fantasy sequences for *Dreamchild*. "Those films were my baptism by fire into the world of special effects and computerized props," Gates reveals.

Following the first season of *Next Generation*, Gates was inexplicably dropped from the cast and just as inexplicably returned in the third season, after her role as ship's doctor had been played for one season by Diana Muldaur. During her absence from the series, among other work Gates had a small role in *The Hunt for Red October* as the wife of the main character. She did not repeat this role in *Patriot Games*, the second film to feature the Jack Ryan character, as a younger actress was chosen for the part in the 1992 sequel.

# LT. COMMANDER DEANNA TROI

Deanna Troi is the ship's counselor. This position didn't exist during the time of the first starship *Enterprise* seventy-five years before. In the twenty-fourth century it has been realized that the success of a starship's mission depends as much on efficiently functioning human relationships as it does on the vessel staying in one piece and having fully functional warp drive.

Counselor Troi is fully trained in human and alien psychology. When a starship encounters alien life forms, the counselor is crucial to the captain and Number One.

While twentieth-century psychiatry and psychology are considered to be more arts than empirical science, in the twenty-fourth century, solid evidence and medical research have radically changed things. Psychiatry has become a field of applied science in which hard evidence has replaced guesswork, supposition, and mere practiced insight. Command ranks aboard starships both respect and actively make use of the skills of the counselor in much the same way that they solicit advice from the medical officers, chief engineer, and other shipboard specialists. With the commissioning of the *Galaxy*-class starships, with the added complexities of families and the presence of children, the Counselor is in even more demand.

A Starfleet graduate, Deanna is half human and half Betazoid. Her father was a Starfleet officer who lived on Betazed with one of that world's humanoid females. Her mother Lwaxana is an aristocratic eccentric who provides Deanna with acute embarrassment whenever she appears onboard the *Enterprise.* She is insistent on pursuing Captain Picard (she thinks he has great legs), or whatever other male she sets her eyes on.

While Lwaxana and all other full Betazoids are fully telepathic, Deanna has telepathic abilities limited to the emotional range; she can "read" feelings and sensations, but not coherent thoughts. Another extreme example of Betazoid ability is the hypersensitive Tam Elbrun, who vanished with the space-faring being dubbed "Tin Man" by the Federation. While most Betazoids develop their full telepathic abilities during adolescence, Elbrun was born with them fully functional, which led him to seek the solitude of space. He was, in fact, Deanna's patient at one time, but she was not able to do much for him.

## OFTEN AWAY

Due to her particular training and inherent abilities, Counselor Troi is often selected as an Away Team member, as she can provide important insights into the motives and feelings of the beings they must deal with.

(Some beings, notably the Ferengi, are impervious even to full telepaths. While some races may be able to intentionally block their minds, the Ferengi probably are resistant due to peculiarities of their brain structure.)

Generally, when dealing with alien life, Deanna can sense something of the moods or attitudes that a being harbors toward Federation representatives. In the case of the Traveler ("Where No One Has Gone Before") she could detect nothing from him, as if he wasn't even there. With humans she is able to sense more when it is a person she has some sort of rapport or relationship with.

For instance, Troi was acquainted with William Riker before either was posted to the *Enterprise.* Neither knew the other had been assigned to this starship until they first encountered one another on board. While Troi did no feel she could become deeply involved with Riker again, she did find their affair meaningful and pleasant. It has not progressed any further, as each feels honor bound to maintain a disciplined and professional status while aboard ship.

## MARINA SIRTIS

A British actress, Marina Sirtis worked in various roles in England for years before she decided to give the colonies a try. She landed the continuing role of Deanna Troi after being in America only six months. "It's taken me years to become an overnight success," she quips. "I had a six-month visa, which was quickly running out. In fact, I got the call telling me I had the part only hours before I was to leave for the airport to return home."

Marina enjoys the irony of being a British actress playing an alien on American television. But viewers won't notice a British accent coming out of an alien being, as she's devised a combination of accents for the character to use. Sirtis states, "In the twenty-fourth century, geographical or national barriers are not so evident. The Earth as a planet is your country, your nationality. I didn't want anyone to be able to pin down my accent to any particular country, and being good at accents, the producers trusted me to come up with something appropriate."

Sirtis initially auditioned for the role of Security Chief Tasha Yar. "After my third audition for Tasha, I was literally walking out the door when they called me back to read for Deanna. While I was looking at the script, director Corey Allen came in and said, 'You have something personally that the character should have . . . an empathy, so use it.' I love being able to play someone who is so deep with that kind of insight into people, particularly since I usually get cast as the hard 1980s stereotype."

Born to Greek parents in North London, Marina demonstrated an inclination toward performing at an early age. "My mother tells me that when I was three, I used to stand up on the seat of the bus and sing to the other passengers." However, her parents wanted their daughter to follow more "serious" pursuits, so after finishing high school, Marina had to secretly apply to the Guild Hall School of Music and Drama, where she was accepted. "My first job after graduating was as Ophelia in *Hamlet* for the Worthing Repertory Company."

## A BIG MTV FAN

Following that, she worked for a few years in British television and musical theater, and in other repertory companies throughout England and Europe. She landed some supporting roles in features, such as *The Wicked Lady* with Faye Dunaway and *Deathwish III* opposite Charles Bronson.

She decided to stay on in the United States and has settled in Los Angeles, where she watches "far too much MTV" and keeps track of her local soccer team in London, in which she owns a few shares. Her brother is a professional soccer player.

Marina has always been interested in the stars and space exploration and believes that she once saw a UFO. "I was working with a repertory company in Worthing, a seaside town in England. One night as I was walking down the street, I saw this huge orange thing in the sky. At first I thought it must be the moon, but it was very off color. It was very close, but too high to be a balloon. Apparently a lot of other people saw it too."

# LIEUTENANT GEORDI LA FORGE

Geordi is trained to work on the bridge and as an Away Team member. His unique prosthetic eyes allow him to perform some of the functions of a tricorder and are actually a visor-like device worn on his head, which can detect the entire spectrum of electromagnetic waves, all the way from raw heat to high-frequency ultraviolet. Other crew persons seem blind by comparison, although Geordi often wishes he could see the way they do, since he has been blind since birth.

Although in his early twenties, Geordi has the maturity of a seasoned Starfleet graduate and has the highest respect for Captain Picard, hoping to emulate the captain when he gets older. His best friend aboard the *Enterprise* is the android Data. Each aspires to be "fully human," because even though they have traits that make them superior in what they can achieve compared to their normal counterparts, neither asked to be different, nor wants to be.

## LEVAR BURTON

Due to the longevity of the original series, the new crew has more than one actor who was a *Star Trek* fan before landing his role, and LeVar Burton is one of them. He states that he has long "appreciated Gene Roddenberry's approach to science fiction. Gene's vision of the future has always included minorities—not just blacks, but Asians and Hispanics as well. He's saying that unless we learn to cooperate as a species, we won't be able to make it to the twenty-fourth century. I think that by projecting that image, we're actually creating a reality for today."

Philosophy has long been an interest of LeVar Burton. At thirteen he entered a Catholic seminary, with the ultimate goal of becoming a priest. But after two years he discovered an interest in existentialism and by fifteen was reading Lao-Tzu, Kierkegaard, and Nietzsche.

"I began to wonder how I fit into the grand scheme of things. The more I thought about it, the less sense it made that the dogma of Catholicism was the be-all, end-all, of the universe," Burton explains. Following what Burton describes as his "pragmatic search," comparing the things he did well with the things that excited him about being a priest, he decided to pursue an acting career.

"What attracted me to the priesthood was the opportunity to move people, to provide something essential. I was drawn by the elements of history and magic. As a priest, you live beyond the boundaries of the normal existence. It's like joining an elite club. You see, it's not that different from acting, even the Mass is a play, combining these elements of mystery and spectacle."

## NIGHT AND DAY

After he left the seminary, Burton won a scholarship to USC, where he began working toward a degree in drama and fine arts. But the contrast between the sedate, introspective life in a small-town seminary and the USC campus, which he calls "Blond Central," was startling. "I'd never had so much freedom, and it was difficult to concentrate the first year." It was during his sophomore year at USC, while only nineteen, that he auditioned and landed the pivotal role of the young Kunta Kinte in the award-winning miniseries *Roots.*

"I think the producers had exhausted all the normal means of finding professional talent and were beating the bushes at the drama schools," the actor ventures. The role would win him an Emmy nomination and subsequent acting roles, which prevented his return to college.

Burton starred in a number of made-for-TV movies, such as the Emmy-nominated *Dummy; One in a Million: The Ron LeFlore Story; Grambling's White Tiger; The Guyana Tragedy: The Story of Jim Jones; Battered; Billy: Portrait of a Street Kid,* and the miniseries *Liberty.* The actor has also been the host of PBS's highly acclaimed children's series *Reading Rainbow* since its inception in 1983. Among his film credits are *Looking For Mr. Goodbar, The Hunter* (with Steve McQueen), and *The Supernaturals* (with Nichelle Nichols).

The actor was born in Landsthul, West Germany, where his father was a photographer in the Signal Corps, Third Armored Division. His mother was first an educator, then for years a social worker who is currently working in administration for the County of Sacramento Department of Mental Health. Burton is single and resides in Los Angeles with his German shepherd, Mozart.

# SECURITY CHIEF TASHA YAR

Tasha grew up on a failed Earth colony where law and order had broken down and the survival of the fittest became the order of the day. An orphan, she spent her nights and days foraging for food and fleeing the roving rape gangs. The colony broke down due to being comprised largely of renegades and other violent undesirables who were being given a second chance. Instead, violence ruled. A sample of what life there was like was briefly seen in "The Naked Now," while later developments were seen in the episode entitled "Legacy."

In her teens, Tasha escaped to Earth, leaving behind a sister who remained by choice, and discovered Starfleet. She worshiped the order and discipline of Starfleet because it was the exact opposite of the chaos she grew up fighting.

At the age of twenty-eight, she achieved the rank of security chief and was handpicked by Captain

Picard. She was one of the few crew members who performed the same duties on and off the ship. When an Away Team was selected to investigate a landing site, whether for a possible shore leave or for a conference that Captain Picard was being called to attend, Yar, as Security Chief, was always a part of the initial contact team.

The young security chief satisfied her need for peace and order in her chosen occupation, and held the Starfleet officers embodying this quality of devotion to duty and decency in the highest possible regard. She came close to worshiping them. This is particularly true in her attitude toward the commanding officers of the *Enterprise*. In her youth, figures of authority had been brutal and deadly.

Captain Picard, having visited Tasha's homeworld—her "hell planet"—understood what she went through and became her mentor. He taught her to apply the cushioning of history and philosophy to her almost obsessive need to protect the vessel and crew.

## TOUGH AND BEAUTIFUL

Natasha was of Ukrainian descent. This, combined with her own strict exercise regimen, gave her a quality of conditioned, subtle beauty that would have flabbergasted males from earlier centuries. With fire in her eyes and a muscularly well-toned and very female body, she was capable of pinning most crewmen. She was also an exciting sensual and intellectual challenge to men who enjoyed full equality between the genders. Neither Number One nor Picard was blind to these qualities in Tasha, but she could never bring herself to view these "saints" as mere mortals.

In "The Naked Now," Tasha revealed a previously concealed interest in Data. She even went so far as to take him into her quarters and seduce him! When the judgment-inhibiting effects wore off, Tasha realized that she had completely violated her personal sense of decorum, and told the literal-minded android, "It never happened." Since she didn't specify what "it" was, Data was a bit confused as to what, exactly, had never occurred.

Tasha's death at the hands of the creature Armus was a senseless tragedy that left her comrades stunned and bereaved. Oddly enough, it seems to be the emotionless Data who cherishes her memory the most; he keeps a holographic snapshot of her among his most cherished possessions.

The *Enterprise* crew later encountered Ishara Yar, Tasha's sister, when they went to rescue a Federation freighter's crew from captivity on Tasha's hellish homeworld. She reminded them of Tasha, but she was using them to get help for her political faction. Perhaps she was as capable of loyalty and friendship as Tasha, but Ishara's loyalties were bound up in the ongoing struggle of her world, and she lacked the courage to turn her back on the chaos and follow her sister's path.

In "Yesterday's Enterprise," a temporal anomaly gave Tasha a chance to die a meaningful death, sacrificing herself to go back to a certain doom in order to restore reality to its proper balance. As it turned out, the doom, while certain, was somewhat delayed.

In the fourth-season cliffhanger "Redemption I," we see a Romulan commander who looks exactly like Tasha Yar. In "Redemption II," we learn that the woman's name is Sela and Tasha Yar was her mother. In this alternate timeline, Tasha Yar had been captured by the Romulans due to the events set in motion in "Yesterday's Enterprise" and taken as a Romulan's wife. Sela was her daughter from that union. When Tasha attempted to flee Romulus with her young daughter, they were stopped and Tasha was executed. Sela does not miss her mother and believes that Tasha deserved her fate.

## DENISE CROSBY

Denise Crosby described the character she played with this thumbnail sketch: "She comes from an incredibly violent and aggressive Earth colony where life was a constant battle for survival. She can fight and she knows her job, but she has no family, is emotionally insecure, and somehow feels that she doesn't quite belong on this ship of seemingly perfect people."

As the granddaughter of the late legendary crooner Bing Crosby, Denise enjoyed the part and even related to it to some extent. "My grandfather was a Hollywood legend. Growing up with that wasn't exactly normal or typical either, and I think that helps me understand Tasha's imbalance and insecurities," explained the actress in a first-season interview.

Prior to getting involved in developing an acting career, Denise went through what she describes as her "European runway model thing. I hated modeling, but I was taken to Europe by three California designers who were trying to launch their fashions there. I loved London, so I just stayed on."

When she returned home for the Christmas holidays, she was almost tapped for an acting role. "Toni Howard was casting a movie called *Diary of a Teenage Hitchhiker* and had seen my picture in a magazine. I looked wild. My hair was about a quarter of an inch all the way around. I wore army fatigues and no makeup." While she didn't land that role, Toni Howard encouraged her to enroll in acting classes. The roles soon followed.

Her feature film credits include *48 Hours, Arizona Heat, The Eliminators, The Man Who Loved Women, Trail of the Pink Panther*, and *Miracle Mile*.

The TV credits for Denise also include *L.A. Law,*

*Days of Our Lives, The Flash,* and the made-for-TV movies *O'Hara, Stark, Malice in Wonderland,* and *Cocaine: One Man's Poison.*

Denise has also appeared in some local Los Angeles theater productions, including the critically well-received *Tamara,* in which she had the lead, as well as the controversial one-act play *Stops Along the Way,* directed by Richard Dreyfuss.

Needless to say, Denise Crosby reprised her role as Tasha Yar in "Yesterday's Enterprise," and returned to the show in its fifth season. The form this character took was revealed in the final episode of the fourth season, "Redemption I." A clue about this occurs in the episode "The Mind's Eye" in which Denise Crosby plays one of the Romulans on the ship that kidnaps Geordi, although her identity in "The Mind's Eye" is obscured unless you look closely. In the fifth season Denise Crosby turned up periodically, such as in "Redemption II," and "Unification I & II," in the latter appearing with Leonard Nimoy in his guest-starring role of Spock. She is one of the few *Next Generation* regulars to ever play opposite Leonard Nimoy or appear with Mr. Spock.

# GUINAN

The mysterious Guinan serves exotic drinks and meals in Ten Forward, but her most important role seems to be that of counselor, as she is also a fount of wisdom, giving advice and support, sometimes unsolicited but always needed, to members of the *Enterprise* crew. She has Captain Picard's complete trust, as when she alone sensed that something was amiss when the time lines shifted in "Yesterday's Enterprise" and Picard believed her. Their shared background has never been revealed. In "The Best of Both Worlds," she says that she was "more than family and more than a friend" to Picard, and elsewhere it is revealed that the two met before the *Enterprise*-D was commissioned ("Time's Arrow, I and II").

What is known is that Guinan is thousands of years old, and that her homeworld was destroyed by the Borg and her people dispersed. She was not there at the time, however, and did not witness the destruction. She is an old nemesis of Q, who obviously fears her. She undoubtedly possesses powers that have never been revealed. Her encounter with Q, two centuries ago, is another mystery, deepened by Q's revelation that she wore a different form at that time. Supposedly, her relationship with Q has something to do with her presence on the *Enterprise*, but, as usual, revelations about the character only deepen the mystery that surrounds her.

More about Guinan's background was revealed in "Time's Arrow," the fifth-season cliffhanger. Here we learned that she had met Data and other *Enterprise* personnel hundreds of years before on Earth in San Francisco in the nineteenth century. She has kept silent about this incident, never speaking of it until she urged Captain Picard himself to pursue Data, who was lost in the past, because his presence was necessary there, as she knew this to be a fact.

Still, to most crew members who encounter her, Guinan is the twenty-fourth-century equivalent of the classic bartender, who not only serves up just the right variety of synthehol, but also lends a caring ear and freely gives a touch of humane wisdom wherever and whenever it is called for.

## WHOOPI GOLDBERG

Whoopi Goldberg describes her character Guinan as "a cross between Yoda and William F. Buckley," but freely admits that she's put a lot of herself into the role as well. Growing up in New York, young Whoopi was inspired by the harmonious message of the original *Star Trek*, and especially by Nichelle Nichols.

When Goldberg learned that her friend LeVar Burton would be on a new *Star Trek* series, she asked him to tell Gene Roddenberry that she wanted to be on the program, too—but the producers of *The Next Generation* thought he was joking. A year later,

Goldberg took matters into her own hands and contacted Gene Roddenberry; the two worked together to create the mysterious alien bartender who runs Ten Forward, a popular gathering place for the crew of the *Enterprise.*

Although Whoopi's first showbiz experience took place at the age of eight, there was a large gap in her career as she raised a child and, at one time, contended with a heroin addiction. She worked at a variety of jobs, including one in a funeral parlor whose owner had a curious sense of humor, and "initiated" his employees by hiding in a body bin and playing "zombie," scaring them witless in the process. Whoopi was not amused.

By the time the 1980s rolled around, however, she was active in theater and comedy, working in southern California with the San Diego Repertory Theater and putting on a number of one-woman shows. (She also washed dishes at the Big Kitchen restaurant, where the menu still carries a special named after her.) In 1985 she got her big break, in Steven Spielberg's film of *The Color Purple,* in a role that earned her an Oscar nomination and the Golden Globe Award. Since then she has starred in *Jumpin' Jack Flash, Burglar, Fatal Beauty, Clara's Heart,* and *Homer and Eddie.*

Her role as psychic Oda Mae in *Ghost* netted her the Oscar for Best Supporting Actress, and she continues to work in such films as *The Long Walk Home* (with Sissy Spacek), *Soapdish,* the hit film *Sister Act,* and *Corrina, Corrina.* She won an Emmy for her 1986 guest appearance on *Moonlighting,* and starred in the CBS sitcom *Baghdad Cafe* with Jean Stapleton.

She is concerned with the plight of our nation's homeless and has, with Robin Williams and Billy Crystal, been a prime force behind the annual Comic Relief benefit concerts. In 1989, her various charity projects resulted in her being named the Starlight Foundation's Humanitarian of the Year.

Still active on stage, Goldberg has performed in *Moms, The Spook Show,* and *Living on the Edge of Chaos,* as well as returning to the San Diego Repertory Theater, a.k.a. The Rep, to take part in fund-raising performances (along with Patrick Stewart) for that organization.

Goldberg continued to reveal new aspects of Guinan in *The Next Generation,* but, as always, each new revelation only raised more questions than it answered—and that's the way Whoopi Goldberg likes it.

CHAPTER

# THE NEXT GENERATION *OVERVIEW*

*In 1987 something controversial was done.* Star Trek *was brought back to weekly television, as* Star Trek: The Next Generation, *without any of the familiar faces who had graced the name since 1966. Now, seven years later, it has graduated to the big screen, but how did this series fare in quality over those seven years?*

# SEASON ONE

During the first year of *The Next Generation*, Gene Roddenberry was asked what he thought of the scripts for the show, and if he felt it was really working out. The creator of the show replied, "We got some good writing in the old series, and we've had some good writing in the new series. Most of the writing comes from a very few, very good people who labor hard, and very often they are staff people."

May of 1988 saw the broadcast of the final original episode of the first year of *Star Trek: The Next Generation*. While it went into reruns and fans caught up with episodes they had missed, it was possible to sit back and look at all twenty-five stories and see how they shaped up. One could determine what patterns could be seen which perhaps weren't apparent at the time an episode first aired and judge just how the year of stories held up.

While an average TV series sets up a premise and repeats it week after week, with little variation in character or structure, *ST: TNG* was not your average show. With an ensemble cast, on a superficial level it could be compared with shows like *Hill Street Blues*, *St. Elsewhere*, or *L.A. Law*, where we could see many characters vying for attention as the series sought to achieve balance. Early on it seemed that while all the characters were getting some attention, it didn't always hold together, as though they needed a focal point. This was finally achieved when Picard and Riker emerged as the main characters, filling out enough so that shows spotlighted them, sometimes to the virtual exclusion of the other cast members (such as in the first year's "11001001").

## THE GROWTH OF *THE NEXT GENERATION*

This series surpassed the original *Star Trek* in the sheer number of episodes, and shows an evolution much different from that found in the *Star Trek* of the sixties. While the first season of the original show is considered the best, with the second a close second and the third a distant third, the opposite has occurred in *Star Trek: The Next Generation*. This series has had growing pains, but grew appreciably better each season.

However, things got off to a rocky start.

The series started off with episodes that were often fair to mediocre, until by the end of the first year, it felt as if one had reexperienced the third season of the old *Star Trek*, when the episodes lurched around in strange directions as though searching for a focal point. Amid the chaos, the first season of *ST: TNG* did manage to produce a handful of gems out of the otherwise undistinguished first cluster. At the time many fans refused to acknowledge this and vociferously defended the new series, but looking back now from the point of view of a hundred and seventy-eight episodes, the weakness of the writing for most of the first year is quite apparent.

## ENCOUNTER AT FARPOINT

The series was launched with the two-hour story "Encounter at Farpoint." Originally written by D. C. Fontana, it was rewritten by Roddenberry and expanded to include the character of Q. This is apparent simply from the internal structure of the episode as there are two parallel stories which are forced to touch at only one point. Q was obviously a character Roddenberry liked very much, but the sad fact is that this omnipotent alien, who was a virtual clone of Trelane, the "child" being in the original *Star Trek* episode "Squire of Gothos," didn't work and wasn't written well at all until his third outing, in the second-season episode "Q Who?," which also introduced the Borg.

Launching the series with a much ballyhooed two-hour adventure was a good idea. Unfortunately the script wasn't entirely up to the challenge. The story careened back and forth between two virtually unrelated plotlines—the intervention of the obnoxious, self-important Q and the mystery at Farpoint Station. When I later learned that Fontana had written a script dealing with the Farpoint mystery and Roddenberry added the Q storyline himself and forced them together, I could see why I felt as I did when watching it. The story tried hard to introduce all the characters while really revealing little about them, other than Picard's willingness to surrender in situations where Kirk would have defied the odds in an attempt to depict Picard's more diplomatic and temperate nature.

Unfortunately, it forced a comparison that was

not in Picard's favor. The story introduced new ideas, such as families living on the *Enterprise*, and then demonstrated what a horrible idea that was when the ship had to perform a dangerous saucer separation to protect the families in the main vessel from threats by Q. While the ending with the interplanetary jellyfish was touching and wrought with some beautiful special effects, it seemed to be an attempt to distract us from what led up to it and leave us with a warm feeling about the show.

## THE NAKED NOW

In hindsight, the early episodes of the first season show a distinct lack of direction and forethought. The second show, "The Naked Now," is an acknowledged remake of the original *Star Trek* episode "The Naked Time," in order to give the characters some dimension, unfortunately forcing a direct comparison between the two episodes: the strengths of the original story cause it to far outweigh its reworking in *The Next Generation*.

"The Naked Now" was written by J. Michael Bingham, from a story by John D. F. Black and J. Michael Bingham. Black worked on the original *Star Trek* episode "The Naked Time," but while the original story examined hidden motives, with many of the character traits revealed having dramatic as well as tragic overtones, the sequel carried little of the original's sense of drama. The characters in "The Naked Now" don't act uninhibited, but simply irrational.

Some of the actors on the show, such as Jonathan Frakes, felt that it was too early to have the characters act out of character since the viewers still weren't sure who the characters were. The point of "The Naked Time" was never to have characters act strangely but rather to have them reveal what they are really like inside and the extent of their private demons. In this way, the characters were to be broadened and deepened through a lack of inhibitions. In "The Naked Now," they acted crazy.

## A QUESTION OF HONOR

The third episode, "Code Of Honor," has structural elements from "Amok Time" in both the climactic fight and its resolution. Using Arabian Nights-style costuming and an all-black culture is an interesting idea for the episode, particularly the matriarchal angle (which would repeat in "Angel One"), but it's sacrificed to stage a fight that has obvious parallels with "Amok Time" in the resolution as the one who dies is revived aboard the *Enterprise*.

Picard makes a lot of angry noise over the kidnaping of his security chief, but in the end seems impotent to really accomplish anything. Why he must follow the alien culture's bizarre protocol while they can flagrantly violate the Federation's at will without reprisal is unclear. In this writer's opinion, the story played like a first-draft script in need of several rewrites.

## ENTER THE FERENGI

Since the Klingons are now in the Federation (just as the Organians predicted in "Errand of Mercy"), a new villain was called for, or so someone thought. The villain must be vile and despicable, but maybe a bit amusing as well. Enter the Ferengi, the midget merchants of space; capitalists of the lowest order. In "The Last Outpost" another old plot is borrowed, this time from "Arena," when a superior alien intelligence sees the *Enterprise* and another vessel bent on combat and renders both of them helpless so that he can see what the personnel aboard the ship are really like and learn who the true aggressor is. Just as Kirk refused to see the Gorn destroyed when he triumphed, Riker turns down the offer to have the Ferengi ship destroyed after he triumphs intellectually.

This episode introduces the Ferengi, who were intended to be the villains to replace the Klingons. That didn't quite work out, did it? In the many episodes made since, they've returned several times, and each time they have been diminished in menace until they were reduced to annoyances at the bargaining table. In the sixth-season episode "Rascals," when some Ferengi attempt to steal the *Enterprise*, the characters had been so diminished by then that it was difficult to take them seriously. Due to their small stature and interchangeable personalities, they became dull quickly. Only with the introduction of Quark on *Deep Space Nine* and in the sixth-season episode "Suspicion" have the Ferengi been explored in more detail and become marginally more interesting overall.

## TO BEYOND AND BACK

"Where No One Has Gone Before" is interesting because none of its elements can be traced back to any of the original *Star Trek* episodes of the sixties. No distracting subplots, just the *Enterprise* hurling itself across the universe to realms humans could not reach in centuries at normal warp speeds. Eric Menyuk as the alien is effective in that he underplays his character as though hinting at gulfs of mystery left unspoken and unexplored. We are left wanting to know more and yet finding him interesting for what we do know.

His interest in Wesley is touching, particularly in what he reveals to Picard. This story deals with some gentle ideas as well as some grandiose special effects. This episode was supposedly rewritten drastically, but somehow that resulted in an interesting story that is better than the four that preceded it.

This was the first story to attempt to elevate Wesley Crusher in importance. Here it was handled well, as is the strange voyage of the *Enterprise* to realms where it should ordinarily take a starship three hundred years to reach. A good story, but a first-season fluke in comparison to so many others from this period. Ideas introduced in it would ultimately be resolved in the season seven episode "Journey's End."

## AN ALIEN AMONG US

"Lonely Among Us" again features ideas from the first series that force unneeded comparisons. The *Enterprise* is transporting two feuding delegations of aliens (remember "Journey To Babel"?). It's all they can do to keep them apart, particularly when one faction is carnivorous and considers the other to be suitable prey. Rather than exploring this further, these aliens remain as a subplot while the main plot shifts to a disembodied alien entity that gets aboard when the ship passes through a strange cloud. The presence of the alien ambassadors primarily serves as a juxtaposition to demonstrate the different kinds of aliens present in the universe: the one that accidentally gets aboard and finally takes over Picard's body apologizes for all the problems it caused, while the ambassadors aboard the *Enterprise* remain belligerent and uncooperative.

The mystery angle as the entity moves from one person to another is well handled. An interesting side note is that a scene in the briefing room shows a model of the *Galileo 7* in the background—the original special effects model of the shuttlecraft used in the sixties series. The model had been unearthed by Paramount and restored by model-maker Greg Jein.

Later, this story of an alien entity that steals aboard the *Enterprise* and causes problems will become an old standby plot device as the series progresses.

## A KIND OF JUSTICE

"Justice" explores the nature of justice and whether a

law is correct just because everyone in a given society supports it. What seems odd is that a landing party would wander so freely, embarking on shore leave on a world where the society has not been strictly charted by the Federation. Laws and customs can vary widely and wildly from country to country on Earth, so another world can have pitfalls of protocol undreamed of, which is just what happens here.

When Wesley accidentally falls on some plants in an area marked off-limits, he's promptly arrested and prepared for execution. We're expected to believe that this is a society that prizes friendship and physical pleasure very highly, and yet allows friends and lovers to be eliminated for even the slightest infraction. That may make it a society with no crime, but the fear quotient must be incredibly high. Picard's defense of justice in the face of an unseen, all-powerful ruling entity is well handled, but we have to wonder what kind of entity allows its subjects to be killed for non-violent, victimless crimes. The people themselves cannot defend their position with any eloquence except to say that it prevents crime and anarchy.

However naive and simple the portrayal of the alien culture is, it demonstrates that drastic differences in perceptions of law and justice will continue to be found when dealing with alien societies. Had Wesley genuinely done something that would be considered bad, even by our standards, but which had been an accident or some other kind of mistake, it would have made the examination of the conflicts of justice a much more fascinating and complex one.

## RETURN OF THE *STARGAZER*

In "The Battle," since the Ferengi are cosmic capitalists to such a degree that profit is not only the bottom line but the only line, it's amusing to see their astonishment when their commander presents Picard with the spaceship *Stargazer* as a gift. Gifts are obviously alien to their culture. The rest of the story is a standard revenge plot in which the Ferengi commander blames Picard for the death of the Ferengi's son.

The most interesting part of the episode is where Picard relates the tale of the battle the *Stargazer* had with a mystery ship, which would have been more interesting had it been shown in flashback rather than re-created in the present as a hallucination of a mentally dominated Picard. The whole story just doesn't hang together, particularly when a different record of the battle is found aboard the *Stargazer* that seems to implicate Picard in piracy. What's never dealt with is why the Ferengi commander, Bok, blames Picard when the records aboard the *Stargazer* prove that Picard was attacked for no reason and was just defending himself. Bok had to alter these records in order to make Picard look like the aggressor. He knows that his son caused his own death by his hostile actions. Maybe the Ferengi think it's bad form to defend oneself against them?

In this episode we're still supposed to be impressed by the Ferengi as villains. This one is better written than "The Last Outpost," as it is the only time the Ferengi are shown having different points of view among themselves until they are featured on *Deep Space Nine* several years later. This story is slightly above average in some respects, particularly in the background it gives on Picard.

## Q AGAIN

Just like "Encounter at Farpoint," this episode, "Hide and Q," comes across as two stories that each work independently of the other. The opening, in which the main characters find themselves battling foes assembled against them by Q on another planet, has nothing to do with the last half, in which Riker accepts Q's gift of ultimate power, but must learn to use it wisely. Although supposedly from a superior culture, Q again comes across as a playmate of Trelane (who romped through "Squire of Gothos" in the original *Star Trek*). Even John deLancie labels this as the worst of the Q episodes.

Riker is given tremendous powers by Q, but only the obvious and the illogical happens as a result. One good scene is when Riker has promised not to use his powers and as a result doesn't bring a child back to life, which he could have done, both accepting the consequences of keeping his word and showing a well-realized emotional response.

## ENTER LWAXANA

In *Star Trek*'s pilot episode "The Cage," Majel Barrett played Number One. In the original *Star Trek* series she played Nurse Chapel. Then, in the newest incarnation of *Star Trek* she turned up as the obnoxious mother of Deanna Troi in "Haven." At least no one can accuse her of playing her characters the same way, because they're all quite different. Unfortunately the plot of Troi being pushed into an arranged marriage dominates the episode while the most interesting part of the story plays a distant second.

Wyatt, Troi's betrothed, has for years been executing drawings of his "dream woman." He's never met Troi, but he believed she was the woman he'd been drawing for so long. However, Deanna turns out to be very different looking from his drawings, and when Wyatt instead sees his dream woman on a plague ship carrying the last few survivors from a colony on a distant planet, he wastes little time in beaming over, thus abruptly ending the wedding plot.

By the end of the first season, the producers learned to concentrate on one storyline and develop it to its full potential, but they hadn't learned that hard lesson yet when they created "Haven." Majel Barrett comes aboard for the beginning of her recurring role as Troi's mother, Lwaxana Troi, but unfortunately she's played primarily for laughs.

## HOLODECK SECRETS

"The Big Goodbye" was the first of the big holodeck stories and it won a Peabody Award, although much better episodes have been done since without garnering any such attention at all. This is a good story, although inexplicably *TV Guide* criticized it for being derivative of "A Piece of the Action" (from the original *Star Trek*) just weeks before it garnered the Peabody Award for originality! What makes it a standout is the idea of the holodeck creating personalities who may well have a life of their own, an idea so ripe for further exploration that it would spawn two memorable sequels ("Elementary, Dear Data" and "Moriarty").

While the holodeck had been introduced in the premiere episode, this was the first time it was used as more than a background gimmick. This salute to hard-boiled detective fiction goes deeper than the superficial idea would at first suggest as it explores the concept that the holograms created by the holodeck might just have self-knowledge, personalities, and identities independent from their programming. This is hammered home when one of the *Enterprise* personnel suffers a real bullet wound and the other visitors to this "imaginary" setting are held captive.

When confronted with the reality (or lack thereof) of their existence, the holograms refuse to accept it, and two of them put it to the ultimate test and are destroyed, although the question is not addressed as to what would happen if the deck re-created these characters. This is a story worthy of the original *Star Trek* and it is one of the top five episodes of this first season.

## DATA'S EVIL TWIN

One of the best of *The Next Generation* episodes is followed by one of the weakest. Virtually every TV series of the past twenty years has done an "evil twin" story. It's become a television cliché and is seemingly treated as *de rigueur* by the story editors, if what we see on the tube is any evidence. People who satirize television invariably zero in on the evil twin syndrome: it's considered common fodder for humor.

When the coming attractions for "Datalore" referred to the character as "Data's evil twin," I laughed out loud, but unfortunately this episode is no joke. The story has all the depth of imagination of an episode of *Land of the Giants*.

The strength of this episode is that it returns to the planet where Data was found and reveals more about his origin. The original writer's guide had Data having been created by aliens, but here it is revealed that an old scientist, Dr. Noonian Soong, built him. Again Roddenberry was forgetting his past as he'd already created a character on the original *Star Trek* named "Khan Noonian Singh," who even returned in the big-screen outing *The Wrath of Khan*. If you can't borrow from yourself, whom can you borrow from? Thankfully, the subsequent writers and producers on *The Next Generation* have only used Lore with great restraint, and then in stories that avoided all the evil twin clichés, almost as though they were embarrassed by how the character had been introduced. "Brothers" in season four is interesting, but then Lore vanished again until the climax of season six.

## PLANET OF THE AMAZONS

Science fiction has its own clichés. The matriarchal society is one of them. This one wasn't done in the sixties because of network censorship—they would have found the idea too disturbing. Women subjugating men? Roddenberry did explore the subject in the seventies TV movie *Planet Earth* and it's explored again in "Angel One," with a few differences. While the men in this culture are portrayed as weaker, the female ruling class are not Amazons by any means, which is one cliché avoided. The story is rather thin, as survivors of a star freighter accident have been living on that world for seven years and have found women who prefer strong men to the souls who cringe and bow before the ruling class. This has created an underclass who oppose the matriarchal society and want to exist separately from it, something those in charge find abhorrent and threatening. Finally the ruler demonstrates she has compassion and spares the men and their wives from execution, exiling them to a region where they can live in peace without disturbing the status quo too much.

"Angel One" is another script where the *Enterprise* is placed in jeopardy; this time a plague sweeps through the crew, as opposed to the crew being in jeopardy from a shipwide power loss, as in "Justice." This type of plot device continued to crop up as Gene Roddenberry believed for the first few seasons that every episode had to place the *Enterprise* in jeopardy.

## 11001001—NOT BY THE NUMBERS AT ALL

"11001001" is a very good episode that combines an interesting plot about the theft of the *Enterprise* (for a unique reason) with a further exploration of the advantages of the holodeck, and the two tie together very neatly. This is a very fast-paced story that has a great idea—get rid of everyone on the *Enterprise* so that Picard and Riker are the only characters left in the story from the regular cast. Stripped down to using just two characters, the story works very well. The Bynars (aliens who work in twos, tied to their computer culture) are interesting and better than most any of the other new aliens seen in the first season.

This episode combines the oft-repeated "things aren't always what they seem" motif by revealing the intentions of the aliens to be strictly benevolent. A good added touch is that the aliens actually return to Starfleet to answer for their crimes. The relationship between Riker and the hologram, Minuet, is very interesting: we feel Riker's sense of loss when she is gone from the computer banks along with the rest of the information the Bynars had stored there.

This is an action-adventure story with an interesting idea behind it and even a new twist on the holodeck. Until now the scripts seemed determined to give everyone equal time, but with the story concentrating on Riker and Picard, these two finally emerge as the strong characters they are. This episode clearly marked a turning point in the first season, and life (and scripts) was never the same again for the rest of the supporting cast.

## TOO SHORT A STORY

Somewhere in "Too Short a Season" is the germ of a good idea, but it is buried under the acting of Clayton Rohner as Admiral Jameson. Instead of a story about a man who takes an overdose of a youth drug for reasons other than the threat he's called upon to face, we get a morality tale about an aging statesman who must face the war he caused with his betrayal of a people forty-five years before. The old-age makeup for Jameson is terrible, and the actor's portrayal of an old man is a parody.

When Jameson and his old nemesis finally come face-to-face, there is no strident debate of principles or fiery oratory—because Jameson drops dead on the spot. This comes across as something that was rushed into production to fill the slot.

## AND SEVEN SHALL SAVE THEM?

The effective story "When the Bough Breaks" has its logic undermined by budgetary considerations. When an ancient, and now sterile, race needs children to continue, they kidnap children from the *Enterprise* to perpetuate their species. The difference in cultural values is handled quite well when the Aldeans find nothing morally wrong with the concept of trading goods or services for children and are annoyed that Picard finds the concept repugnant.

When the children are kidnapped, clearly less than a dozen are taken, hardly enough to perpetuate an entire race. Since the people seem to plan to reproduce the old-fashioned way, it would take decades just for the seven to produce children who would have children, and by that time everyone else who had been alive on the planet before them would have died.

It would have made more sense to kidnap healthy adults to obtain what is needed, but that wouldn't have been as dramatic and emotionally volatile as stealing children. This episode also grandly points up the flaw in the concept of having entire families on the *Enterprise,* since it is so easy to strike at the least defensive members and thus force the ship to do the kidnapper's bidding.

## A TINY PROBLEM

"Home Soil" has the series going into a new area for TV science fiction as it explores the concept of terraforming—using scientific means to alter a planet's atmosphere and chemical balances to make it habitable by (in this case) humans. Is there something similar done by other races that would alter class-M planets into something humans wouldn't find very comfortable? It isn't brought up here. The dynamics of the story depend on the terraformers being so devoted to what they're doing that years into the project they deliberately avoid signs that mistakes were made when the world was scouted and ruled sterile of all indigenous life forms.

It's a good science fiction mystery story, although having the simple colony form of life turn out to be intelligent and capable of communication seems to take it too far to avoid any ethical arguments over whether the project should be halted due to a collection of what would otherwise amount to organized amoebas. By making them intelligent, the questions raised are all reduced to black-and-white extremes. Still, it's an episode that explores interesting ideas in an unspectacular manner.

## FINAL EXAM

"Coming of Age" is an episode focusing on Wesley in which he doesn't save the *Enterprise* from destruction. The scenes with the Starfleet entry program are interesting, although they beg the question of why people obviously this talented are winnowed down to just one candidate. The others are obviously possessed of their own remarkable skills as well. The scene in which Wesley undergoes his "psyche" test, in which he faces his deepest fear, is quite well done; we're left wondering about the deepest fears of the other candidates. Questions we may have had about past episodes are dealt with head-on when Picard is investigated for past decisions he made, including the one in "Justice" that appeared to violate the Prime Directive.

This episode attempts to broaden Wesley's character again in an effective story. The series was improving at this point, and this is a good episode with a strong emotional undertone that elevates it above typical TV science fiction fare. Roddenberry claimed to have rewritten the first dozen episodes of *The Next Generation*, but it is only once we're past that largely unfortunate group that things start looking up. Only "The Big Goodbye" emerged as a carefully written script in that first dozen, and it is stylistically completely different from the other early episodes.

## THE KLINGON WAY

"Heart of Glory" is by far the best episode of the first season. Worf had been largely just a fixture on the bridge up to this point, given one or two good lines per episode or one interesting scene, such as in "Hide And Q" when he confronts and rejects his own Klingon savage nature. In this episode, we learn that not only wasn't he raised among Klingons, but he has rarely associated with them. This contrast is made especially strong when he is confronted by two of his race who hearken back to the warlike days when the Klingon Empire and the Federation were at odds, and who wish those days to return. Had Worf encountered more diplomatic Klingons, the clash of wills would not have been so evident, if at all, but here the character is forced not only to deal with the difference between himself and these two members of his own race, but also with the vast cultural differences between himself and his fellow crewmen, who find that there is more to Worf than they would have imagined.

Interesting touches abound in this story, such as the intensely personal Klingon death howl, which is chilling to behold. The expressions on the faces of Worf's human friends as they witness this scene show their surprise and inner questioning better than any dialogue could. The Klingon throwbacks, in spite of being more like the villains of the original *Star Trek*, are shown to have dimension as well, such as when crewmen are arriving to arrest them and we think they are about to take a child hostage. The Klingons reveal that their sense of personal honor prevents them from warring on children. It's a very good scene, but then this episode has many good scenes.

A new classic, "Heart of Glory" is the standout episode of the first season as it explores the character of Worf in ways that are both powerful and moving. It brings out the previously unrealized potential in the character. Other Klingon episodes that have followed in subsequent seasons have each demonstrated how fascinating these characters can really be. The writing credits on this one go to Maurice Hurley for the script, based on a story by Maurice Hurley, Herb Wright, and D. C. Fontana.

## OPEN FOR BUSINESS

Following "Heart of Glory," almost anything would seem a poor second, but "Arsenal of Freedom" slips back to weaker scripting of earlier shows. The *Enterprise* investigates a planet and finds that everyone on the world has been annihilated by their own weapons systems; a rather obvious allegory. An Away Team is under attack, and the *Enterprise* can't help them due to being under fire itself from orbital systems.

The two parallel stories work, but there is a lack of emotional frisson. An entire planetary population has been destroyed, but we're not made to care for them as people. When Riker encounters a friend and discovers that it's just an imitation, he doesn't show any emotion over registering that this means that the real man must be dead. It's all very cool and by the numbers; action adventure without the necessary human equation to give it real impact.

Picard and Dr. Crusher seem to be approaching a strong moment when he learns that she had grown up in a colony that has a certain tragic history connected to it, but we never learn what that tragedy was.

## INTERPLANETARY PUSHERS

The episode "Symbiosis" is a twist on the drug addiction storylines common to television shows. In this case, an entire planet is addicted to a drug supplied by another world, but the addicts think the drug is "medicine" to prevent them from dying of an ancient plague. The deaths come from withdrawal symptoms. This rather simple story about one culture exploiting another purely for profit turns into a critique of runaway capitalism rather than the anti-drug story it was obviously intended to be. Even explanations about why drugs are bad can't change that the exploited people aren't using the drugs by choice. When the people take the drug and feel good, they believe it's because it's relieving the symptoms of the plague.

Although the people who need the drug are supposedly a scientifically advanced race and are trading technology for the drug, they somehow don't know how to fix their own spacecraft. If these people are so technologically advanced, how come no one ever explored the nature of the plague and learned the truth? While some interesting ideas are explored here, they are not fully resolved.

## EXIT TASHA YAR

"Skin of Evil" is the now well-known episode in which Tasha Yar first dies. The most surprising element in this story is that her death is handled as an aside; it is sudden and not built up to in any substantial way. Most of the story deals with Armus (a black blob creature) and how it torments Deanna Troi, who is trapped in a crashed shuttle. The best part is the funeral for Tasha Yar, in which her previously prepared holographic message says good-bye to those friends she loved. The story with Armus is minor and would have been better replaced by a story that really spotlighted Tasha, rather than seeming to kill her off as an afterthought in the opening minutes of the story.

"Skin of Evil" is really a story about an ancient villain marooned long ago on a planet, an idea repeated in *Star Trek* V: *The Final Frontier*. It's an average episode elevated by the funeral scene at the end of the story. Tasha's death is so offhand that it seems it was finally decided she deserved a better send-off, which she got in the episode "Yesterday's Enterprise" two years later.

## WE'LL ALWAYS HAVE CLICHÉS

We'll always have cliché lines used as story titles on television shows. In "We'll Always Have Paris," Picard and the crew experience momentary time distortions traced to a remote outpost that is conducting dangerous experiments. Picard's old girlfriend is there, which causes him to go to the holodeck to relive a favorite locale in Paris.

The plot involving experiments in nonlinear time is so interesting that you don't need Picard's old girlfriend. The paradoxes are handled in an interesting manner, particularly the scenes in which Data is sent in to do what only he could accomplish. This story spotlights Data in a far more interesting and dramatic fashion than anything in "Datalore." The imagination quotient in this story is quite high and handled so well that the subplot with Picard and Mrs. Manheim doesn't even intrude, but rather forms a relaxing aftermath to the conflict.

"We'll Always Have Paris" is highly entertaining and better than average, even though it is largely an action-adventure episode. Some of these later first-year episodes demonstrate even more solid plotting and complete exploration of scripting possibilities.

## EXPLODING HEADS

This action-adventure episode is so intense it's genuinely scary at times. "Conspiracy" caught some fans by surprise because *TNG* had been playing it pretty safe until this point and seemingly going out of its way to avoid doing anything that anyone would find even remotely disturbing. Then along comes this episode, in which Roddenberry allows the show to depart greatly from his "I never met an alien I didn't like" philosophy and introduces a nasty race of parasitic creatures who like to crawl inside humans through the mouth and control their bodies to undermine and ultimately control Starfleet and the entire Federation.

The slow discovery of this plot begins as Picard is called to a secret meeting by an old friend, and it builds the suspense layer upon layer until we know that it is building up to one strange climax—and it doesn't let us down. Employing state-of-the-art make-up effects, a man controlled by the queen alien is eviscerated before our eyes in a scene that no doubt sent some light-hearted viewers screaming from the room. There is a tangible sense of immediacy, and the graphic violence shown in the climax is startling considering how timid the series had been in that regard until this point.

While at heart this is an old-fashioned alien invasion story, it has a tight plot, inner tension, and a sense that the characters are involved in something life-threatening. This mood of impending destruction has only rarely been attempted since, most notably in "The Best of Both Worlds" and "Yesterday's Enterprise."

## THE ROMULANS RETURN

According to this episode, the Romulans have not been heard from for fifty years. Three twentieth-century humans are found in suspended animation, and the primary plot of "The Neutral Zone" deals with their revival and attempts to adjust to the twenty-fourth century. In shades of "Balance of Terror," there are also Federation outposts being mysteriously destroyed along the Romulan Neutral Zone, only this time it has nothing to do with the Romulans, who are also suffering similar losses and turn up at the end to do little more than announce that they're back and that they won't be hidden anymore.

*The Next Generation* version of a season cliffhanger and the abruptness at the end made it feel as if it was the first part of a two-part story. As it turned out, the elements introduced in this episode would only be followed up on in bits and pieces over the following two seasons, and only in "The Best of Both Worlds" at the end of season three would we understand what it all meant.

This season finale seems uneven because it introduces a mystery that is never specifically resolved. If the mysterious destruction of outposts in the Neutral Zone is being done by the Borg (as we might conclude from a reference in season two's episode "Q Who"), then why are we led to believe later that the Borg were unaware of the Federation until Q brought the *Enterprise* into contact with them? "The Neutral Zone" reintroduces the Romulans to spice things up since the Ferengi proved to be a flop in the villain department. The Romulans at least have some villainous dimensions that can be used as the Klingons were in the original *Star Trek*, and their subsequent appearances in season two and thereafter fill just that role.

# SEASON TWO

T*he Next Generation* didn't start entirely fresh with year two. The premiere episode, "The Child," was reworked from a script for the proposed but never accomplished *Star Trek II* television series which Paramount had been planning in 1977. That series would have featured most of the original cast, with the exception of Spock; Xon, a different Vulcan, would have been on the bridge in Spock's place. In order to work for *The Next Generation*, the script had to be completely rewritten to incorporate the new cast.

The second season of *TNG* was late out of the gate due to the protracted Writer's Guild strike which lasted through the summer of 1988. So rather than having their new season begin in September, which was the normal premiere time, the first new episode of year two didn't air until November. That fact didn't really stand out, though, because most other

TV series didn't begin new episodes that fall until October and November, either. While some series shoot a handful of episodes at the end of one season and hold them over to give them a jump start on the next season, most shows start in fresh. In the case of *TNG*, this meant waiting for the Writer's Guild strike to end during a time when the series would otherwise have been in full production.

That strike, which lasted several months, was quite controversial and resulted in a flood of allegations against producers for attempting to have scripts written during the time of the strike, in violation of industry regulations. Even when a contract expires, certain rules remain in effect. Writer's Guild members face stiff fines if they write for a producer during a strike, just as they would if they wrote for a producer who is not a signatory to the basic guild agreements.

One writer, Mel Gilden (who has since written *Star Trek* novels for Pocket Books), even announced on a radio show that he was supposedly approached by Paramount to pitch story ideas, which he agreed to do—after the strike was over. Gilden was never contacted by Paramount again. The guild investigated various charges of guild violations by Roddenberry and others, but nothing substantial was ever proven.

## AN ADEQUATE LAUNCH

When Gene Roddenberry decided that Gates McFadden just didn't fit as Dr. Beverly Crusher, he replaced her with a new doctor without a word of explanation. Dr. Pulaski was then replaced after the end of the second season, mostly because her character just wasn't written or developed very well, after being on hand to deliver Deanna Troi's baby in this season two opener.

The reworked *Star Trek II* script, which retained its original title of "The Child," deals with an alien entity impregnating Troi in order to experience life in a human body. The child in question matures rapidly, finally dying after a few days because the alien had experienced all it needed. Unfortunately this child is still Troi's son as far as she's concerned, even if the pregnancy and birth took place over a matter of hours rather than months. When her human son dies because the alien has to abandon the body, it's no less wrenching for Troi. Because the alien looks like a cute young boy, it's supposed to be wrenching for the audience as well.

The second episode, "Where Silence Has Lease," has the *Enterprise* caught in a featureless void where it races back and forth trying to get out while an alien entity manipulates events to experience what the crew feels. It's a big special effects extravaganza.

"Elementary, Dear Data," the following episode, is sort of a sequel to "The Big Goodbye," wherein the holodeck gets an extraordinary workout. Data has the holodeck create Professor Moriarty and then gives him all the android's knowledge to create a worthy adversary. The only problem is that now the hologram of Moriarty knows it's a hologram and is determined to hold on to its existence at any price. It's an interesting story that stands up to repeated viewing. Amazingly, it would be four years before this excellent episode spawned a direct sequel.

## MIXED BLESSINGS

"The Outrageous Okona" is when Data creates Joe Piscopo on the holodeck to teach him how to tell jokes. The problem is that they also needed someone to teach Joe Piscopo how to tell jokes, and to get better material. That's only the subplot, but the main plot is even more dull and not worth recounting.

"Loud as a Whisper" features a real deaf-mute actor in the role of a deaf-mute Federation negotiator. The story presents a fresh idea but doesn't do much with it and depends on the originality of the idea itself for the script.

"The Schizoid Man" is one of the strongest second-season episodes and demonstrated the solid writing the series was becoming more and more adept at producing. When a brilliant cyberneticist, who modestly admits to having taught Data's creator everything he knew, transfers his persona into the android, an interesting tale is the result. Although the scientist is initially portrayed as an arrogant buffoon, his true humanity saves Data in the end, rather than anything Picard and the others do. This is a good story.

"Unnatural Selection" is a quick reworking of the old "Deadly Years" story. The episode is the only one that features Dr. Pulaski as a major character as opposed to a minor character. It may have been about this time that Roddenberry started reconsidering his decision to replace Dr. Crusher.

## TOUGH VOYAGING

"A Matter of Honor" is by far the best second-season episode. When Riker is transferred to a Klingon ship as part of an exchange program, personality clashes and vivid portrayals of life aboard a Klingon ship are the result. Great stuff! This is the second of this series' Klingon episodes, all of which are top of the line material. "A Matter of Honor" demonstrates the conflict that can be lost by having everyone aboard the *Enterprise* so gracious to each other all the time.

"The Measure of a Man" is another well-written

entry as the matter of Data's humanity is explored in depth from a legal standpoint. When an aggressive and overbearing Federation officer wants to disassemble Data to find out what makes him so unique, Picard argues against it in a stirring episode that doesn't even have to put the *Enterprise* in jeopardy to be dramatic.

Wesley is the main character being spotlighted in "The Dauphin" that deals with the perils of falling in love with an alien because things are not always what they seem.

"Contagion" is a fine episode in which the Romulans return after the *Enterprise* unsuccessfully attempts to aid a sister ship, the *Yamato*, in the Neutral Zone. The destruction of the *Yamato* is startling and the race by the crew of the *Enterprise* to prevent the same thing happening to them is well wrought. The uneasy truce with the Romulans is very well portrayed here and this episode begins to establish the Romulans as the kind of ongoing adversary that the Klingons were in the original *Star Trek*. While the Romulans are portrayed as antagonists, they are given more dimension than the old versions of the Klingons were.

## INTERSPATIAL TWISTS

"The Royale" is another strange episode showing Hollywood's peculiar and inexplicable fascination with Las Vegas style casinos, with an homage to old movies.

"The Icarus Factor" deals with Riker having a showdown with his father while Worf undergoes a painful ritual in the holodeck, both of which deal with confronting problems head on.

"Pen Pals" is a touching episode in which the Prime Directive is invoked when Data wants to save an alien child whose distress call he's received. The problem is that this world is at a primitive stage in which contact with offworld societies would interfere with the planet's normal cultural development. The way Data deals with the problem shows he has more humanity than we're often led to believe.

A key episode in the entire series is "Q Who," which introduces the Borg and sets up another confrontation that won't take place until over a year later. It's also the first episode with Q in which the character is more than just a cartoon in human form. Although it's made clear in the conclusion that because of this encounter the Borg will now come in search of the Federation, early in the episode a reference is made to the destruction of outposts in "The Neutral Zone" episode from the previous year. That would indicate that a Borg scout ship had previously been in Federation space. The presence of Q this time leads to a loss of life as eighteen crew members die when the Borg slice out a section of the *Enterprise* for examination. While the special effects in the original *Star Trek* were much better than some people make them out to be, they never did anything close to what is seen in this episode.

## THE YEAR WINDS DOWN

Other episodes in the second season continued the variance in quality, although they remained largely above most of what was done in the first season of *The Next Generation*.

"Up the Long Ladder" is interesting, while "Manhunt" is another visitation from Troi's mother.

"The Emissary" is a Klingon episode with a twist. A ship with Klingons in suspended animation from the bad old days defrosts and then goes after the *Enterprise*. It's a fine Worf episode that introduces his old flame, a character who will be killed off in season three.

"Peak Performance" is another good one in which Riker commands a frigate in wargames against the *Enterprise*. If the year had ended with this episode it would have been fine, but the finale, "Shades of Gray," is inexplicably a flashback story filled with clips from previous shows while Riker is unconscious from an alien virus.

# SEASON THREE

By this time Gene Roddenberry had largely turned over the production of *The Next Generation* to Rick Berman and others and the show was well on its way to a long run. The producers and the writing staff had a handle on the characters and they knew what style of television series they were creating. That didn't mean everything was running smoothly; they had decided that a small miscalculation had been made.

Year three saw the return of Gates McFadden as Dr. Beverly Crusher. She had been let go at the end of the first year and replaced by Diana Muldaur. There was the usual Sturm und Drang from the fans when she was replaced, and even a letter-writing campaign ensued, but Gene Roddenberry stated publicly that it was his decision and he wouldn't change his mind. By the end of year two, however, he had changed his mind. It was decided that although Muldaur was good, her chemistry with the other performers wasn't what they were looking for, and that Gates McFadden had worked out better after all. She returned in season three with the same lack of ceremony with which Diana Muldaur had both joined and left the show.

The third season of *The Next Generation* was not the improvement over season two that season two was over season one. The show held its own in the third season, with as many good episodes as the previous season, while also producing the single most outstanding episode of the first three seasons.

## A VERY UNUSUAL ALIEN

The season opened on an only average note with "Evolution," a story about a scientist obsessed with getting the *Enterprise* to a location where he can perform a once-in-a-lifetime experiment. This becomes complicated when one of Wesley's experiments, involving nanites (microscopic "nanotechnology" robots) gets out of control and threatens the ship.

"Ensigns of Command" is a much better episode and more worthy of the lead slot in a season. It deals directly with the concept of having to compromise and accept the inevitable. Relations with an alien race require that the Federation evacuate the human colonists on a planet. The colonists refuse to cooperate and insist that they will stand and fight for their colony even with no military technology available. In a display of brutal honesty over negotiation, Data demonstrates the futility of their resolve by using his phaser, demonstrating exactly what they would be up against. In the face of such overwhelming odds, the colonists are forced to capitulate. This is an excellent episode.

"The Survivors" is another top-notch entry, and continues the attempts to come up with ideas never explored by *Star Trek* before. When the *Enterprise* discovers two human survivors on a planet devastated by an alien attack, their curiosity is only heightened by the fact that the modest dwelling occupied by these two old folks is the only patch of ground on the planet not obliterated. The couple refuse to be evacuated, and finally the man reveals that he is a being of a species previously unknown to the Federation.

The alien had taken human form to marry a human woman he'd fallen in love with, but even though he has massive powers, his kind are strictly pacifists. His wife chose to join the colonists in trying to fight the alien attackers, and when she died along with the others, the man struck out in his grief, destroying not only the attacking ship, but every last member of the race the ship represented throughout the universe! John Anderson, as the heartsick, pacifist superbeing, gives a touching performance as he confesses what he has done and what he must live with. He had created an illusion of his dead wife to remain with him in what is now his self-imposed exile. It is a touching story by Michael Wagner with a rare downbeat ending. The alien portrayed by John Anderson can only be compared with Q, although he is never so identified. His race has never been encountered again. The role was one of Anderson's last. He died a year later.

## WELL-CRAFTED WRITING

Beginning with "The Survivors," the series started doing more location shooting, which added immeasurably to the realism of the planet exteriors. Dark, turbulent worlds can be pulled off on a sound stage, but class-M (earthlike) planets look like sound stages when they're shot indoors.

"Who's Watching the Watchers" deals with the

Prime Directive and how it is inadvertently violated when a primitive people observe some Federation scientists who have been observing them. When they see *Enterprise* crewmen beam in, they assume the obvious—that they are being visited by gods. It's up to Picard to try to undo the mess and keep the planet from developing a new superstition and thereby harming its natural development. The provocative theme is dealt with intelligently. This episode was a personal favorite of Gene Roddenberry's.

"The Bonding," written by Ronald Moore, is an emotionally wrenching story that returns to the fact that the *Enterprise* crew have their families with them, a facet all but ignored throughout the second season. When a little boy's mother dies while exploring an ancient world with an Away Team, Worf feels responsible because he was in charge of the detail. Death is not a subject dealt with often on the show as casualties are often discussed in abstracts. This story deals with the aftermath of such inevitable casualties. Complicating it is an entity from the planet who feels responsible and attempts to undo the harm by taking the form of the boy's dead mother.

Wil Wheaton is given a rare opportunity to do some genuine acting when he's called upon to talk with the boy about his own loss of a parent when he was that boy's age. Wes Crusher resists this encounter until the climax has all involved confronting their inner turmoil and facing that which cannot be avoided, accepting death and the grief that comes with it. In an excellent scene, the show ends with Worf and the boy participating in a private Klingon ceremony, the "bonding" of the title. Coincidentally, it follows close on "The Survivors," another story that deals with death and grief, subjects rare in any action-adventure series, much less in science fiction television that all too often gets wrapped up in exploring ideas more than feelings. *Star Trek* has always tried to do both whenever possible.

## ADVERSARIAL ALIENS

Geordi La Forge is a character seldom used to his full potential, but he is a focal point of "Booby Trap." This episode explores what happens when the *Enterprise* is drawn to investigate an ancient alien craft and is trapped by the same alien mechanisms that caught the other ship ages ago. The scenes of Geordi interacting with the holodeck re-creation of the *Enterprise*'s designer are dramatic as well as touching. It is an interesting and compelling story.

"The Enemy" is a follow-up to last season's "Contagion." When a crashed Romulan scout ship attracts the attention of the *Enterprise*, a Romulan warship soon appears in an attempt to cover up an obvious spy mission. Geordi is lost on the planet with a Romulan survivor he's found. They are forced to help each other to survive. The opposite happens aboard the *Enterprise*. When a wounded Romulan needs a blood transfusion from Worf to survive, the Klingon refuses, many times, because his real parents were killed by Romulans when he was just a child. Worf's character has never been more forceful and compelling than in this story.

The Ferengi are back in "The Price," but unfortunately portrayed as buffoons. The arrogance of the Ferengi is what makes them funny, particularly in the scene when they refer to Worf as Picard's Klingon servant. Troi is the focal point of this show as she meets another Betazoid who has hidden his true nature to use his mind-reading for delicate trade negotiations, such as the one portrayed in this episode.

## THE MANY FACES OF WAR

"The Vengeance Factor" explores the idea of old feuds when Picard mediates a settlement between a planet's leader and a pirate band that had long bedeviled him. This interesting story offers little new.

The Romulans return in "The Defector," which turns out to be a direct sequel to "The Enemy." The *Enterprise* picks up a Romulan defector, an admiral determined to head off a war between his people and the Federation. He reveals plans for a sneak attack slated to be launched from the Neutral Zone, but he turns out to be a deliberate plant. While his reason for defecting is real, the Romulans had manipulated him so that they could lure a Federation starship inside the Neutral Zone and capture it. The surprise which Picard has up his sleeve in anticipation of such a trap reveals him to be as canny as a starship captain should be.

The old Romulan admiral is portrayed in a sympathetic light, and the suicide of the Romulan at the conclusion adds a downbeat note to Picard's victory. There is a nice touch in the form of a letter the Romulan admiral leaves behind for his wife and daughter, a communication that can only be delivered when the Romulans and the Federation at last declare a complete peace rather than an armed truce.

The concept of what to do with super-soldiers after a war's conclusion is explored in "The Hunted." It's an interesting idea, dealing with a society that depended on these men to win a conflict for it. After the war, society is afraid to integrate them in spite of the sacrifices these men made to preserve that society. In keeping with the principle of the Prime Directive, Picard ultimately refuses to solve the problem for them, but insists that the planet's society and the soldiers work it out between them before admission to the Federation will be granted. It raises an interesting question, though: once a planet is in the Federation, if it has a revolution, which side would the Federation support if both sides appealed for aid? That very idea is dealt with in the next episode.

## BENDING THE PRIME DIRECTIVE

When Gene Roddenberry was honored by the Museum of Broadcasting in 1988, near the end of the first season of *The Next Generation*, he stated that he wanted to deal with the subject of terrorists in a forthcoming episode and demonstrate that even they have what they feel is a legitimate point of view (see Appendix). This idea is tackled in "The High Ground," and while the terrorists' point of view is presented, they are nevertheless shown as going too far in their willingness to kill the innocent along with the guilty. This is essentially the twentieth-century conflict in Northern Ireland homogenized for consumer consumption and reduced to a very simplified form.

The terrorists kidnap Picard and other *Enterprise* crewmen not because of anything they've done (other than tending the wounded) but because they believe that Picard is going to side with the oppressive ruling class. With a little work, the complexities of such a situation could have been explored much better. Since this is a civil war, the Federation chooses to help neither side in the conflict and is only drawn into it when its own personnel are kidnapped since the terrorists want to force the issue.

In "Deja Q," we have the exiled Q meet the *Enterprise* again, only now he's been stripped of his powers to teach him humility. Learn it he does, and when his powers are returned he not only solves the problem that had been bedeviling Picard for the entire show (he casually puts a moon back in its proper orbit), but gives Data the ability to understand humor, a concept not yet followed up on since its introduction in "The Outrageous Okona."

## A MATTER OF TIME

"A Matter of Perspective" takes place entirely aboard the *Enterprise* so Riker can be proven innocent of committing a crime by showing the key events from three perspectives. There is little suspense in spite of the ingenious explanation for the destruction of a lab and the death of a scientist that Riker is accused of causing.

"Yesterday's Enterprise" is a time travel story that's the equal of the best shows done on the original *Star Trek*. When the *Enterprise* 1701-C, from twenty years previously, appears in this time line, history is changed and we suddenly find a darker, grimmer *Enterprise* with Picard in command, fighting a continuing war with the Klingons that the Federation is losing. Denise Crosby returns as Tasha Yar, who comes to realize that she isn't supposed to be there, or even be alive. Her sacrifice to help put time right again is a far more fitting send-off than her offhand death back in the first season's "Skin of Evil."

The alternate universe aspect is handled meticulously and the complicated science fiction aspects are presented without stopping to present a blackboard explanation with diagrams such as *Back to the Future II* felt it necessary to do. This is science fiction equal with its complexity to some of the better prose science fiction published today, and the script bears the names of six writers required to pull it off. This show has drama, action, and the kind of details that make any story memorable.

## A MATTER OF HUMANITY

"The Offspring" is a touching story that deals with what would happen if Data created another version of himself, which he dubs his "child." The Federation tries to take possession, just as they did with Data in "The Measure of a Man," although why they seemed on the verge of getting away with it this time and not last time remains unresolved.

"Sins of The Father" is a key episode in the continuing examination of Klingons and their culture. This one travels to the Klingon homeworld, where Worf encounters a younger brother he'd believed long dead. The examination of Klingon politics is complex and interesting. Worf's decision to accept an unfair expulsion from his society for the betterment of all is nothing less than heroic and shows him to be a true Klingon, inside and out. Picard is with him when he goes to the Klingon homeworld, and there are interesting scenes of life among the common Klingons rather than military personnel.

Picard is replaced by a double in "Allegiance," but the double's inability to think precisely the way Picard would, and follow his better judgment, exposes him soon enough.

"Captain's Holiday" is another routine story trying to be overly complex. Picard takes a holiday and winds up in a futuristic takeoff on the *Indiana Jones* movies. It's amusing and diverting, but little else. The time travelers materialize at just the right moment and spoil all the fun.

## TECHNOLOGICAL TRICKS

One of the more unusual episodes of the third season is "Tin Man." Adapted from their award-winning story, writers Dennis Putnam Bailey and David Bischoff craft an interesting tale. The telepath who cannot stand the company of normal beings is extremely well-played by Harry Groener, although his eventual decision to remain with the unusual life-form (the "Tin Man" of the title), which is a living starship, seems inevitable. Still, it remains an effective, moody story, and even the Romulans are back to stir up trouble.

"Hollow Pursuits" tackles an obvious but untried idea using the holodeck. What if a crewman conjured up images of fellow crewmen to use and degrade them? While handled tastefully here, one can imagine more unusual extremes the idea could be taken to. Crewman Barclay spends too much time in his fantasy world on the holodeck because he has trouble dealing with the real world and his tedious job aboard the *Enterprise.* Only his ability to solve a crisis by coming up with just the right idea enables him to start recognizing his positive abilities and putting his own life in order.

In "Allegiance," Picard was abducted and replaced by a duplicate. In "The Most Toys," Data is abducted under cover of his supposed destruction. Data is captured by a crazed collector in a plot all too reminiscent of something from *Buck Rogers* or *Space: 1999.* What elevates it above the dreary and the routine is the way it deals with the consequences of imprisonment and the ethical dilemma of Data finding it necessary to make a decision to kill even though it violates his own personal moral code. Data doesn't actually kill his captor, although the ending makes it clear that he fully intended to by using one of the collector's weapons so cruel that it had been outlawed by the Federation.

"The Most Toys" was originally supposed to star David Rappaport as the villain. Halfway through shooting the episode, the diminutive performer made his first suicide attempt; he was promptly replaced. All his scenes were reshot, although those who saw the original footage labeled Rappaport's performance as brilliantly menacing. Perhaps one day that last performance of Rappaport (he succeeded in a second suicide try a couple of months later) will be seen.

## A TREK CLASSIC CROSSOVER

Mark Lenard made his first of two extremely memorable guest appearances on *The Next Generation* in "Sarek." Other than the cameo by a 137-year-old Dr. McCoy in "Encounter at Farpoint," this was the first true crossover of an original *Star Trek* character on *TNG*. He's the title character, of course, and is forced to come to terms with a rare form of Vulcan senility, showing that the ravages of old age can strike down even the finest of us. It's a compassionate treatment of a difficult problem in a medium (television, not science fiction) which usually treats the afflictions of the elderly with mockery and contempt.

"Menage á Troi" has Troi's mother return yet again, but it is a misfired attempt at humor. Only in the episodes where her character is presented in a dramatic setting is she believable.

"Transfigurations" again deals with the *Enterprise* being pushed and pulled into the middle of the affairs of another culture. This time Picard takes a stand, refusing to turn over an escaped criminal for what would clearly be execution. It's an interesting idea, dealing with the concept of a race evolving and those left behind attempting to destroy those who represent the actual future of their kind.

The season concludes on a cliffhanger that doesn't artificially force events into this all too abused angle. In "The Best of Both Worlds," the Borg return as long feared, and the *Enterprise* is the only vessel on the scene to confront them. This is what the Borg want. Picard is quickly kidnapped, transformed and absorbed into the Borg collective, where he becomes Locutus. The tension is thick, particularly when an Away Team beams aboard the Borg ship in an attempt to rescue Picard; they fail. It is only one of the many surprises. This is a good episode that holds up well even years after it originally aired.

# SEASON FOUR

The highly anticipated "The Best of Both Worlds, Part II" proved to be a fitting conclusion to the third-season cliffhanger. When the *Enterprise* fails to stop the Borg ship, it speeds off toward Earth, where a fleet of starships unsuccessfully attempts to halt it. The scene when the *Enterprise* catches up to the battle site and sees dozens of wrecked starships drifting in space is truly awesome. Scenes like this attempt to convey the immensity of space, but are diminished on the small screen. (This was particularly evident last season in "The Defector," when mixed success in trying to show the *Enterprise* facing two Romulan ships who were in turn surrounded by three Klingon ships that overlapped so much that they almost obliterated the starfield background was achieved on the crowded screen.) The rescue of Picard and the defeat of the Borg is cleverly handled, although the destruction of the Borg ship seemed a bit too conveniently accomplished.

The follow-up episode, "Family," chose not to ignore the consequences of what Picard has just gone through. While the rivalry between Picard and his older brother in their quaint French village seems forced and artificial (and perhaps all too easily resolved), other aspects of the reunion are rewarding, particularly the brief scenes between Picard and his young nephew. The actor who played his nephew would return two years later to play Picard when he's turned into a child in the sixth-season episode "Rascals."

The subplots in "Family," dealing with Worf's foster parents visiting him and Wesley playing a holodeck file recorded for him by his father years ago, seem perfunctory and are dropped as Picard visits home to recuperate from his ordeal in space.

The show offers character stories that involve nothing more than people talking about their feelings, demonstrating the chances the series took. Unfortunately "Family" was the lowest rated episode of the season, which says more about the audience than it does about the series.

## THINGS ARE MORE THAN THEY SEEM

"Suddenly Human" seems like it's going to be a story dealing with child abuse. Even the coming attractions made it out to be this kind of story. It's nothing of the sort. It could be regarded as being a story about how child abuse is assumed when it's not really there.

When Picard discovers that a human child has been raised by the aliens who slew the boy's family eleven years before, the captain is determined to return him to his people. The boy has been so fully integrated into the alien culture that it is all that he knows. While Picard has some success drawing out the boy's human memories and reactions, in the end he realizes that in spite of the unfortunate circumstances, the boy belongs with the foster father who loved and raised him. Essentially the child was kidnapped at age five and raised by his kidnappers. Does that mean his kidnappers are good parents? It's an episode that asks difficult questions and provides uncomfortable answers. Frankly, the original *Star Trek* never would have taken such a downbeat position as this story does, which again shows the risks *Next Generation* was willing to take.

"Remember Me" plays with reality in a manner that brings to mind the works of author Philip K. Dick. When Dr. Crusher notes that people she knows are no longer aboard the *Enterprise*, she finds it difficult to convince anyone else of this when no trace of the missing person's existence can be found. We're over halfway through the story before we realize what's really going on and the pace sustains itself well. It's an interesting idea and certainly one of the most unusual episodes thus far. Unfortunately the suspense and interest hinge completely on us trying to figure out what is happening, and knowing what's going on will make it less interesting as a rerun, unlike other stories that have special and memorable scenes.

Tasha Yar's sister is introduced in "Legacy" when the *Enterprise* journeys to the planet of Tasha's birth to rescue two crewmen from a shuttle. It's a good story overall, but it establishes that Tasha left fifteen years before and that her sister had already joined the rebellion. Unfortunately, the actress playing Tasha's sister looks to be in her late twenties at the most, and somehow I can't accept Tasha having abandoned a thirteen- to fifteen-year-old sister when she left the planet. This is never adequately explained and is a point that is quite conspicuous.

## HAIL AND FAREWELL

"Reunion" is another Klingon storyline. It continues

the tradition of having episodes focusing on Worf that explore his Klingon character and heritage. These episodes have consistently been among the finest the series has produced. In this case, Picard is dragged into a matter where the Klingon ritual of ascendancy to the throne is at hand. The subterfuge behind-the-scenes tells the tale. Here we meet Worf's old lover and a son named Alexander that he never knew he had, and while the idea is not original, it's handled well. The ending, when Worf decides to allow his adoptive parents to raise his own son just as they raised him, is quite touching and clearly leaves an opening for future stories. As it turns out, this episode marked what would be a downturn in the characterization of Worf, or what has been called among fans the "domesticating" of the Klingon.

Another story about the nature of reality, which one could also say owes something to the influence of Philip K. Dick, is "Future Imperfect." This story is done so well that it keeps us guessing right up to the end. Even when we're congratulating ourselves for guessing that Riker is being tricked by a Romulan illusion, we never think that it could be an illusion within an illusion. It's a tale well told and one that holds up on repeated viewing. The characterization and the little details in the story add weight to the underlying premise so that the surprise is clearly not all the story has to offer.

"Final Mission" is the day many *Next Generation* fans had been praying for since the first season. It is the episode marking the departure of Wil Wheaton from the show as a series regular. Even though the character of Wesley Crusher has been largely cleansed of the crimes for which we suffered in the first season, he frankly just never seemed to fit in. Wesley was the character Gene Roddenberry liked the best, and as mightily as they tried to make him work, it always came across as forced.

The actor left the series to attend college and pursue film projects. In the series, Wesley left to attend Starfleet Academy, at last. In a rare story in which Wesley is the focal point, he's given a fine send-off, as we're allowed to see many sides of his character when he's marooned on a small planet with Picard along with the gruff captain of a mining shuttle. Although Wesley must save Picard in the end, at least he doesn't make it look easy this time, which was a common complaint about the way Wesley Crusher was used in the first season's episodes. It will come as quite a surprise in season five when Wesley makes a guest appearance only to get his comeuppance!

## THINGS TO COME

"The Wounded" would turn out to be a crucial episode, as it introduced the Cardassians to the *Star Trek* universe. The Cardassians are relentless, stereotyped villains, similar to the Klingons of the sixties. Roddenberry later felt guilty about creating an entire race that was portrayed as being evil and did penance by reversing himself when he set down the rules for *The Next Generation*, thereby making Klingons an interesting race of characters.

In this story, a starship captain is convinced that the Cardassians are preparing for war again and decides to attack them first. Captain Maxwell had lost his family to the Cardassians in the previous war and refuses to see the miscreants launch another campaign of terror. The story is quite interesting and gives O'Brien good scenes, since he served with Maxwell in the past and fought the Cardassians in the last war. The twist ending of having Picard figure out that Maxwell had guessed correctly is a nice touch. Maxwell's mistake was that he launched a counteroffensive without sufficient proof and against Starfleet orders.

The Cardassians, of course, formed a vital element of the background for *Deep Space Nine.* Their one-note villainy has also been broadened in an episode of *Deep Space Nine* titled "Duet," featuring a Cardassian who felt guilt for his race's war crimes and imitated a known war criminal in hopes that he would be tried for those crimes and thereby force his people to confront their collective guilt.

## NEW IDEAS

"First Contact" is an episode of thrilling ideas. While the Prime Directive was established (if rarely invoked) in the original *Star Trek,* this episode more directly explores the notion of avoiding contact with societies not prepared to confront the reality of life on other worlds. When Riker, who is disguised as an alien, is injured on the surface of a planet in a freak accident, he is exposed when taken to a hospital. The resulting paranoia regarding an "alien invasion" threatens Riker's life. A variety of characters are presented, including a woman who wants to accompany Picard back to the *Enterprise* when Riker is rescued, as well as an official who is terrified of what the existence of the *Enterprise* represents to his people's future.

The original *Star Trek* never approached the idea of first contact in this complicated a fashion. While the story is diminished somewhat by the Bebe Neuwirth character who wants to "have sex with an alien," the rest of the story takes the high road. This episode demonstrates the drama of ideas.

Another important episode is "The Drumhead," which presents a Federation official who sees spies everywhere and is prepared to convict innocent people to protect the Federation. Jean Simmons as

J'Dan is excellent in this story that demonstrates that the Federation isn't all squeaky clean.

## A NEW DIRECTION

Lwaxana Troi, as played by Majel Barrett, has been one of those characters one either finds amusing or obnoxious by turns. Until her appearance in "Half a Life," the character was not particularly interesting. The cartoon characterization of her was abandoned in this episode in which she falls in love with a man who is honor bound by his society to commit ritual suicide when he reaches the age of mandatory retirement. For him to refuse would bring horrible dishonor on his family.

This episode is a little quirky in its use of the Prime Directive. While Picard feels that he cannot interfere with the planet's culture, the Prime Directive only applies to planets not in the Federation. Kaelon II is a member that clearly employs a cruel and unusual cultural practice. Then the story deals with the concept of putting the old out to pasture when they still have much to contribute to society. Majel Barrett is so good in this episode that one wonders why she ever tolerated having her character presented as it was before.

"The Host" is another episode that introduces an element which became a part of *Deep Space Nine*. Here we meet a Trill for the first time: an alien that lives by merging with a host body. When the Trill's current host body is injured, it relocates for a time into Riker. The twist is that Dr. Crusher had been having an affair with the Trill in its previous host body. The ending caused some controversy when the Trill's new permanent host body turns out to be female, whereupon Crusher breaks off the affair, ostensibly because too much is happening in too short a time. She certainly didn't have that objection when the Trill made love to her in Riker's body, something he certainly hadn't consented to when he offered to help save the Trill's life.

## A LANDMARK SEASON

Although Gene Roddenberry rarely granted interviews during his *Next Generation* days, he was quoted in the Los Angeles *Times,* October 28, 1990, on the occasion of the new series surpassing the seventy-nine-episode marker that the original *Star Trek* television series had achieved in the sixties.

Roddenberry also discussed the whole *Star Trek* phenomenon in more depth, in particular as it related to *The Next Generation,* stating, "Many people haven't thought deeply what it is they like about it. They're not crazy about rocket ships or space travel. It's none of those things. What our show does, we take humanity maybe a century into the future. Our people do not lie, cheat or steal. They are the best of the best. When you watch the show, you say to yourself, at least once, 'My God, that's the way life should be!' "

As with season three, this fourth season also featured a final-episode cliffhanger. "Redemption I" involves a power play on the Klingon homeworld. Worf takes a leave of absence to join in the conflict and serve on a Klingon ship commanded by his brother. Worf's aim is also to restore the good name of his family that was besmirched when his dead father was accused of collaborating with Romulans against his own people in "Sins of the Father." It's a good, complicated story worthy of being the season finale.

# SEASON FIVE

The conclusion of "Redemption" as a season opener isn't a letdown: the story keeps moving with all its twists and turns right up to the end. Somehow it was inevitable that the Klingons supported by the Federation would win, but it's a well-written story just the same. The discommendation Worf endured in season three is lifted and he can hold his head high again.

Season five started to move in some more experimental directions beginning with "Darmok," an unusual episode that deals with a race which speaks only in metaphors. As in the original *Star Trek* episode "Arena," the captains of the *Enterprise* and an alien vessel meet face-to-face on the surface of a planet to settle their differences. Here the differences are philological. It's a very unusual and satisfying story, although the average TV viewer may well have found it a bit difficult to follow due to the notion of communication through metaphors.

## A NEW CAST MEMBER

"Ensign Ro" introduced Michelle Forbes as the controversial Bajoran officer. In an increasingly complex story, Ro, released from a Federation prison to assist the *Enterprise* on a vital mission, finds herself manipulated by a Federation admiral who has a secret deal with the Cardassians. In this one episode, Ro is established as a very interesting character and one who is a welcome addition to the *Enterprise* crew.

Michelle Forbes appeared in several more episodes in the fifth season as a semiregular. She was slated to be a regular on *Deep Space Nine* , but her character had been written in without ever consulting her, and she had no interest in committing to a series for several years. She appeared in only one sixth-season episode in spite of the other actors on the show wanting to see her return. Her absence from the series was sorely felt. Whenever she was given a large role, she stole every scene she was in. This is because her character has an argumentative edge to it, something even Worf didn't display much any more.

"Silicon Avatar" brings back the character from the first-season entry "Datalore." A woman whose young son was a victim of the strange alien creature has devoted her life to tracking the thing down and destroying it. She succeeds at the cost of her own career in Starfleet. The scenes between Data and Dr. Kila Marr are quite effective, particularly when Data recalls her son's diary from his extensive programming since he was built in the colony where her son lived.

## THE RETURN OF SPOCK, THE END OF SAREK

Wesley Crusher appeared in two episodes in the fifth season, "The Game" and "The First Duty," and in the latter the character was taken down a few notches. In "The Game," Wesley figures out that the *Enterprise* is being invaded and conquered by an insidious new game that becomes physically addictive. Although Data saves everyone, that's only because Wesley reactivated Data after he had been shut down to insure he couldn't interfere.

In "The First Duty," the story is set at Starfleet Academy where Wesley is a real hotshot nearing graduation. When he becomes involved in a cover-up of the death of one of his friends, Wesley's pristine image comes crashing down. Even though he finally confesses, it is clearly under duress and isn't something he would have done without outside pressure from Captain Picard. It's doubtful Wesley will ever be perceived as being quite so pristine again.

Year five also marked the long-rumored crossover of Mr. Spock on *The Next Generation* in the two-part "Unification." While the story seemed a bit weak in part two, it still had some interesting moments throughout, although few of them involved Spock. The episode had a rushed feeling to the script, as though the story was hastily concocted to get it into production to air in the November "sweeps month" ratings period early in the season. It achieved the ratings success it set out to accomplish, but dramatically the story left a lot to be desired. Spock doesn't appear until the last scene in part one and yet the writing in part one is better than it is in part two. This storyline also features the death of Sarek, which happens offstage. Mark Lenard's scenes with Patrick Stewart are excellent and one can only wonder how much better they might have been had they involved Spock more directly.

## A TIME FOR CHANGE

Matt Frewer, a fine comic actor who starred in the series *Doctor, Doctor,* as well as having roles in films like *Honey I Shrunk the Kids*, plays a strange, fussy scientist whose time machine encounters the *Enterprise* in "A Matter of Time." There is so much clever misdirection in the storyline that you guess everything but the truth when the climax arrives. Frewer is excellent as an unscrupulous scientist who knows how to take advantage of even the most extraordinary opportunity.

Worf was all but domesticated this season when his son Alexander returned to live on the *Enterprise* in "The New Ground." Seeing Worf more as a father than a warrior dilutes much of the edge this character had until this season. Unfortunately, this didn't last for just the duration of this episode, as subsequent storylines involving Worf and his son, Alexander, make Worf out to be no different from any human father.

## DATA'S WAY

The character of Data has been explored in many ways, often to show contrast between him and the humans he works with. In "Hero Worship," Data demonstrates that he understands the human psyche better than was thought as he is able to guide a young boy through a traumatic situation and out the other side again. When a young boy loses his parents in an accident aboard a ship that the *Enterprise* finds drifting in space, the child blames himself. To escape the guilt and pain, he begins to imitate Data, since androids don't feel pain. The teleplay by Joe Menosky is very sensitively and intelligently handled and is one of the best episodes of year five, a season that contained many strong episodes.

"Conundrum" is an excellent mystery: the memories of the *Enterprise* crew are all selectively blanked and they are led to believe they are at war with the Lysians. One amusing sequence has Worf deciding that he must be the captain since he's the only Klingon aboard the *Enterprise*.

"Power Play" is a bravura performance in which some of the regulars are given the opportunity to play very different characters. When Data, O'Brien, and Troi are taken over by alien entities, they ruthlessly try to take over the *Enterprise* so they can rescue their fellow entities imprisoned on the planet the ship is orbiting. The ending seems a little convenient, but overall it's a captivating episode that is just as powerful in subsequent viewing.

## IT'S ALL A MATTER OF POINT OF VIEW

"Ethics" is more or less a Klingon episode in which Worf suffers a crippling spine injury due to a freak accident. Interesting touches include Worf demanding the right to commit ritual suicide rather than live on as a cripple. Riker refuses to help him: he points out that by Klingon law the oldest son must commit the killing. Worf does not want to involve Alexander. The subplot, which involves a visiting medical doctor onboard, explores the questions of medical ethics involved in experimental procedures.

The most controversial episode of the season, though, was "The Outcast," the story of an alien race in which some members realize they are sexually different from their fellow androgynes. In spite of how incredibly careful the scriptwriter strove to be, some people were still offended by the story's plea for compassion and its slam against prejudice that seemed to strike a bit too close to home. The androgyne race is portrayed entirely by actresses, which makes the condemnation of one of their members' involvement with Riker come across as a race of lesbians condemning relations with men. It is easily the bravest story in twenty-six years of *Star Trek*.

Time travel gets a new twist in "Cause and Effect." This time the *Enterprise* is caught in a time loop that begins repeating each time the starship is destroyed. What could have been boring and repetitious was fascinating, and direction by Jonathan Frakes shows that he has a firm grasp on the series. The episode begins with the time loop and the destruction of the *Enterprise,* and then after the commercial break picks up at the beginning of the loop again. What makes it all work is that events don't repeat exactly, but rather there are differences and coincidences that the crew begin to notice in spite of having no conscious memory of the previous time loop experience. It's another experimental episode that is fascinating to watch.

## DATA'S HEAD

The Borg were presented in a different light when "I, Borg" showed one that was capable of human compassion. This may well lead to changing the one-note characterizations of these villains into something more complicated. This episode has also formed the background for events that began to unfold in the season-six cliffhanger and when "Hugh" the Borg reappears at the beginning of season seven.

Fans still discuss "Inner Light" as experimental. When Captain Picard is zapped by an alien space probe, he is seemingly drawn a thousand years into the past, where he lives out the remainder of his life as a husband and father, only to reawaken on the *Enterprise* and find that he's been unconscious for twenty minutes. This might well have been titled "Conundrum" (another episode in the fifth season), as it was a real mystery that still has fans arguing over what was really going on during the climax of the story when Picard, on the alien world, sees people who had died during his years spent there. The *very* unusual story took many worthwhile risks.

The season cliffhanger, "Time's Arrow" hooked us with a story about how Data will die. Rather than a battle story, such as the cliffhangers from seasons three and four, this was a more complicated story involving nineteenth-century San Francisco, Mark Twain, Guinan before she'd ever met anyone on the *Enterprise*, and strange aliens stealing the life force from humans. The episode is sometimes referred to by fans as "Data's Head," a parody of the original *Star Trek* episode title "Spock's Brain."

Overall, season five turned out to be one of the best seasons yet and promised high hopes for year six.

# SEASON SIX

Year six got off to a rocky start with the disappointing conclusion to "Time's Arrow." The meandering storyline in part two undercut the excitement established in the first part while it lurched from one scene to another, dragging Mark Twain along for the ride. The buildup to part two turned into a big letdown as the alien life-force thieves were never given any personality beyond being the bad guys. While all the loose ends are tied up, it is done in a rather perfunctory manner.

## OLD ACQUAINTANCES

"Realm of Fear" features the return of Barclay, the crewman first seen in "Hollow Pursuits." Barclay still has emotional problems, including a phobia against using the transporter. Thus, when he reports seeing something while inside the transporter beam, his observations are treated with large amounts of skepticism. His observations not only turn out to be true but form a surprising twist to the end of the story.

Surprisingly, the original *Star Trek* Scotty's crossover appearance on *The Next Generation* in "Relics" is better written than Spock's was in "Reunification." James Doohan is given some meaty acting to do, particularly in his portrayal of a man out of time. The manner in which he finds a way to fit into the twenty-fourth century opens up future possibilities, particularly now that Paramount is planning another *Star Trek* television series, *Star Trek: Voyager*. The scene fans are still talking about is the holodeck scene when Scotty resurrects the bridge of the original starship *Enterprise:* it is an amazing thing to see again. In the novelization of "Relics," the author added elements to the holodeck scene, including Scotty talking to Kirk and Spock.

"True Q" managed to come up with a new twist on the old reprobate when a woman stationed aboard the *Enterprise* reveals that she has fantastic powers. The reason she does is that her father was a Q who fell in love with a human. The resulting child grew up an orphan, following the mysterious death of her parents. While Q tries to get the young woman to agree to become a Q with the others, Picard determines that her parents were executed by the Q for refusing a directive from them. It's a change of pace Q episode and works well.

## HOLLOW PURSUIT

"Rascals," on the other hand, is a light, amusing episode. When Picard, Ensign Ro, and a few other crewmen are turned into children by the transporter, it happens just in time for them to outsmart some Ferengi who attempt to steal the *Enterprise*.

"A Fistful of Datas" is another episode that must have been fun to create. When a programming glitch causes Data to infect the holodeck, Worf and Alexander find themselves trapped in a Western scenario in which all the characters look like Data—even the women. They must play out the program to its conclusion before the holodeck will shut itself down.

Year six had quite a variety of episodes, and "Schisms" is certainly one of the most unusual episodes of *The Next Generation.* Essentially this is a Riker episode in which he suffers from strange dreams and when awake he is tired all the time. The secret behind this mystery is indeed a strange one, as Riker and other crewmen periodically disappear off the *Enterprise* into a dimensional pocket where aliens experiment on them in a sort of futuristic "alien abduction" scenario. The scene where Dr. Crusher announces that microscopic analysis reveals that Riker's arm had been surgically removed and reattached is certainly disturbing.

"The Quality of Life" is a strange episode in which Data determines that a new type of android has achieved the definition of true life, since the robots have knowledge of their own existence and are unwilling to risk their "lives" because of that self-awareness.

## A DEEP SPACE CROSSOVER

Season six was a season of continued episodes, and the first of these was the two-part story "Birthright." During a visit to *Deep Space Nine,* Worf encounters a man who offers to sell him information about the whereabouts of his Klingon father, who supposedly died years before at Khitomer. Worf forces the information from the man and it leads to a moon under the control of Romulans: a prison planet where

Klingon prisoners have grown old and their children have grown up unaware of many of the old Klingon customs. It's an interesting story that gives Worf the chance to act like a true Klingon for the first time in two years.

This was also the season that decided to show that Captain Kirk wasn't the only *Enterprise* commander who was a man of action. "Starship Mine," in which Picard finds himself trapped aboard the *Enterprise* between two deadly points of opposition, is clearly *Die Hard* on a starship. Picard, alone on the ship when he discovers criminals stealing a deadly waste product for use in a weapon, must battle and elude them. Complicating the matter is a decontamination ray slowly sweeping the length of the supposedly evacuated starship—a beam that is lethal. Picard resorts to new and old weapons as he proves himself as ruthless as the criminals he fights. Just as interesting is a scene in which Data listens to a boring diplomat whom he deliberately engages in pointless conversation to learn how to talk endlessly without saying anything worth listening to. It's quite a funny scene, especially if you're a fan of good humor.

Picard is the focal point again in "Lessons," a character study of what happens when a commander falls in love with a member of his crew. When it becomes evident that he is granting her special dispensation, she insists on being treated like everyone else, up to and including being made part of a dangerous mission. It's an effective story, particularly when Picard believes that she has died. When she chooses to leave the *Enterprise* because of the complications evident in their relationship, it demonstrates the complexities of command. The final scene in the episode is of Picard, rather than of the *Enterprise*, as is otherwise standard.

## KEY EPISODES

Some fans have expressed disappointment with year six, yet the season emerges as at least as good as season five. There are some weak episodes here and there, but many strong ones as well, including some which are quite imaginative.

"The Chase" has so much in the storyline that it could have easily been stretched into a two-part adventure. Thankfully it wasn't as it is written tightly and works perfectly as a single-episode thriller. The reason it works is that it features no subplots to slow things down.

Norman Lloyd is perfect as Picard's old archeology teacher, Professor Galen. Thirty years ago Picard had been an extraordinary student of the professor's, and Galen never got over Picard's decision to pursue starship command instead of archaeology. When Galen visits the *Enterprise,* he tries to get Picard to leave with him on the archaeological adventure of a lifetime—but he won't reveal what that adventure is. Picard refuses, and when Galen is murdered as a result of this mysterious study, Picard chooses to find Galen's killers and solve the mystery. The riddle involves the origin of many of the races in the Federation. It is a key episode in the entire *Star Trek* milieu.

"Chain of Command," an unusual two-part episode, introduces a replacement for Picard who manages to get on Riker's bad side. When Picard is sent on an espionage mission, it turns out to be a Cardassian trick. Picard is tortured in sequences that give Patrick Stewart the chance to present some of the finest acting he's ever done. It is inexplicable that his work in this season wasn't nominated for an Emmy. This episode also demonstrates that humanity in the twenty-fourth century isn't as perfect as we may have assumed. Ronny Cox, as the new captain of the *Enterprise*, and Riker don't agree at all and continually clash over styles of command. The new captain even labels Riker as unfit to be a first officer, which is quite a switch.

## A SEQUEL FIVE YEARS LATER

"Ship In a Bottle" is the long-awaited sequel to the first-year episode "Elementary, Dear Data." In that earlier episode Data used the holodeck to create a representation of Sir Arthur Conan Doyle's Professor Moriarty, the notorious enemy of Sherlock Holmes. Few recall that Professor Moriarty appeared in only one Sherlock Holmes story, "The Final Problem." He was such a well-rendered character, complete with a detailed criminal background, that Moriarty was used often in Holmes movies and elsewhere years after Doyle died.

While Doyle portrayed Moriarty as a black-hearted villain, on *The Next Generation* he is something more. Moriarty becomes a man obsessed with remaining alive and who exhibits human feelings of love and compassion. He's still seemingly willing to go to any length in order to preserve his existence.

A contradiction exists in this episode. While Data argues for recognizing true life in the small androids in "The Quality of Life," Moriarty clearly qualifies even more as he is aware of his own existence and is more than just a program on the holodeck. "Ship In a Bottle" has many interesting twists and turns, particularly the conclusion. While a sequel may one day be done to this episode as well, it would be unnecessary. Though done five years apart, these two *TNG* episodes form a perfect, self-contained story.

## SOLO OUTINGS

"Aquiel" is one of those rare episodes that spotlights Geordi. In this case he meets an African-American woman and falls in love with her, even though she is a suspect in a murder. The ending is interesting enough, but the writing is a bit slack overall. It looks particularly weak in comparison to the following episode.

The character of Troi has never been given an episode built around her that was particularly interesting. The closest *TNG* had ever come was in "Power Play," which showed what the actress could do when given more substantial material to work with. She's really given something substantial in "Face of the Enemy." The teaser when Troi awakens and discovers that she has been turned into a Romulan shows that we're in for something pretty unusual. The episode then takes us into Romulan life aboard a ship. No episode since "Balance of Terror" has done anything even remotely like this about the Romulans. It's quite impressive.

Picard certainly had plenty of starring venues in *TNG*, but nothing like "Tapestry." When Picard is the victim of an assassination attempt, he apparently dies—and meets Q. Does this mean that Q is God, or something along those lines? Q even gives Picard the chance to relive part of his life as well as to endure the consequences. The ending leaves the story open to interpretation whether Picard was hallucinating or not, particularly since Q doesn't reappear after Picard awakens. It's a damn good story though, and includes a particularly violent scene where the young Picard is stabbed in the back and the blade protrudes from his chest.

## NEW TWISTS

Dr. Crusher gets her own episode in "Suspicions," a story that is more interesting for some of the secondary elements than for its primary murder mystery. For the first time we meet a Ferengi scientist, and he's completely unlike the Ferengi businessmen and starship personnel we've met until now. Another interesting touch is that a shuttle in the episode is named the *Justman*, a reference to Bob Justman, a producer on the sixties *Star Trek*.

Worf starred in his second Klingon episode of the sixth season, perhaps to make up for the fact that there were none in the fifth year. "Rightful Heir" deals with the biological resurrection of Kahless, an ancient Klingon warrior who is legendary among even the modern warriors. Because of what Worf encountered in "Birthright" when he met Klingons who were out of touch with their past, Worf has been feeling inadequate and trying to get closer to his own heritage. This leads him to the world which Kahless promised to return to, and Worf is just in time to witness the reappearance.

Once we're shown the ancient knife that is stained with the blood of the 1500-year-old warrior, it's easy to guess where the story is headed. It is still well done, and unlike other Klingon episodes where humans were at least peripherally involved, ninety percent of the scenes in this story involve only Klingons. The scene when Worf threatens to kill Koroth and the Guardians on the spot if they don't admit the truth about the origin of Kahless immediately shows that Worf isn't a wimp anymore. Lest you think that the idea for Kahless was just pulled out of the air, a very different version of the character was originally done in the third-season *Star Trek* episode "The Savage Curtain," not to mention all archtypical hero myths of both eastern and western literature.

"Second Chances" used an idea pioneered in the original *Star Trek* episode "The Enemy Within" and managed to produce something which in its own way is just as original as what Richard Matheson did back in 1966. When a freak accident with the transporter beam created a duplicate of Riker eight years before, one can only imagine how they felt when they met. Many interesting questions are raised, such as which is the duplicate. In the end, it doesn't matter. For eight years they've lived very different lives and "Thomas" and "William" Riker are thus different people now. Both remain alive at the end. It turns the cliché on its head, particularly since neither of them is an evil twin. This is a delightful episode that plays to our expectations and then does the opposite. The second Riker, who calls himself "Thomas," was seen again in the third season of *Deep Space Nine*, following the conclusion of the seven-year run of *The Next Generation*.

## RETURN TO TOMORROW

In the original *Star Trek* blooper reel there's a scene from 1966 where a 10-year-old boy wearing pointed ears walks onto the bridge and says to Mr. Spock, "Hi, Daddy." That child was Leonard Nimoy's son, Adam. Twenty-seven years later, Adam Nimoy, an entertainment attorney turned director, is at the helm of "Timescape," one of the more challenging episodes of the sixth season. Time travel has been explored in various ways on *The Next Generation*. In "Yesterday's Enterprise" time throughout the galaxy is altered. In the fifth season, in "Cause and Effect," the *Enterprise* became caught in a time loop that begins and ends with the ship's destruction. In "Timescape," the destruction of the *Enterprise* takes place again, but time is manipulated in a different manner.

The fragmentation effect which Picard, Troi, and Geordi discover in the shuttle is quite interesting. The *Enterprise* becomes involved with a Romulan ship on a friendly basis (following the unfriendly encounter in "Face of the Enemy"). The directing by Adam Nimoy is quite good, particularly considering the complicated requirements of the story. This episode is both suspenseful and imaginative and keeps you guessing right up to the climax. It's quite an accomplishment.

## A CLIFFHANGER SURPRISE

Since the end of season three, *The Next Generation* had been striving to craft cliffhangers that would keep the viewing audience on the edge of their seats throughout the summer as they awaited the fall premiere. This had never been better accomplished than with "Descent," the sixth-season climax. While setting us up for the return of "Hugh" the Borg from the fifth season, we instead encounter Lore, Data's "evil twin," last seen in the fourth season. Just when we'd practically forgotten the miscreant, he returns leading a contingent of the Borg.

Data began acting strangely earlier in year six when he began having a recurring dream in "Birthright." Then in "Descent," Data becomes angry during a fight with the Borg, an emotion he is surprised to have. Data works at duplicating the experience to better understand its origins. His explorations led to his uniting with a splinter group of Borg now led by Lore. It was an unexpected twist. It certainly promised interesting developments for the seventh season of *Star Trek: The Next Generation*.

# SEASON SEVEN

Seven years after a bridge full of new faces entered the *Star Trek* universe, the *Enterprise*-D is warped off television and onto the big screen in *Generations*, but the final year of first-run TV episodes was certainly an eventful one, marking the return of some familiar faces and the introduction of new ones. Season seven opened with part two of "Descent," the episode that featured the return of Lore, Data's evil twin. "Descent" adds the Borg to the mix, and parts of "Descent, Part II" are riveting.

The following episode,"Liaisons," is an odd little story about people who aren't what they seem.

"Interface" is remarkable largely for the virtual reality probe device which Geordi employs to explore areas too dangerous for a person to enter. It introduces his parents for the first time, only to have his mother immediately killed off. It's an interesting storyline, but Geordi so rarely gets character episodes that one would have thought that the story could have served him better than it does.

## PICARD UNDERCOVER

The two-part story "Gambit" is a good story involving Captain Picard going undercover (without telling anyone) to join a gang of space pirates. He uses the cover name Galen (the name of his late professor, seen in the episode "The Chase"), and the story has many interesting twists and turns which make it worth repeated viewing. Robin Curtis, who played Saavik in two *Star Trek* feature films, appears here as a Romulan who is a Vulcan who is a Romulan. This is also the only *Next Generation* episode that reveals something new about Vulcan history.

"Phantasms" is a mystery with enough bizarre dream imagery to give viewers restless nights, particularly the Deanna Troi living cake which is having pieces cut out of it. This is a Data episode and is certainly one of the more unusual and imaginative ones.

"Dark Page" is a Deanna and Lwaxana Troi episode that offers the first dramatic turn for Lwaxana in a *Next Generation* episode since the fourth season's "Half a Life." This very good story involves suppressed memories of a sister Deanna never consciously knew she had.

"Force of Nature" is a key episode that reveals that the warp drive used by starships can cause damage in certain quadrants of space. This good story has a surprising, explosive climax.

## DID DATA HAVE A MOTHER?

As Data became more popular, more Data episodes were done, and "Inheritance" is the third one in season seven to concentrate on him. It is one of the key Data episodes in the entire seven-year run of *The Next Generation*. Here, the android meets his mother, Juliana

Tainer. She had been Dr. Soong's assistant when Data was created, but Juliana harbors a secret that even she doesn't know she possesses. This is an excellent episode that shows *The Next Generation* creative crew working at the top of their craft.

"Parallels" may well emerge as the single most popular episode in the final season of *TNG*. Ostensibly a Worf episode, it also manages to involve the rest of the crew in crucial scenes. *The Next Generation* has managed to explore the concepts of alternate realities in exciting ways that are comparable to what the original *Star Trek* achieved in "Mirror, Mirror." What *The Next Generation* does in "Parallels" is like "Mirror, Mirror" squared, as Worf keeps shifting into one parallel universe after another, causing the parallel Worfs to shift as well. The climax, where we see what some of these other universes are like—including one in which the Borg have conquered the Federation—is genuinely mind-bending.

In its own way, "The Pegasus" is as exciting as "Parallels." It explores the past of Commander Riker. The Romulans appear in this episode, along with some of the most interesting special effects scenes presented in the series to date. This is a wonderful mystery story with a very satisfying payoff that should not be spoiled for anyone before they experience it.

"Journey's End" features the return of Wesley Crusher in a story which ties in to elements introduced in the first season of *TNG*. It resolves issues introduced seven years before and writes a finish to the character, whom Paramount has decided not to include in the feature films.

## THE RETURN OF ENSIGN RO

"Homeward" is an episode that shows a distinctly dark side to the Federation. When the Prime Directive dictates that the last survivors of a race of intelligent people on a doomed planet must be left to die, Worf's brother intervenes and saves them. In a third-season episode, "The High Ground," a character criticized the Federation for hiding behind the Prime Directive when it comes to making certain difficult ethical decisions. "Homeward" proves the truth of that accusation.

"Lower Decks" introduces several new characters in an intriguing story that ably demonstrates how much we can get involved in the lives of well-rendered characters we've only just met. When was the last time you saw an episode of *The Next Generation* that introduced several new crew members and told a story that focused on them to the virtual exclusion of all the other regulars? The episode is an interesting experiment that works quite well, demonstrating that even previously unknown characters can be compelling if written well.

The Maquis, a group of Federation anti-Cardassian terrorists introduced on *Deep Space Nine*, figure prominently in one of the best episodes of season seven. "Preemptive Strike" features the long-awaited return of Ensign Ro, an important regular during the fifth season. Ro Laren agrees to go undercover to help the Federation destroy the Maquis and prevent a border war with the Cardassians. Ro discovers that the Maquis may be fighting the good fight after all. When she sees a friend slain by the Cardassians in a sneak attack, her decision is made. This is a fine character episode and a good drama that opens a variety of possibilities.

## FINAL BOWS

"All Good Things" is the end of *Star Trek: The Next Generation* on television. Although some cast members openly complained that they didn't understand why the series was being canceled at the height of its success, it is possible that Paramount can make more money by doing a series of motion pictures and making room for the new series, *Star Trek: Voyager*.

"All Good Things" is not as compelling as "Preemptive Strike." The plot is complex and it is enjoyable to see one possible future and what it is like, both for the characters and the Federation. This is a fun story the first time you see it, but doesn't hold up to repeated viewing as "Parallels" and "Preemptive Strike" do. "Gambit" is better written, but isn't as cosmic in scope. The strength of "All Good Things" involves the use of time travel and seeing Picard interacting with the same people in different times, including Tasha Yar. Seeing the future version of Data with his several pet cats is also a hoot.

In seven years, *The Next Generation* accomplished a great deal, and this was well exemplified in seasons six and seven. Although Roddenberry had frozen the show into an unrealistic idealism where the crew of the *Enterprise* existed in perfect and absolute harmony, "Chain of Command" aptly demonstrated just how that harmony could be ruptured. That one episode showed many of the unrealized potentials that still exist in the characters on the series.

## CHARACTER QUIRKS

In the original *Star Trek*, Kirk and McCoy, and McCoy and Spock had realistic disagreements. Under stress human tempers would flare and Spock would come close to expressing the Vulcan equivalent of exasperation. On *TNG* there is no apparent stress—except with people who are not regular members of the crew. Visitors seem to easily rub people the wrong way, as evidenced by Lwaxana Troi. Riker's encounter with his estranged father is another example. In season six, when Scotty gets on Geordi's nerves, La Forge explodes and tells Montgomery Scott off. This never happens between Riker and

Picard, or Picard and anyone in the regular cast. It's a strange schizophrenic approach to the characters on *The Next Generation*, and it can all be traced back to Roddenberry. He made it very clear that the new crew of the *Enterprise* was "perfect."

This seems to be changing now. Rather than demeaning Roddenberry's dream, it is broadening it into a more believable reality. After all, if someone is "perfect," then what goals could they have? The future depicted in *Star Trek*, whether in the original or *The Next Generation*, is not a perfect world. It is an improved future hundreds of years beyond our own, but it is also more complex, with just as many difficult problems as we have today.

By showing a humanity that has moved beyond certain shortcomings of today is admirable, but to proclaim that they have abruptly triumphed over millions of years of emotional strife is unrealistic. Better that we see they have left some of that strife behind, just as twentieth-century humanity has in many respects left behind the kind of strife they lived with three hundred years before. While not close to perfect, we are attempting not to repeat the mistakes of our ancestors. Better that *The Next Generation* films and *Voyager* continue with this approach as well.

In 1968, when the original *Star Trek* series was canceled, many people wrote a finish to the saga. Fans, however, wouldn't let it die. It was a battle in the 1970s to bring about the revival. Not even the most die-hard fan of twenty years ago would believe the 1980s would see a new *Star Trek* series that would last 178 episodes and usher in additional spin-offs. *Star Trek* would never again solely live in the province of reruns.

PART

# DEEP SPACE NINE

*One good spin-off deserves another. While* Star Trek: The Next Generation *got off to an uneasy start in 1987, it soon found its wings and has been at or near the top of the syndicated ratings ever since. It was only a question of when Paramount would decide to try to catch lightning in a bottle for the third time, for now they had the confidence of repeated success behind them and the people on staff with the proven know-how to do it.*

# THE THIRD GENERATION

## INTRODUCTION

*Deep Space Nine* features several regular characters. The commander of the space station is Benjamin Sisko, a Starfleet captain who was serving with his wife, Jennifer, onboard one of the vessels attacked by Picard when the *Enterprise* captain had been transformed into Locutus of Borg. Sisko's wife was killed in the attack, and he had been rotated back to Earth in semi-retirement to recover from the ordeal. His command of the space station is his first active-duty post since his wife was killed three years before. He finds it difficult to accept that Picard was *completely* helpless to stop the attack. But Sisko's feelings about Picard were explored in the premiere episode, "Emissary," thereby resolving that conflict immediately rather than continuing it into the series. Along with Sisko on *Deep Space Nine* is his son, Jake, played by Cirroc Lofton.

"We felt that a father-and-son relationship would be a different relationship than any other *Star Trek* kind of hero that we've seen before," series cocreator Michael Piller explains. "He has found himself at a place in his life that he can't quite get beyond and he's sent to this space station, and he really doesn't like this assignment because this space station was built by the Cardassians, who have just abandoned it. The Bajorans are struggling with the potential of civil war." Piller's description of the Bajorans has proven to be somewhat exaggerated, as thus far the planet Bajor has been talked about a lot more than it's been visited and seen.

Although Sisko wasn't initially happy with his assignment, all this changed when the stable wormhole was discovered. The importance of *Deep Space Nine* became elevated immeasurably in the eyes of the Federation. In further describing this character, Piller said, "He is sent on a quest and in this whole pilot episode it is a personal quest for this man who has lost his way and must conquer the dragon, but in this case he must conquer his personal dragons in order to move on with his life and to grow as a man and to be a good father and to be a good officer. And so what we will find in this show is a man who is coming to *Deep Space Nine*, but is coming to find himself."

## AN ALIEN FOR ANY OCCASION

Another character is a shape shifter, Odo, who is also the security chief. Odo came from a world on the other side of the wormhole, but he does not remember his past, having been found aboard a drifting spacecraft fifty years before. In order to fit in among the people who found him, he has chosen to adopt a humanoid form, but his efforts at maintaining this form are imperfect. The producers have stated that this character will be used to explore the nature of humanity and what truly defines one as being human. In this way he will occupy the position of Spock and Data, as those characters have been used to act as a mirror of humanity in the other two *Star Trek* series. But being neither part human nor an android, the approach has been completely different from that taken with either Spock or Data.

Odo is played by Rene Auberjonois and is already being touted as one of the main characters to emerge from the series. "He is the curmudgeon of all curmudgeons," Piller states. "So instead of Data, who worships humanity and wants to be that, and Spock who would deny it, Odo has been forced to pass as a humanoid all of his life, to look like us and act like us because it's a lot more socially acceptable, and he resents it. So he has now found a way to use it as a defense mechanism and keep a distance from it and find ways to be critical of the human condition. . . . He is one of a kind," Piller revealed. "He was found near where this wormhole shows up, as an infant in a spacecraft, which we are going to assume probably came out of the Gamma Quadrant. But he has no idea where he came from and he's always searching for his identity."

Regarding the makeup that disguises him, the actor explained, "It's a mask, but it feels what I feel is in the script for the character, and I find it very evocative." One plot thread regarding Odo was revealed when Majel Barrett appeared as Lwaxana Troi and became a romantic interest for the alien shape shifter. When he reveals to her that he has to turn into a bucket of liquid every night, she unhesitatingly replies, "That's okay. I can swim."

Odo had emerged from the wormhole fifty years before and had served the Cardassians on the space station long before Starfleet determined that *Deep*

*Space Nine* had any strategic importance. The alien is just as willing to assist Starfleet as he did the Cardassians for the past half century. With Starfleet planning to explore the galaxy through the wormhole, he believes that he may at last uncover the clues he needs to unlock the secrets to his past. A shape shifter similar to this alien appeared in *Star Trek VI: The Undiscovered Country.*

## TROUBLESHOOTER AND A TRILL

Colm Meaney, whose role as Miles O'Brien, the transporter chief, had been growing on *The Next Generation,* was transferred from the *Enterprise* in the premiere episode of *Deep Space Nine,* where he became Chief of Operations on the station. His character changes are explored as the viewers compare his *Enterprise* duties with his duties on *Deep Space Nine.*

"We've always thought he was a terrific performer," Piller states, "and now we're giving him something much more interesting to do as a leading character on the new show. He is pulling his hair out from one minute to the next because everything is breaking down. He can't get the replicators to make a good cup of coffee; his wife Keiko is terribly unhappy about having been taken off the *Enterprise* and over to this dreadful space station. So he finds himself in an uncomfortable position." The subplot with Keiko was mostly resolved early on when she opened a school for the children living on the station, and in fact her character has largely been relegated to the background ever since.

The science officer aboard the space station is played by Terry Farrell. Lieutenant Jadzia Dax is an alien known as a Trill. The Trill were introduced in the *Next Generation* episode "The Host," where we were shown that the Trill are a dual species that join to become a single entity. Since the sex of the host body is unimportant to the Trill, the three-hundred-year-old Dax now inhabits the body of a young woman. Previously Dax inhabited the body of an older man, Curzon Dax, who was a mentor of Captain Benjamin Sisko's. But in its new body, Sisko finds that he's physically attracted to Dax.

Originally they had conceived Dax as being a very serene and focused character, but according to Piller, "The more we've written her, the more we're finding that she is not what she appears to be. That underneath this placid exterior, there's all these various personalities that she's gone through that are in turmoil and there's a lot of inner conflict. You know all the voices we hear inside of ourselves are all made up of different subpersonalities; well she's got them all screaming at her in a variety of different ways."

## A DOCTOR AND A QUARK

Siddig El Fadil plays Dr. Julian Bashir, a twenty-seven-year-old Starfleet medical officer. His youth and inexperience will be emphasized, since he has just graduated from Starfleet Medical and this is his first post outside of the Sol system. Dr. Bashir thinks he knows it all and has a knack for rubbing people the wrong way, although he means well and is a very likable character. Piller speaks highly of the actor, stating, "He's able to take this character, who can be very grating on the nerves, and make him charming."

Armin Shimerman plays the Ferengi bartender, Quark. Quark is one of the shifty, untrustworthy aliens introduced in year one of *The Next Generation*. He has his hands into all sorts of illegal and improper activities going on behind the scenes aboard *Deep Space Nine*. His ongoing presence is intended to create constant conflicts aboard the space station, but as a series regular he'll be in a position to have a more fully developed role than any Ferengi who has been presented to date. In fact he forges a friendship of a sort with Benjamin Sisko, and will be liked (but not entirely trusted) by his compatriots. The actor explains that, like *The Next Generation,* in *Deep Space Nine* the staff has created "fascinating aliens that have three sides." One of the more interesting relationships on the show is that between Quark and Odo, as they're sworn enemies who have an ongoing verbal conflict. Before the series aired, those involved with the show were predicting that Quark would emerge as the most popular character. The fact that he has been thus far written and portrayed as pretty much of a cartoon rather than a character has tended to limit that possibility a great deal.

*Deep Space Nine* is not noticeably different from *The Next Generation* in style and approach. And like any new series, it suffered from growing pains in its first season. The characters, who seemed so clearly defined in "Emissary," became subservient to the plots. Major Kira, who was clearly antagonistic to Commander Sisko initially, was suddenly completely accepting of him and the Federation presence. In fact for the first season she seemed no less a Federation representative than Sisko himself. By the end of the first season, and into the second and third, the supporting cast, especially the character of Odo—due primarily to the acting experience of Auberjonois—continued to mature into a much stronger element for what have been increasingly more demanding storylines.

## UNFRIENDLY ALIENS

The Cardassians form the continuing threat in the series, as the space station is right on the edge of Cardassian space. The Bajoran homeworld, the planet around which *Deep Space Nine* is in orbit, was ravaged by the Cardassians before they left it after being overthrown by the Bajorans in a war. This left the Bajorans in a sorry state, as the planet had been so severely damaged in the war that the Bajorans were left with nothing to rebuild with. This is why the Bajorans have turned to the Federation and requested admission, although many of them continue to resent the fact that the Federation maintained a neutral distance while the Bajoran people were being exploited and brutalized by the Cardassians.

The presence of warring cultures was also key to the basis of the series. "Our whole goal was to create more conflict everywhere you turn in this series. So what you have as a result are people who have different agendas. You've got Major Kira, who is a Bajoran, who really doesn't want the Federation to be there, and as a result she and Sisko are in conflict. You've got Odo and Quark who are in conflict. You've got Sisko and Quark who are in conflict. Everywhere you turn you've got conflict in the show. But what we found as a result of that is not only good drama, but a lot more humor than we expected to have."

While humor is always a good idea when kept in balance, it has largely replaced the initial conflict presented in the series premiere. Odo and Quark have a humorous conflict rather than a dramatic one, just as Sisko and Kira do with Quark. In "The Passenger," even though Quark is shown providing hired mercenaries at the behest of a brutal murderer, he's portrayed almost as though he is being forced to do it.

Berman and Piller had been pushing for a spin-off from *The Next Generation* for two years, and when they worked out the details of *Deep Space Nine*, Paramount was quite enthusiastic in their support of the series concept and gave the producers a great deal of latitude in the casting. Michael Piller states that, "There is absolutely no truth to the rumor that the arrival of *Deep Space Nine* is the end of *The Next Generation*. *The Next Generation* is continuing." Majel Barrett was once quoted as stating that *The Next Generation* was projected to run for six seasons, whereupon the syndication package would be considered complete. But it did continue, ending in its seventh season.

## BAJOR—A PLANET ABUSED

*Deep Space Nine* is set aboard a space station in orbit around the planet Bajor. The space station was being used by the Cardassians to exploit the mining resources of the Bajoran homeworld. When the Bajorans finally overthrew the despotic rule of the Cardassians, the Federation placed personnel aboard *Deep Space Nine* to oversee its operation and make sure everything stayed cordial and cooperative. But while the Federation personnel will not be officially acting as police, their presence is consciously there to discourage the Cardassians from trying to bother the newly liberated Bajorans. Since the Bajorans have applied for membership in the Federation, their presence there is by the invitation of Bajor.

The Bajorans have been encountered previously, as they are the race to which Ensign Ro belongs. While Ensign Ro is an ex-terrorist who was more or less drafted into Starfleet due to her expertise in certain matters, *Deep Space Nine* deals with a different aspect of the Bajorans. While the character of Ensign Ro was initially announced as appearing in this new series, the actress, Michelle Forbes, chose to bow out to pursue other projects, while remaining as an occasional character on *The Next Generation*.

The space station *Deep Space Nine* was established by the Cardassians and the Bajorans in conjunction with other alien races. As a result it reflects cultural needs and biases often unfamiliar to some Starfleet personnel. The station was considered of remote interest until the first stationary wormhole was discovered near the star system where Bajor is located. In fact this wasn't discovered until after Commander

Sisko was posted to the space station. This discovery, in fact, caused the Cardassians to consider retaking *Deep Space Nine* and Bajor for its strategic importance.

Bajor has been described as a stripped mining planet, but one whose culture is very conscious of the spiritual and the mystical. The Bajorans even believe that the stationary wormhole was created through divine intervention. Its existence has saved what was a dying, backwater world. One of the semiregular characters is a religious leader from Bajor who holds very strong views on the purpose of the wormhole. Kai Opaka, as the series bible indicates, is to be a semiregular character and provides a fairly detailed description of her. She is the spiritual leader of Bajor, and is intended to provide a sharp counterpoint to the secular nature of Starfleet. The Kai can supposedly explore her guests' "pagh" (which refers to a person's energy meridian) through deep-tissue massage of their ears, and this can supposedly reveal a person's true nature. I expect Quark would particularly enjoy this encounter.

In the premiere episode, it is the Kai who reveals to Sisko that he's fated to find the celestial temple, the source of the mysterious and wondrous orbs that are a vital element of the Bajoran religion. According to the *Deep Space Nine* series bible, "The Kai seems to have an awareness on a higher plane of consciousness, and knows things she cannot possibly know. Although our people do not accept her 'powers' at face value, we cannot always explain them either. She speaks in vague, mystical and indirect language, forcing the listener to seek her meaning." As the series continues, successor Kais have been elected, showing more detail of Bajoran culture.

## THE FUTURE OF *STAR TREK*

The stories, many of which are confined to the station, often create a claustrophobic sensation on the show. This has caused rather confining situations on the plots, as well. It wasn't until episode eleven, "Vortex," that we finally got out and about again like we did in "The Emissary," as Odo went through the wormhole and into the Gamma Quadrant. Granted, all we saw was a rocky asteroid, but there was also a space battle that in some respects was a reprise of the one seen eleven years ago in *Star Trek II—The Wrath of Khan*. Now if only we could visit those mysterious archaeological sites referred to in "Q Less," we might finally see some real otherworld excitement. The addition of a small ship to be docked at *Deep Space Nine* in the third season is promising.

Set in the year A.D. 2360, the new series is contemporary with *The Next Generation*. While the extent of crossovers between the two series has yet to be fully determined, *Star Trek: Deep Space Nine* was launched with a two-hour premiere, "Emissary," that included a stopover from the *Enterprise* and Jean-Luc Picard. But Starfleet personnel accustomed to the clean, modern conveniences of starship life find very different things to contend with aboard the space station. These include a casino and a holographic brothel, as the station also serves as a port of call for merchant ships. But once the station was cleaned up in early episodes, any "darker" aspects to the show all but vanished.

A crossover between *Deep Space Nine* and *The Next Generation* took place in March 1993 in the two-part *TNG* episode "Birthright." Worf stops over on *Deep Space Nine* and encounters someone who claims to know where his long-lost Klingon father is. The station actually plays just a peripheral element in the storyline, as the *Deep Space Nine* regulars are not involved in the drama or the action that follows.

By establishing *Deep Space Nine* as being contemporary with *The Next Generation,* characters from that series will still turn up on the new series even though *TNG* has gone off the air. With the highly rated appearance of James Doohan on *The Next Generation* in the fall of 1992, Doohan has reportedly been urging Paramount to add him to the cast of *Deep Space Nine.* Less certain are rumors wherein Shatner has expressed interest in participating in *Deep Space Nine* in some respect, which would be a surprise since he has steadfastly refused to be involved in *The Next Generation* (which has thus far been visited by Dr. McCoy, Mr. Spock, and Montgomery Scott), and in fact Shatner claims never to have watched the show.

*The Next Generation* was slated to go into production as a new series of feature films once the seventh season ran out, *Generations,* which is a crossover between the original *Star Trek* and *TNG* but does not include *DS9.*

It's hard to believe that back in the seventies, many people were saying that *Star Trek* was just old news and that nothing would ever be done with the premise again. *Deep Space Nine* has shown that there are many more directions in which the concept created by Gene Roddenberry and company can be spun, and with the success of *Deep Space Nine* and plans for yet another *Star Trek* TV series in 1995, *Star Trek: Voyager,* there will no doubt be even more spinoffs in years to come.

CHAPTER

# THE BACKGROUND

*When Paramount announced the launch of* The Next Generation *almost eight years ago, there were more doubters than believers. Following its unqualified success, it was inevitable that they'd return to Roddenberry's realm for yet another run at the stars.*

# BEHIND THE SCENES: THE CREATION

January 1993 marked the deep-space launch of *Star Trek: Deep Space Nine*. Ironically the announcement of the plans to produce this series came shortly after the death of Gene Roddenberry in late 1991. The timing led to speculation that had Roddenberry lived, this series might not have. Suspicions along these lines were raised particularly after descriptions of this new series filtered out. "It's going to be darker and grittier than *The Next Generation*," executive producer Rick Berman stated in the March 6, 1992, *Entertainment Weekly*. "The characters won't be squeaky clean."

To the fans, *Star Trek* has always meant just that—squeaky-clean heroes. What would Gene Roddenberry have thought of this? After all, people close to him have stated that Gene hated *Star Trek VI* merely because it postulated *Enterprise* crew members who were anti-Klingon bigots. In the future that Roddenberry made, humankind had outgrown such pettiness. Gene overlooked the fact that in the 1966 *Star Trek* episode "Balance of Terror," an *Enterprise* crewman was presented as being an angry anti-Romulan bigot who transferred his feelings of mistrust and suspicion to Mr. Spock when it was discovered that Romulans and Vulcans were of the same race. As it has turned out, though, the only character on the new series in its first season who had a real dark side is Quark. Major Kira is a former terrorist, but she fought on the "correct" side of the conflict. At worst, Dax had an affair with a married woman when the Trill was in her former host body, that of the man Curzon Dax. The characters couldn't be much more well scrubbed than this.

Rick Berman and Michael Piller were originally at a loss for a title for the newest addition to the *Star Trek* canon. They toyed with calling the series "The Final Frontier" and having the space station rechristened with a Starbase number after the Federation took over the day-to-day operations of the station. Having a series with a Cardassian or Bajoran name was not considered a terribly good marketing ploy. In the course of the series' development, the station was dubbed *Deep Space Nine*, a temporary appellation that not only became permanent but also became the title for the fledgling series itself, despite Piller and Berman's dissatisfaction with the name.

Even though the announcement about *Deep Space Nine* seemed to come from out of nowhere several weeks after Roddenberry's death, Michael Piller and Rick Berman had actually been discussing ideas for a new series for some time. It was always planned to be a spin-off from *Star Trek*. Even though the ideas were discussed with Paramount, it never went beyond the planning stages. When Brandon Tartikoff moved from being the head of NBC to being the head of Paramount, he told Rick Berman that he wanted to see a spin-off from *Star Trek* to launch into syndication. Berman and Piller returned to their series notes and worked up a proposal for *Deep Space Nine.*

The reason that Paramount wanted a new *Star Trek* television series to run concurrently with *The Next Generation* was to help establish *Deep Space Nine* so that when *The Next Generation* went into reruns, a new and different *Star Trek* series will already have been established and be in place in the syndication market. Originally, *Star Trek: Deep Space Nine* was syndicated with another new Paramount series, a revival of the fifties series *The Untouchables,* which was quickly canceled. The ratings success of *Deep Space Nine,* which has put it neck and neck with *The Next Generation,* has thus far shown Paramount's judgment in launching the new series to be a sound one. As plans for a Paramount television network are further developed, further series will likely be planned.

## RODDENBERRY'S INFLUENCE

Rick Berman insists that *Deep Space Nine* is not going to be his and executive producer Michael Piller's own personal take on *Star Trek.* He states that this series is just another way of expressing Gene Roddenberry's vision, and it is fitting and consistent with everything that has been done with *Star Trek* before. *Deep Space Nine* was initially announced as having been developed under Gene's guidance and with his input. However later statements contradicted this and indicated that while *Star Trek*'s creator was aware of the plans for *Deep Space Nine,* he wasn't directly involved with it at any time.

Regarding Roddenberry's influence on *Deep Space*

*Nine,* Piller explained, "Every writer knows that we have a responsibility to maintain his vision. We take it very seriously. I got a letter from twenty-five grade-school children, and the teacher, who said, 'Please, we use *Star Trek* as an example of life in the future and the optimistic view and the hope that Gene gave us. We've heard that this is going to be dark and dreary.' And the truth is that it is not."

But by the time Roddenberry created the backdrop for *The Next Generation,* he had adopted the philosophy that all the members of Starfleet should be in harmony, particularly those who work together on a starship. "He had very clear-cut rules about Starfleet officers having any tension or conflict between themselves. His futuristic humans were too good for that," Berman told *Variety* in the January 25, 1993, issue. "As a result, it's very difficult to write for these people, because out of conflict comes good drama."

## THE DARK LIGHT YEARS?

Producer Rick Berman sees the show as a means of escaping the somewhat limiting constraints of Gene Roddenberry's original *Star Trek* concept. "We set about creating a situation, an environment, and a group of characters that could have conflict without breaking Gene's rules. We took our characters and placed them in an unfamiliar environment, one that lacked the state-of-the-art comfort of the *Enterprise,* and where there were people who didn't want them there."

On *Deep Space Nine,* set in a rough-and-tumble corner of the known universe, Berman sees a lot more room for conflict. "By putting Starfleet characters on an alien space station with alien creatures, you have immediate conflicts."

"The truth is that there is more conflict," Piller says, trying to put the show and its various elements into perspective, "that we're in a part of the universe that is giving us more conflict. And the fact that we are on an alien space station instead of the *Enterprise* will allow us to do that. But it is the same Gene Roddenberry optimism for the future of mankind that drives the vision of this show. There is not going to be any more shooting, more weapons or battles or anything like that. Certainly we're going to have action. It's going to be an adventure show and it's an entertainment show. We wanted to find the camaraderie that existed in the original *Star Trek*, like that relationship between McCoy and Spock, and in order to do that you have to have differences, and differences between the characters on *The Next Generation* are not so clearly defined."

One character whose personality is explored more is Miles O'Brien. He has more room to be curt and unpleasant from time to time. Less regimented than a Federation ship, the space station, from which *Deep Space Nine* draws its title, leaves its inhabitants more room to express the less agreeable aspects of their personalities. On the other hand, this also leads to scenes in which O'Brien and Commander Sisko discuss matters in a considerably more relaxed and informal fashion than O'Brien would ever have been able to employ while speaking with Captain Picard.

"There are characters who come through much darker than the *Next Generation* characters, but I don't know that I could say this is a dark series," Piller says reflectively. "It's still Gene Roddenberry's vision. It has an optimistic view of mankind in the future. Reason and dialogue and communication are still the key weapons in the fight to solve problems. I think the label of darker is probably exaggerated."

## A NEW ORDER

Michael Piller never had any doubt that there was room for a third *Star Trek* series. He feels that Gene

Roddenberry created a huge universe of characters and concepts. "Gene used to say, somewhat in kidding, but in a way to communicate what he wanted to do with *Star Trek*, that space was like the Old West, and that *Star Trek* was like *Wagon Train*. In that whole genre of the West there were dozens of television shows. In the universe that Gene has created there is room, not only for a *Wagon Train*, but also for a *Gunsmoke*. In essence, what I think we're doing is the counterpart to the kind of shows you saw on the Old West where you have a Ft. Sheridan on the edge of the frontier, and a frontier town in a very active area with a lot of people coming through it."

Among the other ideas Berman and Piller discussed was the concept of creating a sort of futuristic Hong Kong on a planet surface and building a set in the desert north of Los Angeles where they'd film the series.

"We felt that would be extremely expensive and difficult to produce," Piller stated in *Variety*, "so we took our Hong Kong and put it on a space station, then we scaled it back in order to make it cost-effective."

Berman explained that coming up with *Deep Space Nine* after working on *The Next Generation* was like living in a house for several years and then deciding to remodel.

"This was how we felt about *Star Trek*. It was very close to us, but there was a lot of 'wouldn't it be nice.' Developing *Deep Space Nine* gave us the opportunity to rebuild the house."

## ORIGINS AND IDEAS

The groundwork for *Star Trek: Deep Space Nine* was created in a couple of episodes of *The Next Generation:* "Ensign Ro" and "The Wounded." Viewers met their first Bajoran in the person of the troublesome Ensign Ro (portrayed by Michelle Forbes), and got a glimpse of the difficult conditions on Bajor after a century of occupation by the genuinely disagreeable Cardassians. Just prior to the premiere of *Deep Space Nine, The Next Generation* featured a two-part episode in which Captain Picard was captured and tortured by Cardassians.

But it seems that much of what would lead to the ideas for *Deep Space Nine* grew out of the political situation that was created for the fifth-season *Next Generation* episode "Ensign Ro."

"We did not create Ensign Ro as a potential spin-off, but for all intents and purposes, that's where the tableau was set for this. We had intended to bring that character with us to *Deep Space Nine,*" Michael Piller explained on the QVC cable channel during his appearance there December 5, 1992, "but the actress, who we love, Michelle Forbes, simply wasn't interested in doing a series. So after we had actually written a bible and created a script, we had to write that character out of it. But it all grew out of that character." A different actor, Nana Visitor, was cast in the role of the Bajoran regular on the series, Major Kira Nerys. She is Benjamin Sisko's first officer and the station's Bajoran attaché, and of her role she states, "The thing that is the most exciting is the script, and the fact that the women in the show are very strong, very powerful, and that it's a lot to do with what's going on in the world right now." Kira Nerys is portrayed as a strong action hero of the kind who would lead rescue missions.

Berman and Piller wrote several different versions of the series bible while it was being developed. The series bible is called that because it serves as the basis of development for the entire series. All of the characters and their relationships are outlined in it as well as the background of everything used in the series. When they finally showed a later version to Paramount, the studio provided its own input into the project, and in fact Brandon Tartikoff (before he left Paramount) suggested that the show might be something like *The Rifleman* in outer space, although Berman and Piller didn't quite feel that this idea particularly fit in with what they were trying to develop. But the studio's suggestions were weighed and incorporated into the series concept to produce the final result used now. In fact the father-and-son idea that Brandon Tartikoff was talking about did appeal to Berman and Piller, and that element is very much a part of the series.

## PITCHING THE SPIN-OFF

These two veterans of *Star Trek: The Next Generation* had been thinking about creating a new series together for some time. It was Rick Berman, in fact, who first presented Gene Roddenberry with the notion of a *Next Generation* spin-off. But Roddenberry died in October of 1991, before he and Berman could discuss the idea at any length. In a famous meeting with Tartikoff and studio executive John Pike, Rick Berman revealed that, by a happy coincidence, he and Michael Piller already had a series concept in the works. Actually, they had more than one: another, non-*Star Trek* concept involved a series with a medieval setting for its science-fiction plots. This was a handy alternative in case Piller and Berman were unable to sway the Paramount studio from its reluctance to do a spin-off of *The Next Generation*.

It was back in October of 1991, when Piller and Berman began developing the show, that they decided to set the series in the same time frame as *The Next Generation*. "That was a decision made consciously to take advantage of all of the alien races; the universe that has been developed over the last five years of *The Next Generation*. We have characters we want to bring onto *Deep Space Nine* that we've seen on *The Next Generation*. We've got political situations. We've got relationships with the Romulans and the Klingons, and most of all, of course, the Cardassians."

When approval for the spin-off was handed down, the team of Berman and Piller had already done plenty of work on the concept, but now the time had come to really knuckle down. It wasn't as if they had a lot of spare time, either; both men were still actively involved in their respective jobs on *Star Trek: The Next Generation*, then in its fifth season. In addition to developing *Deep Space Nine* and writing the pilot, they had to keep working on *Star Trek: The Next Generation* as well.

## VETERAN PRODUCERS

Rick Berman is the absolute boss on *Star Trek: The Next Generation* in the wake of Gene Roddenberry's passing. On *Deep Space Nine*, he shares the helm with Michael Piller.

Rick Berman and Michael Piller are both veterans of *The Next Generation*, and Piller came onboard following experiences writing on staff for the television series *Simon and Simon* and *Miami Vice*. Piller got involved in television as a journalist. He began in CBS Hollywood checking the accuracy of docudramas. His ambition was to become a producer to protect what he wrote because of all the rewriting that is done to television scripts. Piller had also previously worked on the short-lived science fiction series *Hard Time on Planet Earth*.

Michael Piller's job as executive producer of *Deep Space Nine* primarily involves overseeing the writing and development of ideas for the series. In this capacity he oversees the staff writers and works with the writer of each and every script. Rick Berman participates in that somewhat while he also contributes to his specialty, which is overseeing the production, editing, post-production, music, and other aspects of the series.

*Deep Space Nine* producer Michael Piller began his association with the *Star Trek* universe when he took charge of the scripting staff for *Star Trek: The Next Generation* during the third season. He became acquainted with producer Maurice Hurley, who invited him to meet with Gene Roddenberry. This led to an episode assignment on *The Next Generation*. Shortly after, Hurley left *The Next Generation*, and Piller was invited to join the production staff. "For the next year or so," said Piller, "Gene was really on my case and certainly Rick was on my case. Day after day, we went through the creative process as I began to learn to see life through Gene Roddenberry's eyes. And even as he became sick and trusted Rick and me more and more to execute this vision, to this day, even in death, he is an extraordinary influence on both of us." He is generally credited with being responsible for the subsequent changes in *Next Generation* story development as well as general script improvement. When the shift over to *Deep Space Nine* came, one of Piller's first tasks was to hire Ira Behr as one of his main writers; he hired Peter Allan Fields away from *The Next Generation* to write as well.

With the advent of the new series, Piller bowed out of some of his *Next Generation* tasks, but still maintained control over script development along with executive producer Jeri Taylor. His main focus was on his new project: his goal for *Deep Space Nine* was to oversee the production of eighteen scripts for the first, short season.

## WRITING "EMISSARY"

Piller admits that he was influenced slightly by the *Next Generation* pilot, "Encounter at Farpoint," for the *Deep Space Nine* pilot, "Emissary." Piller took his cue from "Encounter at Farpoint" in delaying the introduction of some key characters until later in the story. (Geordi and Riker only came in much later in the *Next Generation* pilot, for instance.)

"Emissary," scripted by Piller from a story by Berman and Piller, would cost as high as twelve million dollars to film (two million of which went to building the standing sets for the series). Obviously, Paramount was more than willing to bank on this project.

Another key plot ingredient inspired by "Encounter at Farpoint" was the necessity of having the lead character (in this case, Benjamin Sisko) explain or justify humanity to an alien race. This may already have become a bit of a cliché in the *Star Trek* universe. How many times did Jim Kirk face the same basic problem during his career? It must have run a close second to outsmarting malevolent computers. This time around Piller managed to give the idea an interesting spin. Sisko must communicate with aliens who do not understand humans and their ilk because they do not, themselves, experience time in a linear fashion (if at all). Sisko is thus faced with the difficult task of explaining time, human consciousness, and the importance of humanity's past experiences to an utterly uncomprehending alien form of consciousness. (One might suspect that these aliens were in fact Kurt Vonnegut's Tralfamadorians out on a lark, but no evidence to support this idea can be found in the pilot as filmed, alas.)

Unfortunately, Piller was dissatisfied with his early versions of the script for "Emissary" and continually involved a somewhat reluctant Rick Berman in constant rehashing of their original story ideas. The basic plot with Sisko explaining humanity to the unseen aliens was, Piller thought, too talky, and the other aspect of the story—the transition to Federation command of the space station—seemed to be suffering.

In the early concepts of the series, the setting of *Deep Space Nine* was to have been a dilapidated, seedy space station with technology that lagged somewhat behind that of the Federation. In the course of series development, this notion had been scrapped in favor of a more high-tech look. Now, however, Piller was forced to rethink his whole approach.

The Los Angeles riots of 1992 gave Piller his breakthrough idea. While the station would still be a fairly advanced piece of alien technology, Piller decided that the departing Cardassians would ransack the place, leaving a shambles that Sisko would be faced with rebuilding. Now the new commander's job would involve convincing the merchants of the Promenade, and other inhabitants of the station, to stay and pull things back together.

This, in turn, helped Piller to develop the relationship between Security Chief Odo (Rene Auberjonois) and the Ferengi huckster Quark (Armin Shimerman).

## RICK BERMAN

Rick Berman is quick to insist that the creation of *Deep Space Nine* has in no way diminished the quality of *Star Trek: The Next Generation,* claiming the last seasons of *The Next Generation* as the best.

Ignoring the theory, expounded by certain cynics, that *The Next Generation* was made worse intentionally in order to draw bored fans' attention to *Deep Space Nine,* Berman was hopeful that both series would claim a sizable audience, pointing out that there are considerable differences between the two series. *Deep Space Nine* is not, after all, a carbon copy of *The Next Generation.*

## HERMAN ZIMMERMAN

The designer Herman Zimmerman came to *Deep Space Nine* with a strong *Star Trek* background: after all, he designed the first season for *Star Trek: The Next Generation,* as well as worked on the feature films

*Star Trek V: The Final Frontier* and *Star Trek VI: The Undiscovered Country.* After five years away from television, he responded eagerly when Berman asked him to work on the set design for the new series.

Sets for "Emissary" cost more than those for *Star Trek VI: The Undiscovered Country.* And under Zimmerman's guidance, the *Deep Space Nine* sets were created from scratch. This was, after all, to be a new setting for a series. With no reference point for Cardassian architecture, it was necessary for Zimmerman and his team to invent it out of thin air.

## CARDASSIAN POSTMODERN

In designing the Cardassian architecture, Zimmerman was inspired by the Cardassian look already established on *The Next Generation.* Unfortunately, even this was limited, as the interior of the Cardassian ships had never been seen at that time. So Zimmerman drew primarily from Bob Blackman's design for Cardassian costuming, an armored look that was somewhat crustacean in appearance. Part of the theory was that the Cardassians were big on structure, and if Cardassians felt structure was of vital importance, they would (like a crab, Zimmerman reasoned) keep structures on the outside. Zimmerman visualized a space station whose basic framework was not concealed inside, as in most human architecture, but one where all supports and structures were clearly visible both inside the sets and with outside views of the entire station.

Working with Zimmerman's basic concept, Nathan Cowley and Joe Hodges melded the desired crustacean concept with the heavy-handed impressiveness of Fascist architecture for the show's sets. As finally realized, the sets are quite imposing, but they still have their own unique appeal, a strangely alien sort of streamlining. Cardassian postmodernism if you will.

As the Cardassians are very military, their Command/Ops center (which combines all the features of Transporter Room, Engineering, and Command functions in one central location) was placed by Zimmerman in such a fashion that the commander's office can look down on it and see everything that is going on. There are literally windows everywhere in that office, so that the Cardassian commander would have had no blind spots whatsoever. The Cardassian commander's staff must have been very uncomfortable indeed under his watchful gaze.

## A HOSTILE ENVIRONMENT

Part of Zimmerman's design concept was that the sets and devices on the Cardassian-built station were not as "user-friendly" as those on, say, the *Enterprise*. Perhaps most notable are the automatic doors on *DS9*. These are large, round, cog-wheeled doors that roll noisily out of the way and then roll ominously shut. One gets the feeling that, while the smooth, almost soundless doors onboard the *Enterprise* would not, and almost certainly could not, close on you, it seems likely that Cardassian safety features were not so rigorous, and that being caught in the way of one of these portals would really hurt.

In fact, this ties in with another underlying design concept. This is, after all, an alien space station, and it is doubtful whether any of the Federation personnel onboard will ever be able to get used to living on *DS9*. Another factor contributing to this feeling is the imposing size of the sets for the show: looming bulkheads and support beams at odd angles everywhere, windows not quite shaped or set at the right level for humans and those damned doors just waiting to catch the heel of a slow-moving Ferengi.

To further enhance this off-balance sensation, Zimmerman designed a large view screen (larger than the one he created for the *Enterprise* of *The Next Generation*) that could be seen from both sides of *DS9*'s operations center. This device is turned on only when needed. Gone is the *Enterprise*'s familiar view of the stars, which always cuts back in when communications are terminated. On *DS9*, you actually see the view screen go off. A ring of blue neon (which necessitates shooting the effect with a green screen) gives a blurred edge to the view screen image, enhancing the alien look to its technology.

## DETAILS, DETAILS, DETAILS

Another aspect of on-set effects that sets *Deep Space Nine* apart from *The Next Generation* is its use of real-time video monitors with actual video images. This was made feasible by the development of techniques that can reduce video speed (a standard thirty frames per second) to the motion picture standard (twenty-four frames per second). With the image speeds matched in this fashion, it is now possible to film live video monitors without any image distortion. This is so effective that there are nearly seventy on-line video screens in use on the sets of *Deep Space Nine*. The total cost: nearly forty-five thousand dollars!

Another interesting detail can be found in the holosuites above the Promenade. Paramount's PR people insist (a bit too loudly, perhaps) that they are not being used for any sort of sexual activities. Unfortunately the actors state otherwise, particularly Armin Shimerman. Plus the episode "Move Along Home" makes it very clear in the dialogue that this is exactly what the holosuites are used for. Again, in keeping with the Cardassian design concept, they reveal the bulky holograph-producing machinery when they are shut off, as opposed to the clean yellow grid pattern seen when an *Enterprise* holodeck shuts down on *The Next Generation*.

## DESIGNING EFFECTS: RICHARD DELGADO

The opening title sequence of *Deep Space Nine* was visually realized by special-effects maven Dan Curry (whose *Next Generation* credits are lengthy). The sequence itself was designed and storyboarded by Richard Delgado, an illustrator whose bosses are Herman Zimmerman and Rick Sternbach. Preproduction illustrations are Delgado's specialty. Much of the look of *Deep Space Nine* can be directly attributed to this talented artist, who came to the new series with no previous experience working on a *Trek*-related project.

Influenced largely by the work of French artist Jean Giraud (a.k.a. Moebius), Delgado designed many of the essential but unobtrusive background details of many of the show's sets in his meticulous designs. An interplanetary banking station and a twenty-fourth-century ATM were incorporated into the Promenade set and built directly from Delgado's designs. In fact, much of the Promenade was the creation of Delgado, from alien plants to shop designs. The only complaint Delgado seems to have about his job is that his boss, Herman Zimmerman, seems to find Delgado's sketches more effective when turned upside down.

Bunks in the former Cardassian quarters were also Delgado's design. Cardassian bunk beds come equipped with a force field, in case someone tries to assassinate the sleeper. This too was Delgado's idea.

The actual design of the space station exterior (the largest version being a six-foot model) was the work of many hands. Other hands beside those of Delgado contributed to its design, including those of Rick Sternbach, Mike Okuda, set designers Joe Hodges and Nathan Crowley, and scenic artists Denise Okuda and Doug Drexler.

## FILMING *DS9:* MARVIN RUSH

*Deep Space Nine*'s chief of photography is none other than Marvin Rush, who held that same position on *The Next Generation* for three seasons. (Rush's job on *The Next Generation* having been assumed by the talented cameraman Jonathan West.) In switching shows, Rush found himself faced with a job of an entirely different scale.

The sets for *Deep Space Nine* are radically different from those for *Star Trek: The Next Generation.* They are much larger. Utilizing sets on three sound stages at Paramount Studios, including Sound Stages Four and Seventeen, *Deep Space Nine* boasts two large, multilevel sets: the Ops Center and Quark's Promenade. These sets are built more in the manner of feature film sets. Paramount has been more than willing to lavish large sums of money on the series they hope will be another smash syndication success for them.

These sets present a wide range of filming options. Camera moves on the large, sometimes complicated sets of *DS9* are not so simple. This presents a much wider range of options in terms of camera movement and techniques than was generally permitted by *The Next Generation*'s format rules.

On one hand, *Deep Space Nine* has much more room for crane shots than *The Next Generation* ever allowed. On the other hand, the cameras on *Deep Space Nine* may on many occasions be obliged to make a sudden transition from the wide-open spaces of the Promenade to the dim, cramped spaces of one of the many small shops that fill that space. While very large, the space station *DS9* has many obscure corners. All in all, there are still many challenges waiting for Marvin Rush and his *Deep Space Nine* camera crew.

## MICHAEL WESTMORE: ALIEN CREATOR

Like producers Rick Berman and Michael Piller, Emmy-winning makeup artist Michael Westmore at one point had two full-time jobs: *The Next Generation* and *Deep Space Nine*. Fortunately, he has an able staff of assistants to help him out on *DS9:* Craig Reardon, Jill Rockow, and Janna Phillips. Janna Phillips is the daughter of Fred Phillips, the very first *Star Trek* makeup artist—the man who designed the ears of Spock himself!

*Deep Space Nine* calls for so many aliens that Westmore is no longer constrained by *The Next Generation*'s rule that new aliens must be designed for a specific script. On *Deep Space Nine,* he can create aliens at will. Some will wind up as characters, and some will become an essential part of the background scenery.

One such character is the hulking Lurian, an alien who has been seen but not really included in any plot lines yet. Thus far he/it seems to be one of Quark's most reliable bar customers—sort of the Norm Peterson of the twenty-fourth century. Some creatures created for *Deep Space Nine* have also shown up in Ten Forward on *The Next Generation,* raising the interesting question—are some of these creatures simply intergalactic bar hoppers out on a never-ending binge?

Some aliens from *The Next Generation* have also shown up on *Deep Space Nine.* Viewers of the pilot episode, "Emissary," undoubtedly noticed that one of Benjamin Sisko's command officers during the battle with the Borg was a blue-skinned Bolin, a race first encountered on *The Next Generation* in the character of Captain Picard's talkative barber.

The most prominent *Next Generation* alien crossover (after the Ferengi and the Cardassians) is the character of Jadzia Dax, who is a member of the Trill—a race first encountered in the *Next Generation* episode "The Host."

The Trill ambassador featured in that episode had a significantly different appearance than Dax does: it was more of a nose and forehead makeup effect, which was dropped for the Trill character on *Deep Space Nine*. For her portrayal of Jadzia Dax, Terry Farrell, fortunately, does not need to hide her attractive features behind any sort of appliance. In her case her "Trillness" derives from her spots, which start at her hairline and run down the side of her face, her neck and presumably beyond. In "Emissary," a glimpse is had of more of her spots, at least as far down as the top of her shoulders. Westmore applies the spotting himself on a daily basis.

As if to compensate for the change in Trill appearance, Westmore's facial appliance for Rene Auberjonois's shape-shifting character of Odo is quite an extensive prosthetic, one that effectively "runs" his facial features together.

And so, with a brilliant team at work, all the elements needed to get *Deep Space Nine* on the air are in place: script, sets, special effects, actors, and their makeup. A major investment for Paramount, and a labor of love for all involved, the new series looks great, and promises to be a worthy addition to the ongoing legacy of Gene Roddenberry's lasting creation.

*Fully a year and a half before* Deep Space Nine *went on the air, the groundwork was being laid to expand the* Star Trek *universe in ways that a third series could take advantage of.*

# *LAYING THE GROUNDWORK—* *FROM* THE NEXT GENERATION *TO* DEEP SPACE NINE

While *Deep Space Nine* is the latest addition to the *Star Trek* canon, its roots can be found in the series that preceded it, *The Next Generation*. Many key elements of *Deep Space Nine* are encountered originally in episodes of *The Next Generation:* the Ferengi, the Cardassians, and the Bajorans all first appeared in that series. A brief look back at their previous histories will undoubtedly shed some interesting light on the goings-on under Benjamin Sisko's command on the space station designated *Deep Space Nine*.

## DEVOLUTION OF THE FERENGI

Gene Roddenberry had great hopes for the Ferengi: he envisioned them as the villains of *The Next Generation* and put a great deal of thought into their character. Motivated primarily by greed, they were to be utterly ruthless in their pursuit of material gain, deadly foes despite their somewhat comical appearance.

Viewers of *The Next Generation* got their first glimpse of the Ferengi in "The Last Outpost," which was the fifth episode of the series' first season. Armin Shimerman played Letek, one of the Ferengi, marking his first—but not last—time out as a member of this race. Shimerman would eventually be cast as Quark on *Deep Space Nine*, a reward for his long association with the Ferengi.

In "The Last Outpost," the Ferengi have never been seen, although there have been a few encounters with their ships—as would be seen in a later episode. Here they come across as fairly ruthless, attacking Riker and an Away Team with deadly whips. The episode also involves a slumbering alien consciousness that eventually awakens. In typical *Star Trek* fashion, it judges the character of the persons disturbing it, finding Riker to be civilized. The entity even offers to destroy the Ferengi, but Riker passes on this. The Ferengi remind him of how humans were two centuries earlier.

The Ferengi reappeared in "The Battle," another first-season episode. Here they were still pretty much villains. We also learn that it was a battle with a Ferengi ship that led to Picard's loss of his previous command, the *Stargazer*. A Ferengi ship returns the wreck of the *Stargazer* to Picard, ostensibly as a peace offering, but actually as part of a revenge plot. DaiMon Bok, commander of the Ferengi ship, is the father of the captain of the ship that attacked the *Stargazer* years before. His son died at the Battle of Maxia, as it came to be called. His plot to discredit Picard, and to drive him insane, almost works, but it is thwarted. Bok is relieved of command by a subordinate because his private vendetta violated Ferengi ethics in one crucial way: it was not profitable.

## THE FERENGI: FEARSOME OR ANNOYING?

By this time Roddenberry and his associates had come to the conclusion that the Ferengi were not the heavies that he'd hoped they would be, and they disappeared for quite some time, making only one appearance during the second season.

Notable in the fact that Armin Shimerman again appeared as a Ferengi, "Peak Performance" was perhaps the best episode so far to feature the Ferengi, although here they were not so much villains as greedy buffoons who stumbled into a wargame exercise between the *Enterprise* and another ship commanded by Riker. Thinking that the wargame is a real conflict between two Federation ships, the Ferengi suspect that something valuable is involved, and cut in, complicating matters. This established the tone of future Ferengi encounters: although their interference provided danger, they themselves were more irritating than threatening.

The third season saw no less than three Ferengi outings, all of which cast the Ferengi as greedy buffoons who figure in plot development but are in no way true antagonists—just nuisances. In "The Price," they interfered in important trade negotiations by inducing an allergic reaction in a Federation negotiator. In "Captain's Holiday," Max Grodenchik (who would eventually be cast as Quark's brother on *Deep Space Nine*) portrayed à Ferengi who, along with a few other characters, undermines Jean-Luc Picard's plans for a quiet vacation. "Ménage a Troi" revealed another aspect of the Ferengi personality: they're extremely horny (and their ears are erogenous zones). In this particular outing, perhaps the most farcical episode of *The Next Generation,* a Ferengi captain falls head over heels in lust with Lwaxana Troi and kidnaps her, Deanna, and Riker.

After a complete dearth of Ferengi episodes during the fourth season of *The Next Generation,* they returned briefly in the fifth season episode "The Perfect Mate." Here, two extremely stupid Ferengi, motivated by greed, set the plot in motion but have nothing more to do with the story.

## ONE LAST STAB AT VILLAINDOM

Then, the Ferengi actually returned as villains of a sort in the sixth-season outing "Rascals." In this tale, some very serious Ferengi outlaws actually succeed in hijacking the *Enterprise.* By a fortuitous plot coincidence, however, Picard and three other regular characters have been turned into children, while retaining their adult minds, use the Ferengi disregard for children to their disadvantage and save the ship.

As can be seen from this brief survey, the Ferengi have suffered a great deal at the hands of the creators of *The Next Generation,* who seem unable to make up their minds about what to do with them. But they saw fit to cast a Ferengi as a regular on *Deep Space Nine.* This may actually be a good move; with a single actor playing the same Ferengi every week, there is at last an opportunity to develop the character of that race and its interactions with the Federation.

## ENTER THE CARDASSIANS

For the villains of *Deep Space Nine,* Berman and Piller chose the Cardassians. They are a warlike race who were introduced in the fourth-season episode "The Wounded." Directed by Chip Chalmers from a script by Jeri Taylor, "The Wounded" examined the aftermath of a recently resolved conflict between the Federation and the Cardassians. It is revealed that

Chief O'Brien had once been involved in face-to-face combat with Cardassians and had in fact killed one in self-defense, which goes against his genial nature.

## ENSIGN RO

Drawing on the Cardassian background, Rick Berman and Michael Piller began to use the fifth season of *The Next Generation* as a means of laying the groundwork for *Deep Space Nine*.

They decided to create a new character for *The Next Generation* who would provide an introduction to the culture of the Bajorans. This character, portrayed by Michelle Forbes, would debut in the episode that bore her name, "Ensign Ro." Scripted by Michael Piller from a story by himself and Rick Berman, this episode introduces the planet Bajor and reveals its long-standing troubles with the Cardassians.

The character of Ensign Ro was well received, and Michelle Forbes would reprise it throughout the fifth season as well as (briefly) the sixth. However, any plans to have her step over to *Deep Space Nine* were scuttled when the talented actress proved unwilling to commit to full-time series work. While perfectly willing to appear as a frequent guest star, Forbes wanted to keep her options open for any possible film work that might come her way (such as the feature movie *Kalifornia*). Her last appearance as Ensign Ro in *The Next Generation* was in the seventh-season episode "A Preemptive Strike," where she returns to the *Enterprise* in order to infiltrate the Maquis—a terrorist group located in the Demilitarized Zone between the Federation and Cardassia. The episode also provided a strong link with episodes ending the second season of *Deep Space Nine*.

Actually, the role of Ro, although created as part of the groundwork for *Deep Space Nine*, had not specifically been intended to cross over to the new show. Efforts to talk Forbes into committing to a single season (there was talk of killing her off at the end of the first year!) yielded nothing, leading Michael Piller, already rewriting the pilot for *Deep Space Nine,* to create a new character to take her place.

Still, Michelle Forbes remained a part of the *Star Trek* universe. In her second appearance on *The Next Generation,* she was one of the *Enterprise* crew members stranded on the bridge in "Disaster." Things really got complicated for her in "Conundrum," when the entire *Enterprise* crew suffer a mysterious amnesia; all Ro Laren recalls is her attraction to Commander Riker, which leads to a steamy romance amidst all the other confusion—and considerable embarrassment for Riker when normalcy is restored. In "Power Play" she was Geordi's primary ally in the struggle to free Deanna Troi, Chief O'Brien, and Data from the alien entities that possessed them. After a largely supporting role in "Cause and Effect," she again teamed with Geordi La Forge in "The Next Phase," in which a Romulan plot causes both characters to vanish to the eyes of everyone but each other. While struggling with a Romulan in the same situation, they try to somehow get Data's attention, and actually attend their own funerals before they are restored to their proper place.

Ro Laren's part in the sixth season of *The Next Generation,* limited mostly to being turned into a child along with Picard, Guinan, and Keiko O'Brien in "Rascals," was brief. And only her initial appearance in "Ensign Ro" had anything to do with the fact that she was Bajoran. One can only imagine what *Deep Space Nine* would have been like with her participation. Perhaps she will return as a guest on one program or another. Until then it is to be hoped that she will find success in her career, wherever it may lead her.

## INTO DEEP SPACE

And now, *Deep Space Nine* goes forward. With the strong backgrounds of the Cardassian and Bajoran races to draw from, there should be many opportunities for exciting drama on the new series. And the Ferengi, as usual, are a wild card. It would be impossible to guess what Quark will be up to in the future, as he is a completely amoral character, acting always to his financial advantage. Certainly, *Deep Space Nine* could have been created out of whole cloth. By utilizing pieces of *Next Generation* back-history, the new series has not only a surefire audience, but a consistent link with the ongoing saga of the *Star Trek* universe.

*What is the corner of the galaxy like where the space station* Deep Space Nine *resides? What are the Bajorans like as a culture and how does their recent history affect what is happening now?*

# SPECIAL CORNER OF THE GALAXY: THE REALM OF DEEP SPACE NINE

When *Deep Space Nine* opens, it is at a turning point. Bajor has just regained its independence following a long, despotic rule, and has requested admission into the Federation. Bajor was annexed by the Cardassians four decades before. But the Cardassians were anything but benevolent despots. [Note: Some sources, including the *Deep Space Nine* writers/directors guide, incorrectly state that the Cardassians ruled Bajor for 100 years. But in the fifth-season *TNG* episode "Ensign Ro," it was established that it was forty years. This takes priority over all subsequent mentions.]

The longer the Cardassians controlled the planet, the more difficult the Bajorans became to control. They increasingly resisted the exploitation of their world with nothing being returned to benefit its people. This inevitably led to violent resistance in the form of an underground of Bajoran terrorists. The presence of the terrorists, combined with the Cardassians' completing their stripping of Bajor of all its useful resources, made the conquerors decide to withdraw and leave the Bajorans to fend for themselves. After forty years of plundering, the planet had nothing left worth stealing, or so they believed.

However, the Cardassians didn't leave quietly. As though their brutal rule was not enough, before they left they destroyed everything they could. Water supplies were poisoned, cities ravaged and burned, and even the ancient monastery, the heart of the Bajoran planet's religion, was desecrated. If the Bajorans were finally going to achieve freedom, it would be at the greatest cost the Cardassians could extract.

## BAJOR—STARTING OVER

Once the Cardassians finally withdrew, the Bajorans reluctantly turned to the Federation and requested admittance. But this was hardly a popular decision. Decades of alien rule had made many Bajorans mistrustful of foreign entanglements. Some of the terrorist underground fear that the Federation, with all its might, could all too easily step in and pick up where the Cardassians left off. Age-old political factions, once united in opposition to the Cardassians, have splintered once again and resumed old conflicts. They've taken sides both for and against admittance to the Federation.

It is only because of the obviously weakened state of Bajor, and its desperate need of assistance, that the most radical elements of these political factions have been held in check. Even so, some individuals are not above attempting to display their contempt for the Federation and any sort of alien alliances. Better to be free-standing than to be ruled by even a benevolent dictator. Starfleet has remained true to its promise to have only an advisory presence, although its scientific expertise has placed it in a command position aboard *Deep Space Nine.*

Starfleet's mission to Bajor is to spearhead the arduous diplomatic and scientific efforts that accompany the lengthy entry procedure into the Federation. All of this was complicated infinitely when the stable wormhole was discovered near Bajor.

## THE SECRET OF THE WORMHOLE

A wormhole is essentially a shortcut through space. Upon entering one end of the wormhole one almost immediately exits from the other end billions of kilometers away. A trip that would take months, years, or perhaps be otherwise impossible can be made in seconds. Previous wormholes proved to be unstable. They would disappear almost as abruptly as they appeared, with entrance and exit points changing. But the first stable wormhole, which is discovered near the Denorios asteroid field, turns out to be close to Bajor and is not discovered until after the Cardassians have left. Like any wormhole, it is visible only when an object enters or exits it.

The Bajoran wormhole will take a starship, or even something as simple as a runabout shuttle, to the Gamma Quadrant, which would otherwise have been a sixty-year journey at warp nine, presuming that one could build a starship capable of maintaining warp nine for six decades. Upon entering the wormhole, brilliant colors appear, which surround the ship. Inside, strange visual distortions affect the perceptions of the passengers as they plunge through the space-time continuum.

This newly discovered wormhole opens up a passageway to the hundreds of unexplored worlds in the Gamma Quadrant. Not only is the Federation sending ships through to make contact with them, but ships from the Gamma Quadrant are coming through to make contact with *Deep Space Nine*. This has turned the backwater commerce-starved planet of Bajor into a crossroads of both trade and scientific exploration. This is attracting travelers from all over the galaxy who otherwise would have had no reason to come there. For a planet depleted of its natural resources, this is a godsend that will insure that Bajor will be able to rebuild after the long years of destructive Cardassian rule.

The reason that this wormhole was unknown until after the Cardassians left is that it was artificially created by a species of aliens who live on a world inside the wormhole. They do not occupy the same time-space continuum as the rest of the known inhabited planets do. In fact they have no concept of past or future, as for them all of time exists simultaneously until Ben Sisko makes them understand how his species lives in a linear time line. These aliens have been sending out mysterious orbs (one every century for a thousand years) in their attempts to contact other life forms. Sisko was the first who used one to contact them. These orbs have become important religious artifacts to the Bajorans and are among the fundamental sacraments of the Bajoran religion.

## CREATION OF *DEEP SPACE NINE*

The Federation managed to prevent the Cardassians from returning to Bajor once the wormhole was discovered. But due to the continued turmoil on Bajor among its political factions, the Federation doesn't consider it safe to establish a physical presence on the surface of the planet itself. At the request of the provisional government, Starfleet takes command of the abandoned Cardassian space station which is in orbit around Bajor. The station is moved into a larger orbit which places it close to the entrance of the wormhole. This way it can be guarded against undue exploitation or control by any hostile species. But the station, called *Deep Space Nine,* remains the property of Bajor even though it is administered by Starfleet in the form of Commander Benjamin Sisko.

*Deep Space Nine* had been haphazardly assembled by the Cardassians over several years using Bajoran work teams. It was used primarily by the Cardassians to monitor mining operations on Bajor and to service the incoming and outgoing crews. About two hundred people, mostly Bajorans, still reside there, plus about fifty Starfleet officers and crewmen.

When the Cardassians abandoned Bajor, they stripped the station of all advanced technology and defense capabilities. This left Starfleet with the demanding task of making the station fully operational once more. But because the Cardassians knew what to take, not everything on the station can be made fully functional without running into recurring glitches.

The Operations Control Center (Ops), the heart of *Deep Space Nine,* is a multilevel facility lined with computer and life support systems, tactical controls, the master communications panel and a transporter pad to beam on and off the station. It is always a hub of activity as ships move in and out of the wormhole. There are shuttle bays for smaller vessels while the larger ships must dock while the starship crews have access to the space station via airlocks and interconnecting tunnels.

## A HUB OF ACTIVITY

Due to the presence of the wormhole, anywhere from ten to three hundred visitors arrive at the station as vessels arrive carrying merchants, scientists, explorers as well as spies and others who have criminal intent. While most visitors remain quartered aboard their ships, the station also has some special guest quarters. All visiting ships have to stop off at *Deep Space Nine* in order to be retrofitted with special impulse energy buffers which allow the vessels to travel safely through the wormhole. This is because the ordinary power sources the vessels use are destructive to the ionic field where the aliens who created the wormhole live.

The spacecraft available for general use by the personnel of the station are called runabouts, and Starfleet has stationed three midsize runabout-class patrol ships at *Deep Space Nine*. These ships have the capability of carrying personnel to star systems within this sector as well as through the wormhole itself. The runabouts are twenty meters long and have both impulse and warp capabilities. The runabout can achieve a maximum warp speed of 4.7. They are small, like shuttles, and are sometimes referred to as shuttles by the personnel. They are generally operated by a two-man crew, but a single person can pilot one when necessary. A runabout is capable of transporting up to forty people in a tight squeeze. The sleeping quarters in a runabout will fit six people but are both cramped and uncomfortable.

The runabouts are not built for luxury by any stretch. Directly off the cockpit is a multipurpose room that can be used for either meetings or dining. The runabouts are the only overt symbol of Federation presence in the sector. Due to the politically charged atmosphere on Bajor, no starship is on permanent duty. The powerful armaments would make the recently independent Bajorans nervous as such a vessel would seem to be a silent symbol of the restrictions that Starfleet could easily impose if it chose to do so.

## LIFE IN THE PROMENADE

In some ways life aboard *Deep Space Nine* is very similar to the way it was when the Cardassians were in charge. The Cardassians had sold the rights for commercial concessions on the station to the highest bidder. Those who won the concession rights were able to provide exclusive services to the mining crews who passed through the station on their way both to and from the planet. Since the Cardassians were stripping the planet of all its wealth, that took a lot of miners to operate a lot of machinery. The focal point of this commerce on *Deep Space Nine* is the Promenade.

The Promenade is supposed to be something between a free port and a flea market, bustling with aliens of all sorts. There's gambling, smuggling, and the worst sort of chicanery going on. The Cardassians didn't care what happened there so long as they were paid their cut. But as a nod toward keeping the peace with their unwilling servants, the Cardassians allowed a Bajoran temple there as well. Other delights included a kiosk that serves live food, a specialty that the Ferengi particularly enjoy.

The hub of activity on the Promenade is Quark's place, a bar and gambling emporium that has a brothel upstairs in the form of holodeck suites whose programming can satisfy the desire of any known intelligent species. A Ferengi, Quark owns and operates the club. He fits right in with the atmosphere the Cardassians created, because Quark was just as ruthless and untrustworthy as the average Cardassian. They respected Quark and therefore didn't trash his establishment the way they did everything else on the station when they left. The Cardassians liked Quark, which is one of the reasons Sisko and Odo continue to mistrust him.

When the Cardassians declared Bajor a loss and pulled out, Quark was considering leaving as well, believing that the Federation would put too many restrictions on him to make his business profitable. But Commander Sisko assured Quark that he would not be bothered so long as he didn't get too out of hand or engage in flagrantly illegal activity. In other words, so long as he didn't get caught. But the Federation doesn't have guards posted to insure that no one is cheated. Sisko made the deal with Quark in order to keep all of the merchants on the Promenade from leaving, and thereby devastating the economy of the station and making it unattractive for visitors. By staying, Quark showed that what was left was worth saving, as everyone knew that where a Ferengi does business has to be profitable or he wouldn't bother staying around. This was, of course, before the wormhole was discovered. After that, no one needed to be convinced to keep their businesses open on *Deep Space Nine*.

## BAJOR

The world that the station is closest to, and which it had until recently been in a tight orbit around, is Bajor. Bajor is an ancient society dedicated to spiritual pursuits. The mysterious orbs seen in "The Emissary" indicate some of what that religion involves. An old planet with an ancient culture, its people are just coming out from under the brutal Cardassian domination and are rebuilding what had been damaged or lost under that ruthless dictatorship. Bajor is a world of striking architecture with rounded domes and other spherical shapes marking the landscape. The ancients of Bajor were gifted architects and engineers even while life on Earth was just entering the Stone Age.

The Bajoran system includes several planets, with Bajor the largest and most populous. Bajor has three moons and provides access to the only known stable wormhole, connecting the Alpha Quadrant with the

Gamma Quadrant, tens of thousands of light years away. (First suggested in *The Next Generation* story "The Price.")

But Bajor is a world of contradictions. Although ancient, it is not powerful. It did not develop the technologies that led to warp drive and the weapons that could thereafter be created, and so it could not stand up to the might of the Cardassians when they arrived. Instead the Bajorans had turned inward, becoming a deeply mystical people with an ancient religion that bound them together as a people. They are a culture that believes in spiritual phenomena and is devoted to a non-secular philosophy that goes against the Federation's logical, scientific way of life. Their religious leader, known as the Kai, is curious and insightful and helped Commander Sisko when he first arrived on *Deep Space Nine*.

Due to the decades of conflict under the Cardassians, political factions have arisen. Many of these factions have different views on what is best for Bajor, particularly now that it is rebuilding. Some look outward to the promise of space and what the wormhole holds for them, while others wish to return to the insular life they knew before the Cardassians came. This political situation remains precarious and the only stabilizing influence is the Kai, who remains honored and respected.

## TERRORISTS WAIT AND WONDER

During the reign of the Cardassians, a terrorist underground had flourished, and Major Kira Nerys was a part of it. But like all terrorists, she found herself committing acts against the Cardassians which were just as revolting as the things that the Cardassians had committed against Bajorans. Eventually she found that she could not deal with this dichotomy and turned away from the terrorists. The terrorist underground still exists in scattered pockets, some on nearby worlds in the Bajoran system. The terrorists mistrust the motives of Starfleet and are willing to commit the same acts against them that they did against the Cardassians.

Although Major Kira is considered a turncoat by some in the underground, she depends on her old alliances to keep the terrorists largely in check so that *Deep Space Nine* does not erupt into a battleground of warring political factions. Thus far most of the underground has been willing to adopt a wait-and-see attitude regarding the Federation. Since the provisional government of Bajor, which all political factions recognize, has requested admission into the Federation, the underground is willing to wait and see if Starfleet is as good as its word and will indeed protect and assist Bajor without dominating or otherwise attempting to unduly influence it.

This is a corner of the universe that has known war, suffering, and deprivations of every sort. But some Bajorans who had escaped the domination of the Cardassians had already joined Starfleet in the hope of influencing the Federation into taking up their cause. The fact that the Federation considered what was happening on Bajor as "an internal problem" did not go down well, as the Bajorans considered the Prime Directive merely a tool that could be used against them by their oppressors. The Cardassians were able to so use it because they were not in the Federation, and neither was Bajor.

With Bajor abandoned by the Cardassians, and requesting admission to the Federation, Bajorans are finding that the Prime Directive can be invoked on their behalf as now any interference in their culture from another world would be considered a violation of the Prime Directive. They are not amused by the irony in that any more than they were when Bajoran refugee camps, which existed on several small worlds, would be given humanitarian assistance by the Federation only on a limited basis, i.e. food, clothing, and medical supplies. "Just enough to keep us miserable," as one Bajoran remarked.

The resentment for the Federation's aloofness in the Bajorans' time of need will not be forgotten by many for a long time and so they feel that now it is the Federation and Starfleet who have something to prove to them. How Starfleet handles their stewardship aboard *Deep Space Nine* will determine how Bajor will respond to the rest of the Federation when the planet finishes rebuilding and takes its position with the other members of the Federation council.

Star Trek, The Next Generation, Deep Space Nine—*three series all set in the same universe and following a cohesive time line. How do the main characters on these shows compare?*

# COMPARING TREKS

**BY KAY DOTY**

From the moment the news of a possible third *Star Trek* series leaked to the public, fandom was abuzz with rumors, guesses, speculation, and gossip. Objections came thick and fast. Many fans were aghast at the very thought of a *Star Trek* without the *Enterprise.* How could a series be *Star Trek* and not "go where no one has gone before"? Did this mean the end of *The Next Generation?* Fans wrote letters of protest, saying, We like what we have. In other words, if it ain't broke, don't fix it.

Paramount, well aware that similar objections had surfaced when *The Next Generation* was announced, and having watched the new series become a fan favorite and ratings winner, went ahead with its plans.

Executive Producers Rick Berman and Michael Piller put writers to work on scripts and designers on drafting plans for the set, while they searched two continents for just the right actors. Hundreds were auditioned before the regulars were cast.

As with the casts of the preceding series, most of the selected actors and actresses were relatively unknown. Only Colm Meaney, who transferred from the *Enterprise* to *Deep Space Nine,* was well known to *Star Trek* fans. Now, with the series well established, fans are accepting the new concept and developing favorites from among the characters.

So how do they compare to their predecessors?

## THE COMMANDING OFFICERS

Commander Benjamin Sisko (Avery Brooks) is a rank below the two ship's captains, James Kirk (William Shatner) and Jean-Luc Picard (Patrick Stewart). Sisko is an experienced Starfleet officer, and a veteran of the Wolf 359 massacre at the hands of the Borg. He is his own man and has his own method of command, but he also has some of the characteristics of both of his predecessors.

Sisko is not quite as likely to "rush in where angels fear to tread," as Kirk did, nor does he call staff meetings, in the manner of Picard, to discuss an imminent crisis, an almost daily event on the space station.

Kirk commanded landing parties, something that Jean-Luc Picard has done much less frequently, due in part to a command directive that captains can best serve by remaining aboard their ships. Sisko will, however, lead a foray into the wormhole if he feels he is the best man for the job, but he prefers to delegate authority. Like Kirk, he is inclined to make quick, on-his-feet decisions, and he expects them to be carried out immediately.

He has an office but spends much less time there

than Picard spends in his ready room. Standing in the circle of the Operational Control Center, generally referred to as Ops, Sisko is surrounded by his senior officers, whom he asks for reports and suggestions before making decisions.

Instead of the state-of-the-art ships that the captains enjoy, Sisko's command is the stationary space station *Deep Space Nine,* located above Bajor in the far reaches of Federation territory. Despite his crew's best efforts, there are usually more nonoperational systems than functional ones at any given time.

Explorers and protectors of Federation territory best describes what Kirk and Picard's positions are, but Sisko's is much more multifaceted. Not only is he the *Deep Space Nine* commander, but first and foremost he is charged with preparing the Bajoran world for entry into the Federation. He must help develop the newly discovered wormhole into a viable enterprise that will allow the Bajorans to restore their war-torn world. While Kirk and Picard went to seek out new life forms, Sisko waits for them to come to him.

Unlike Kirk and Picard, who never married, Sisko is a widower with a teenage son. His wife, Jennifer, died at Wolf 359 three years prior to his taking command of *Deep Space Nine.* He is at last coming to terms with his grief over Jennifer's death and is determined to be as successful in his present post as Kirk and Picard have been in theirs.

## THE FIRST OFFICERS

Commanders Spock (Leonard Nimoy) and William Riker (Jonathan Frakes), first officers under Kirk and Picard respectively, graduated from Starfleet Academy with high honors. Major Kira Nerys (Nana Visitor) was a terrorist and freedom fighter who helped to free her world from the conquering Cardassians.

Spock and Riker have great respect and genuine affection for their commanding officers. It would not occur to them, except under unusual circumstances, to question or disobey a direct order or go to a higher official. Sisko has earned Kira's grudging respect, but she has questioned his orders, has disobeyed them, and gone over his head.

Kira doesn't want the Federation on the space station, but she has come to realize that if Bajor is ever to develop the wormhole and regain its independence, it must depend on Starfleet and the Federation for help. It is a constant irritant to Kira that Bajor doesn't have the capabilities for developing the wormhole's possibilities by itself. This leaves her testy much of the time.

As time has passed and Sisko has convinced her that he does have the best interests of Bajor at heart, she has become a better first officer. However, if put to the test, and she must make a choice between Sisko and Bajor, it is very probable she would choose the latter. This would be something more critical than just the support of one of her former comrades in the Bajoran terrorist movement, as she has turned her back on those days and will not support such tactics used against the Federation.

## CHIEF MEDICAL OFFICERS

When Doctors Leonard McCoy (DeForest Kelley), Beverly Crusher (Gates McFadden), and Katherine Pulaski (Diana Muldaur) first began their tours of duty on the *Enterprise*, their medical careers were well established. They were in their late thirties to early forties, and were considered among the best medical officers in Starfleet.

Lieutenant Julian Bashir, CMO (Siddig El Fadil), newly graduated from Starfleet Medical Academy at age twenty-seven, was granted his request to be stationed on *Deep Space Nine*, possibly because not many doctors were anxious to spend a large chunk of their careers on the remote station. His youth gives him a naïveté and brashness the others have lost, but his skill as a physician is equal to that of his predecessors. In his specialty, alien anatomy, his knowledge and ability to diagnose and treat the nonhuman species he encounters is unmatched.

McCoy, Crusher, and Pulaski, despite their considerable skills, have all agonized over the loss of an alien patient simply because they knew too little about the species to properly treat it. As Bashir gains experience, it is very probable that he too will become one of Starfleet's most respected doctors.

While the *Enterprise* sickbays were the latest in modern technology, Bashir has to work in a facility stripped of many necessities by the departing Cardassians. His computers don't always work and his space is limited. But as hurriedly ordered state-of-the-art supplies arrive, it is safe to predict that Bashir's sickbay will be one of the showplaces on *Deep Space Nine*.

## SCIENCE OFFICERS

It is interesting to note that Starfleet and the Federation seem to prefer nonhumans as science officers in their most prestigious and/or important postings. Spock (Leonard Nimoy) was a Vulcan, Data (Brent Spiner) is an android, and Lieutenant Jadzia Dax (Terry Farrell) is a Trill—a joined species that is two separate entities.

It is true that Spock was half human, but he did everything within his power to subjugate that part of himself. He fought a frequently losing battle to suppress all emotion, and Data was not programmed with emotions. Dax, on the other hand, has over three hundred years of emotions from other hosts to contend with. She is a new host to a symbiont that for over fifty years resided inside the body of a man. She is still struggling to separate her own emotions from those of the former host.

Dax is not the "computer" that Data is, nor has she reached the level of logic that Spock obtained, but her 350 years of real memories, plus her many science degrees and her ability to manipulate a computer, have put her on equal footing with Spock and Data.

## CHIEF ENGINEER

Lt. Commander Montgomery Scott (James Doohan) earned a reputation as a miracle worker by putting his beloved engines back together, usually under stressful conditions following a battle. Using the twenty-third-century equivalent of baling wire, shoelaces, and glue, he frequently gave Captain Kirk that "little extra" to take them out of harm's way. Lt. Commander La Forge (LeVar Burton) is equally ingenious at returning his damaged ship to operational status through the manipulation of his computers, clever use of the holodeck, and the ship's systems.

Chief Miles O'Brien (Colm Meaney) takes twenty-two years—five on the *Enterprise* 1701-D—of experience on starships with him to his new post as chief of operations on *Deep Space Nine.* After his promotion and transfer from the *Enterprise* to the Federation's most recently acquired space station, O'Brien soon realized that he'd be calling on every minute of that experience to keep the station up and running.

What he inherits is a vandalized station. Many components are either damaged or destroyed. He doesn't always understand instructions that are written in the Bajoran or Cardassian languages. Nothing works, and when he gets a system up and running, it doesn't always last. More times than he can count, his mind goes back to the pristine work areas of the *Enterprise.*

O'Brien fields more complaints than anyone else on the station, and despite his harried state of mind, somehow manages to handle each new crisis. His chief emotions are fatigue and frustration. All of his problems aren't the result of the sabotaged station. His wife Keiko (Rosalind Chao) was not happy at leaving the *Enterprise.* At first she hates the deplorable conditions under which they and their three-year-old daughter, Molly, are forced to live. This often creates friction between the couple—one problem that Scott and La Forge never encountered.

Despite his many problems, Commander Sisko and Starfleet Command are fully convinced that O'Brien is the man to bring order out of the chaos of *Deep Space Nine.*

## CHIEF OF SECURITY

Like his counterparts on the *Enterprise,* Lieutenants Tasha Yar (Denise Crosby) and Worf (Michael Dorn), Constable Odo (Rene Auberjonois) is not a native of Earth. Odo is considered to be one of a kind, a shape shifter who has no idea where his homeworld is or who his people are. He was discovered alone in a spacecraft a half century earlier. The Bajorans raised him and accepted him without question. Odo had little, if any, training in the field of law enforcement. Like his friend Kira, he learned his craft while defending himself, and his adopted world, from the Cardassians.

Circumstances also forced Yar and Worf to spend their lives with people not of their own kind. Yar escaped from the rape gangs on her native planet, Turkana IV, after her parents and most government officials were killed. Anarchists, who placed little value on the lives of others, became the rulers of her world.

Yar eventually overcame her fears and hatred

enough to be accepted at Starfleet Academy. Upon graduation she was prompted by the horrors she had witnessed as a child to become a security officer.

Worf's parents were also victims of war. His parents were killed by Romulans at the Battle of Khitomer. A Starfleet officer rescued him and, later, along with his wife, adopted the lonely child. Worf attended Starfleet Academy and became the first Klingon to serve as a Starfleet officer. His warrior blood led him to become a security officer.

Odo, Worf, and Yar shared an ingrained belief in justice, but where Yar and Worf were quick to resort to phasers, Odo bars them from his domain. He does have one added advantage—his ability to change shape permits him to keep ahead of the many, many crooks and criminals who come his way. This ability is a shield against violent attacks.

## HOSTESS/BARTENDER

Except that neither is human, there are few similarities between Quark (Armin Shimerman), the greedy owner/operator of the bar and gambling emporium on the *Deep Space Nine* Promenade, and Guinan (Whoopi Goldberg), genial hostess of the *Enterprise* Ten-Forward lounge.

Quark, a Ferengi, is well endowed with his race's propensity for taking devious advantage of his fellow beings, if he can see a possibility for profit. Although he tries to keep his patrons under control, fights and loud disagreements are not uncommon. He is one of the least liked or trusted people on the station, and no one in their right mind would seriously consider confiding in him.

Guinan's origins are known only to her, the inhuman Q, and to a lesser degree, Picard. She runs Ten Forward with grace and dignity, but is quick to spot, and just as quickly subdue, trouble. She has the well-known bartenders' knack of listening to her customers' problems, frequently helping them find a solution. The antithesis of Quark, Guinan is one of the most popular beings on the *Enterprise.*

## KIDS

Jake Sisko (Cirroc Lofton) is approximately the same age that Wesley Crusher (Wil Wheaton) was when he accompanied his mother, Dr. Beverly Crusher, aboard the *Enterprise* after she became the ship's CMO. Both are half orphans being raised by a single parent. Wesley's father and Jake's mother were killed in the line of duty.

Wesley is a genius whose ability earned him a field promotion to the rank of ensign before he attended Starfleet Academy. His goal is to eventually become a ship's captain. Jake is bright, but not too happy about living in space. He is an obedient young man, but while Wesley was learning to become a Starfleet officer at the same age, Jake's boredom will occasionally lead him into trouble, especially when he teams up with Nog, Quark's nephew.

Quark's nephew was caught attempting to steal ore samples just minutes after Sisko assumed command of the space station. At the urging of Keiko O'Brien, Quark grudgingly enrolled the boy in her new school, " . . . for a few weeks to see how it works." He is a Ferengi, and the only reason Quark allowed him to attend was his own secret hope that school might teach the boy to be a smoother con artist than his father. He may, at times, be a bad influence on Jake, but it is very probable that Jake's honesty will be a good influence on Nog: a typical relationship between teenagers that hasn't changed much over the centuries.

Although initially Nog seemed to be the controlling member of the duo, influencing Jake in some negative ways, Jake Sisko has taken a stand amid refusal to let Nog push him into doing what he knows is wrong. In fact, when Nog's father pulled the Ferengi boy out of school because of the negative influence of the Nagus (a Ferengi leader), Jake secretly began to tutor Nog. The boy recognized his ignorance in important areas and didn't want to be the intellectual inferior of his friend and those he deals with.

CHAPTER

# CHARACTERS AND CAST

# COMMANDER BENJAMIN SISKO

**BY ALEX BURLESON**

Sisko met his future wife, Jennifer, at Gilgo Beach in California. This was soon after graduating from Starfleet Academy and before he received his first posting as a young ensign on a starship. They married and after five years produced a son they named Jake.

They took Jake along with them when Sisko was promoted to full commander and assigned as first officer aboard the USS *Saratoga*. The starship was transporting civilians when Admiral Hanson ordered the ship diverted to Wolf 359 to intercept the Borg. At that engagement the Borg were led by a kidnapped Jean-Luc Picard, who had been turned into "Locutus," spokesborg in the race's dealings with humans.

The *Saratoga*'s Vulcan captain, Storil, was killed in the initial attack, and Sisko was forced into command. He found all of the bridge officers (Garcia, Delaney, Tomamoto, and Storil) dead, with the exception of

Second Officer Lt. Hranok, a Bolian. They managed to evacuate the survivors, but Sisko was shattered by the death of his wife. She was killed during the engagement with the Borg. Benjamin was separated from Jake on the ship but was reunited with his son in the escape pod, which launched seconds before the Borg destroyed the ship. Sisko had been forced away from his wife's body by the strength of the Bolian, and later had to face the fact that he never truly left.

He was assigned to the Mars Utopia Planetia Shipyards (where the *Enterprise*-D was constructed). Three years after Wolf 359, Sisko was ordered to take command of an abandoned Cardassian space station in orbit of the planet Bajor, which had recently overthrown the multidecade occupation of their homeland. Sisko was prepared to reject the order and quit Starfleet altogether. He'd requested an Earth assignment as a single father with a son to raise. He decided to give Bajor a try, which proved key to overcoming his grief. He is a man who carried with him the guilt and anguish of the death of his wife. Until he had an emotional passage in the premiere episode, as he confronted aliens in the guise of people from his past, he could not move on with his life. His important work on *Deep Space Nine* gives him a new direction, but his is still very much a life framed by tragedy.

Had Sisko not been able to expunge the guilt, he may have ended up like another Maxwell. Benjamin Maxwell was taken into custody by the *Enterprise* after he killed hundreds of Cardassians, in an attempt to extract revenge for the death of his wife and children at the hands of the Cardassians. (*Deep Space Nine*'s Chief of Operations, Miles O'Brien, was tactical officer to Captain Maxwell on the USS *Rutledge* before being transferred to the *Enterprise*.)

Sisko had a very tense meeting with Captain

Jean-Luc Picard when the *Enterprise* arrived at Bajor. (Picard: "Have we met before?" Sisko: "Yes, we met in battle.") Sisko was still unable to separate Picard from Locutus. He later realized that Picard was victimized by the Borg when he was kidnapped and that his own anger was misplaced. He learned that lesson after an unplanned stop in the middle of a wormhole. Ben and Lieutenant Jadzia Dax (who was once Ben's elderly male mentor, Curzon Dax, before the Curzon host body of the Trill died) traveled into the wormhole and became the first known visitors to the Gamma Quadrant. (It is later discovered that an archaeologist named Vash preceded them, with help from the "Q" entity.)

Sisko negotiated with the aliens who live in the wormhole, and his own tragic story proved instrumental in teaching crucial facets of humanity to the aliens who have to struggle to understand how linear time operates. They also allowed him to finally release the grief he had stored up inside. The catharsis was most apparent in his next meeting with Picard, in which he withdrew his request for a transfer.

Commander Sisko was happy to see O'Brien's wife, Keiko, open a school on *DS9* and has learned to balance the needs of a civilian population with a Starfleet facility. He has found peace of mind on Bajor, and seeing Jennifer again allowed "her" to help him learn to accept the loss. Sisko's character has developed and deepened considerably over the first two seasons of the show.

## AVERY BROOKS

Born and raised in Indiana, Avery Brooks attended Oberlin College, Indiana University, and later Rutgers University, where he was the first black MFA graduate in the fields of acting and directing.

Brooks spent more than ten years in the theater performing the title role in the biographical play *Paul Robeson,* written by Phillip Hayes Dean. He performed the role on Broadway, at the Westwood Playhouse in Los Angeles, and at the Kennedy Center in Washington, D.C. He also played Paul Robeson in the play *Are You Now Or Have You Ever Been?* in 1978, both on and off Broadway.

His stage credits include the lead in Shakespeare's *Othello,* which he performed at Washington, D.C.'s Folger Shakespeare Theater. Brooks also appeared in Ntozake Shange's *A Photograph* and *Spell #7* for the New York Shakespeare Festival. His musical abilities and powerful voice landed him the role of Malcolm X in the American Music Theater Festival production of the Anthony Davis opera *X: The Life and Times of Malcolm X.* Avery Brooks has also performed with such jazz artists as Butch Morris, Henry Threadgill, Jon Hendricks, Joseph Jarman, and Lester Bowie. Brooks was also the host of *The Musical Legacy of Roland Hayes,* an award-winning documentary.

Avery Brooks is perhaps best known to the public at large for his portrayal of Hawk in the ABC series *Spenser: For Hire.* The performer has also done extensive work with the Smithsonian's program in Black American culture. On PBS's *American Playhouse* he had the title role in the film *Solomon Northup's Odyssey.* Brooks played Uncle Tom in the Showtime production of *Uncle Tom's Cabin,* for which he received a CableACE Award nomination.

Avery Brooks was actually one of the last members of the main *DS9* crew to be cast. Speculation was rife regarding who would ultimately portray Commander Benjamin Sisko, the crucial, leading role on the show. *MacGyver*'s Richard Dean Anderson was rumored to be in the running at one point. The racial background of the character was not determined until Brooks was cast in the part. Tryouts for the role of Sisko involved actors of varied backgrounds, from both Europe and the United States, including Siddig El Fadil, who would be cast for *Deep Space Nine* in a different role. At one point, serious thought was given to the idea of making the commander a woman, a concept that was ultimately watered down to having a woman as Sisko's second-in-command.

Avery Brooks differs from previous *Star Trek* leading men in that he had already been part of a high-profile television series before his involvement in *Deep Space Nine.* The roles of Hawk and Sisko are worlds apart. Brooks retains his hair for his role on *Deep Space Nine*, and Sisko is, without a doubt, a much nicer guy than the bald-pated Hawk.

Brooks won the role of Ben Sisko in a field of hundreds of applicants of all racial groups (even using actors made up as aliens was considered for the role). Rick Berman confirmed that Tony Todd auditioned for the role of Sisko. Todd played the title role in the horror film *Candyman*, and was Worf's brother Commander Kurn in *The Next Generation*'s third-season "Sins of the Father" and in "Redemption." Carl Weathers and James Earl Jones were also considered.

Outside of television, Brooks has been associated with Rutgers University for twenty years and also taught at Oberlin College and Case Western Reserve University. Avery Brooks is also a tenured professor of theater at the Mason Gross School of the Arts.

# JAKE SISKO

Jake is a military brat who doesn't remember life on Earth. The fourteen-year-old boy has been aboard four different starships and stationed on two different planets before arriving on *Deep Space Nine* with his father. The transient lifestyle has taught him how to scope out a new terrain and assimilate into it quickly. At the same time he has an inner fear of forming intimate friendships because he loses them so quickly. He has found a kindred spirit in an unlikely place—Quark's nephew, Nog. He's become close friends with the Ferengi boy, and when Nog was barred from attending the Federation school by his father, Rom, Jake took upon it himself to secretly tutor Nog, who may well grow up into a very different kind of Ferengi.

Jake dreams of going to live on Earth. He collects holodeck programs of various Earth locales, which he uses to try to fulfill his fantasy. Deep inside he knows that his mother would still be alive if they had not been living in space. His father promised that there would be other kids on the station, although it turned out that there are only a few. But Nog, regarded by Jake's father and others as a bad influence, has more sides to him than the adults normally see.

Jake is very close to his dad, and they're buddies to such a degree that the commander is plagued with feelings that he's not doing the job of parenting very well, and that maybe more discipline is required. But as with many adolescents, Ben is discovering that his son is growing up faster than he realized, particularly when he discovers that Jake and Nog like to watch girls arriving on the station.

## CIRROC LOFTON

Cirroc was born in Los Angeles. He entered acting at the age of nine when he appeared in an educational program entitled "Agency for Instructional Technology." In describing his acting debut, Cirroc says, "I have always loved to act, in fact I starred in our elementary school plays—I even portrayed Martin Luther King, Jr."

Cirroc has appeared in a number of commercials for McDonald's, Tropicana Orange Juice, and Kellogg's Rice Krispies. He made his feature debut in 1992 in the Universal comedy *Beethoven*, which was a surprise hit.

Lofton enjoys basketball and bike riding. He is continuing his schooling while working on *Deep Space Nine* and hopes to someday become a doctor. Cirroc compares himself to his character Jake Sisko. "Jake is very close to his father and they are just like buddies. My father and I are buddies, too." Cirroc lives in Los Angeles with his mother and sister.

# CHIEF OPERATIONS OFFICER MILES O'BRIEN

**BY KAY DOTY**

Graduating fourth in his class, Miles O'Brien applied for, and was given, an assignment in deep space. His first ship was a small passenger liner, an assignment that gave him ample opportunity to hone his transporter skills. He didn't, however, get as deep into space as he would have liked. That came several years later when he transferred to the USS *Rutledge* under the command of Captain Benjamin Maxwell.

O'Brien, a likable, jovial man with a quick wit and ready smile, has a talent for repairing any malfunction. The captain observed the young technician for several months before promoting him to the post of bridge tactical officer, with the rank of lieutenant junior grade.

While serving on the *Rutledge*, the ship was ordered to Setlik III, where an outpost was under attack by Cardassian marauders. O'Brien was a member of the party sent in to defend the residents, but the *Rutledge* had arrived too late. Over a hundred people at the outpost, including Captain Maxwell's wife and children, had been murdered.

During hand-to-hand combat with two of the raiders, O'Brien stunned one and killed the other. He had never previously been forced to kill anyone, and he was profoundly shaken by the incident. He'd been forced to take a life and witnessed the worst sort of butchery of innocent civilians performed by the ruthless marauders. O'Brien was left with a deep-seated resentment of all Cardassians.

Soon after the Setlik III incident, O'Brien earned the rank of full lieutenant and transferred to the USS *Enterprise* under the command of Captain Jean-Luc Picard.

Lieutenant O'Brien served at various posts, including bridge con officer and transporter technician, and occasionally filling in as a security officer. A couple of years after O'Brien joined the *Enterprise,* Geordi La Forge, who had been responsible for overseeing the transporter operation, became the chief engineer with the rank of lieutenant commander. He immediately recommended that O'Brien become the new transporter chief.

The arrangement worked well, for not only was the new transporter chief one of the most knowledgeable in Starfleet, but his congenial personality made him a favorite of officers and crew alike.

O'Brien has two passions: his love of women and gambling, not necessarily in that order. After joining the *Enterprise,* word of his skill with a deck of cards earned him an invitation to join the officers' weekly poker game.

If O'Brien had visions of cleaning out his fellow officers' credit accounts (and he did), his plans received a jolt in the person of the ship's first officer,

Commander William Riker. Riker and O'Brien were both shrewd masters of the game and equally adept at bluffing. There were times when their fellow players threw in their cards and watched while the two went head to head. By the end of the first session in which O'Brien participated, no one, including Riker, considered him a patsy.

As the man most responsible for transporting people on and off the ship, O'Brien was seldom part of an Away Team. His duties included the maintenance and operation of the ship's transporter systems—to have them ready for use at a moment's notice, and to be damned certain he didn't put anyone down inside a solid wall.

On the opposite end of the pleasure scale from his gambling was O'Brien's marriage to Keiko Ishikawa, the ship's chief botanist. With Geordi as his best man, Data filling in for the father of the bride, and Captain Picard officiating, the pretty Japanese/Irish ceremony was held in the specially decorated Ten Forward. The couple later became the parents of a daughter, Molly.

After serving twenty-two years aboard a variety of ships, O'Brien was again promoted, and accepted a transfer to *Deep Space Nine* as chief operations officer. Keiko and their three-year-old daughter accompanied him.

Upon arriving at the space station, O'Brien found that it had been trashed by the Cardassians when they'd been forced to leave. This meant that all the electronics on the station had to be checked out and repaired. O'Brien proved he was up to the demands of his job.

His wife, Keiko, didn't embrace the new assignment as readily as Miles did. She found the adjustment a difficult one to make. But when she was able to establish a school for the children who live on *DS9*, she at last found a fulfilling role for herself.

Miles O'Brien has made important contributions to the running and operations of *DS9*, such as when he helped to find subspace shunts hidden by a criminal who was hiding on the station, as well as when he recognized Q as being present and reported the sighting to Commander Sisko.

## COLM MEANEY

Meaney was born and raised in Dublin, Ireland, and began acting at the age of fourteen. After finishing public school, he applied for admittance to the Irish National Theatre, part of the National Irish Theatre drama school. While waiting to be accepted, he worked on a fishing boat. The day he was accepted at the school he gave up the professional fishing business forever. He spent eight years appearing in many theatrical productions in England, including *Accidental Death of an Anarchist* and *Fish in the Sea*. It was then that Colm made his first television appearance, in the BBC show *Z Cars* and the independent British production of *Strangers* before he relocated to New York.

A versatile actor who is seldom out of work, Meaney has portrayed a wide variety of roles on stage, big screen, and television. He first came to the United States in 1978 and spent the next four years dividing his time between roles in London and New York before settling permanently in his adopted country. The next three or four years found him working in off-Broadway and regional theater. His decision to move to Los Angeles in the mid-1980s brought a change to film and television.

On American television he appeared on various series in guest-starring roles, including *Moonlighting, Remington Steele, Tales From the Dark Side*, and in the pilot episode of the Jane Seymour series *Dr. Quinn, Medicine Woman*.

Because of his accent, Meaney was frequently cast as a villain, but admits he likes the nice-guy roles. As Chief O'Brien he has become a household name, at least among *Star Trek* fans, but despite appearing in nearly sixty episodes, he has not been typecast and continues to appear in other roles.

When Colm Meaney's agent suggested he audition for *Star Trek: The Next Generation*, the actor not only had never seen any of the original series episodes or movies, but he wasn't even a science-fiction fan.

When Colm Meaney first came in to try out for *Star Trek: The Next Generation*, the producers were looking for someone to portray the role of Data; obviously Meaney was passed over for this, but he was eventually cast in the part of a nameless transporter technician in such early episodes as "Encounter at Farpoint" and "The Naked Now."

Meaney began his *Star Trek: The Next Generation* career as a bridge officer in the first three episodes of the series. Believing that he wouldn't be used again in the series, he returned to New York to do a play, *Breaking the Code*, with Derek Jacobi. When *Code* closed a year later, the writers' strike was in progress and *The Next Generation* was in limbo. He accepted a short-lived role on the daytime soap *One Life to Live* that lasted until the fall of 1988 and the end of the strike.

When the strike ended, Meaney was called back by Paramount to reprise his role as the character who, after four or five episodes, was given the name O'Brien. Beginning with the strike-shortened 1988/89 season, Meaney's character was given a regular job on the ship and appeared in seventeen episodes. In the fourth season episode "Family," he was given a full name: Miles Edward O'Brien.

The actor, who describes himself as an "irregular

regular," has not appeared in as many episodes as viewers might believe. Frequently orders from the bridge to "Energize, Mr. O'Brien," continue the illusion that the actor is indeed in the episode. But unlike Lieutenant Kyle, his counterpart on the old *Enterprise,* Chief O'Brien has been featured prominently in several episodes.

One of these was the second-season "Unnatural Selection," in which O'Brien was instrumental in reversing Dr. Pulaski's (Diana Muldaur) rapid aging by skillful use of the transporter. He was also featured in season four's "The Wounded," when O'Brien talks his former captain, turned renegade, into surrendering. Meaney even gets to sing a bit in this one.

A talented comic, Meaney enjoys adding a sense of humor to his character whenever possible.

The Irish actor has slowly been insinuating his presence into a number of movies in recent years: his big-screen appearances have included a part in Warren Beatty's *Dick Tracy,* his role as Dennis Quaid's brother in the Alan Parker film *Come See the Paradise,* the part of an airline captain in *Die Hard II: Die Harder,* and as one of Tommy Lee Jones's villainous henchmen in the Steven Seagal action thriller *Under Siege.* He's also appeared in *The Gambler III, Far and Away* with Tom Cruise, and *The Last of the Mohicans.* Colm also appeared in the role of Jimmy Rabbitte, Sr., in *The Commitments.*

Meaney demonstrated his well-developed ability at playing the villain in "Power Play" during the fifth season. In that episode he, Counselor Troi, and Data were possessed by criminals long held on the prison moon Mab-Bu VI. The trio were excellent as they terrorized the ship's crew, while Meaney gave a chilling performance when he menaced his own wife and child.

The theme was again fear in "Realm of Fear" during the sixth season when O'Brien assisted Lieutenant Barkley to overcome his fear of the transporter, while explaining how he had conquered his own aversion to spiders.

Perhaps Meaney is best remembered by *Star Trek* viewers when, in his role of O'Brien, he became the first regular *Enterprise* crew member to be married onscreen. His beautiful bride, Keiko, was played by Rosalind Chao.

Fans have frequently asked about the similarities between Meaney and James Doohan (Scotty in the original series) and their *Star Trek* roles. Both O'Brien and Doohan's Scotty are in engineering, and both characters are very good at their jobs. The similarities end there.

Doohan was, and is, well known for his ability to portray a variety of accents, while Meaney's accent is his own. Meaney hails from Ireland and Doohan was born in Canada. One thing the actors do have in common—both are well-received guests at science-fiction conventions.

As his presence on the series became more frequent, Colm Meaney's character began to take on a more prominent role, emerging as an important supporting character. When Rick Berman and Michael Piller began casting *Deep Space Nine,* Meaney agreed to jump ship and become a regular on the new show. So now Meaney has moved on to the more crucial leading role as the chief of operations on the ramshackle space station *Deep Space Nine.*

Meaney is married and has a preteen daughter, who is an ardent fan of *Star Trek.* He helped Tom Cruise with his Irish accent during *Far and Away*'s filming. Meaney's wife Barbara and eight-year-old daughter, Brenda, often accompany him on location.

# KEIKO O'BRIEN

The wife of Miles O'Brien, she has a three-year-old daughter by Miles, whom she met and married while both were stationed on the *Enterprise*. When Miles was offered the assignment of chief of operations on *Deep Space Nine*, it was not welcome news for Keiko. On the station Keiko has found that her expertise as a botanist is not much in demand, and initially she was angry and frustrated because she did not feel as though she was doing anything useful. What had been a good career move for him had put Keiko's career on hold, seemingly indefinitely. But finally she found a useful place for herself by opening a school for the children who live on the station.

Although Keiko has been a semiregular on *The Next Generation* and now is on *Deep Space Nine*, the experiences of her character have largely been mundane. In the episode "Disaster," the pregnant

Keiko gave birth in Ten Forward without a doctor to assist and Worf acting as midwife, using what he learned from a computer simulation. When her husband was taken over by a threatening alien entity, it was all she could do to protect her baby. The character did no real interacting with the transformed Miles O'Brien other than to cower. For a semiregular, Keiko has been very underused and barely has a recognizable personality. Thus far on *Deep Space Nine* this situation has not improved, and in fact she did not appear in several episodes during the first season, ostensibly because her character is away on Earth visiting her aged mother.

## ROSALIND CHAO

Rosalind Chao appeared on the TV series *Beauty and the Beast* and has been seen in several films and miniseries. Her *Next Generation* appearances include "Data's Day," "The Wounded," "Disaster," "Power Play," "In Theory," "Rascals," "Night Terrors," etc. She is a semiregular on *Deep Space Nine.*

# MAJOR KIRA NERYS

## BY ALEX BURLESON

Kira Nerys grew up fighting the ruthless Cardassian overlords on her home planet of Bajor and became a terrorist to help win independence. She is a former major in the Bajoran underground. She finally quit the organization after finding out what tactics they used, up to and including chemical biological warfare. She proved her loyalty to the Federation when she destroyed an explosive that had been designed to destroy the wormhole. Having fought for freedom all her life, it has angered her to see the older leaders throw it away through their petty dissensions. At that time, she tried without success to reach the Kai herself to air her grievances. It's very possible that she was sent by the government to be the Bajoran administrator at the station simply to get her outspoken voice out of earshot.

At first, Kira was not a supporter of Federation involvement at *Deep Space Nine*, preferring that Bajor remain independent of all outside interests. She initially viewed the Federation's arrival with suspicion, as it seemed that the Bajorans were exchanging one powerful overlord for another. As the representative of the Bajorans onboard the space station, she has no confidence in Sisko when he arrives. In fact she's working in his office when he gets there, clearly having taken charge. She steps down from that position with ill-disguised reluctance.

She considers herself an administrator more than an adventurer, but proves her worth at Red Alert, and once even tried to hold off an entire Cardassian fleet in the unarmed space station. Sisko's arrival with a Cardassian warship in a runabout's tractor beam took the fight out of the fleet and saved Kira from the humiliation she would have borne in surrender. She also learned not to try to go over Sisko's head (even if it is to Spock's wife—Susan Bay). Major Kira (Bajorans' family name is first) is proud of Bajor.

Kira loathes the Cardassians and she committed atrocities against them in the name of freedom, some of which bother her now. When others in the Bajoran underground begin a new wave of terrorism, she is forced into a moral quandary about tracking them down and bringing them to justice. Former terrorists consider her a turncoat because she won't join with them in violently opposing the presence of the Federation on Bajor. Kira will come to respect and bond with Sisko, although they will continue to have different agendas as new issues arise.

## NANA VISITOR

Nana Visitor was born and raised in New York City on the West Side, in and around the theater district, where her father was a successful choreographer on Broadway. Her mother ran a dance studio and was a ballet teacher. So her interest in performing was clearly in the blood. At age seven, Nana began to study ballet at her mother's studio.

Following high-school graduation, Nana began appearing on the professional stage in such productions as *42nd Street*, *Gypsy* (with Angela Lansbury), *My One and Only*, *The Ladies Room* at the Tiffany Theater in Los Angeles, and *A Musical Jubilee*. While still living in New York, she also secured regular roles on the daytime dramas *One Life to Live* and *Ryan's Hope*. She had an early movie role in the 1977 film *The Sentinel*, a horror movie based on a bestselling novel.

While working as a fledgling actress she was also employed as a dancer, although becoming a successful actress was always her first goal. She pursued this seriously by relocating from New York to Los Angeles in 1985. Soon after she found guest-star roles on such TV shows as *Jake and the Fatman; Baby Talk; Murder, She Wrote; L.A. Law; Empty Nest; In the Heat of the Night; Matlock;* and *thirtysomething*. She also had the supporting role of Bryn Newhouse on the short-lived NBC television series *Working Girl*.

While growing up in New York, Nana Visitor watched reruns of the original *Star Trek* every day at six o'clock. What she felt made the original series work were the relationships, and this is what she feels will also be a strong point of *Deep Space Nine*. The actress feels that the reason that Major Kira and Jadzia Dax were made such strong characters was in response to the constant lobbying of Marina Sirtis on *The Next Generation* to make female characters stronger and less traditional on that show. While Berman and Piller could only change things to a degree on *The Next Generation*, the possibilities were wide open on *Deep Space Nine* when it came to the characterizations.

Nana Visitor is looking forward to a long run on the series and appreciates the opportunity the series offers due to how difficult it is for actors to find work in the very competitive film and television industry. "To be working is great, period," the actress told *Starlog*. "There are so many actresses my age who aren't working. They're really talented, really beautiful. I'm just thrilled and grateful to be working, and to be working on *Star Trek*. We're part of the futurists' thoughts and ideas. Many people are putting a lot of creativity, effort, care, and love into this show every day, so I'm really looking forward to the experience that's ahead of all of us."

# LIEUTENANT JADZIA DAX

Dax is a member of a joined species known as the Trill. She combines the host body of a twenty-eight-year-old female with an ancient creature who survives into its seventh lifetime. The symbiotic relationship is extremely complex. Jadzia shares Dax's wisdom and experience and can recall all its memories over more than three hundred years. Dax has been a mother three times and a father twice. Its last host was Curzon Dax, who served as Sisko's mentor. Benjamin was Curzon Dax's friend for nearly twenty years.

A Trill is comprised of two separate but interdependent entities: a host and a symbiont. The host provides a humanoid body. The symbiont is an invertebrate, androgynous life form that lives within the host. It looks like a short, fat snake. Centuries ago the symbionts lived underground while the humanoids thrived on the surface of their world. But due to an environmental disaster, they were forced to unite in order to survive. As time went on this mutual support evolved into a biological interdependency and thus two individuals became one. They speak with one voice (you can't ask to speak with the symbiont or the host, only the combined life form). The symbiont's life span is much longer than that of the host body, and as a result one symbiont will be combined with several hosts during its lifetime.

Dax was implanted into Jadzia's body when Curzon died. Jadzia relived the incident during her research on the Bajoran orbs. When a host dies, doctors surgically remove the symbiont. The worm then burrows itself into the new host. Dax's host was joined with her symbiont when she was an adult. The symbiont part of her is three hundred years old, and is a brilliant scientist with an innate wisdom who can draw upon a library of knowledge built from six lifetimes of experience.

Jadzia trained long and hard to pass the various mental, physical and psychological testing required to serve as host—the highest honor her people can receive. Jadzia was quite the academician and scholar, with doctorates in several separate scientific disciplines, including premiere distinctions in exobiology, zoology, astrophysics, and exoarcheology. She earned all of these degrees as Jadzia, before being joined with Dax.

Jadzia wanted to be a Trill host since childhood. She won many scholarships and competed with other young Trill candidates. Jadzia excelled in all character profiles as well. Both personalities are blended together. Neither is suppressed. Jadzia Dax made legal history when an attempt was made to prosecute Dax for crimes that Curzon Dax was accused of, including treason and the assassination of General Tundro. Trill Minister Selar Peers testified in the extradition hearing. Dr. Bashir explained how the symbiont and host are biologically interdependent. Ninety-three hours after they are joined, neither can survive without the other.

The result of the joining is a serene character who brings a calm, centered voice to any discussion: patient, confident and wise. Dax could be thought of as something like an ancient Zen master in the body of a twenty-eight-year-old woman. There is a subtle conflict within her, a generation gap of sorts. The older symbiont suppresses the youthful instincts of the host. And so, sometimes she will seem controlled when a part of her really would like to let go. For example, the three-hundred-year-old worm has no use for sex or passion except as it serves procreation, but occasionally the youthful instincts of the host overcome that resistance, as revealed in the episode appropriately titled "Dax."

Dax and Ben Sisko have worked together before, as Curzon Dax was Ben Sisko's mentor years before. The only trouble is that back then, Dax was still in the host body of an elderly man. Her sexually attractive new form creates a certain amount of unspoken tension between her and Sisko, which they both resist. After all, he's still having a hard time getting used to the fact that she's a three-hundred-year-old worm, but he doesn't hide the respect and affection he has for her.

Julian Bashir, even though he understands perfectly the symbiotic relationship of a Trill, is still very much attracted to Jadzia Dax and imagines that he can, perhaps, get her to respond to him.

## TERRY FARRELL

The role of Jadzia Dax went through a number of drastic changes during the preproduction work on *Deep Space Nine.* As originally conceived, Dax was to have been a character from an alien world who, due to differences in the relative gravity of *DS9* and her home planet, would require a high-tech wheelchair in order to function outside of her special office. (This is what is referred to in the twenty-fourth century as being "gravitationally challenged.") When this notion was thought through, it was seen to present considerable production challenges, and so the original idea was scrapped, and Piller and Berman cast around for another alien until they hit upon the Trill, a symbiotic race that had been introduced in the Rene Echevarria-scripted *Next Generation* episode "The Host."

With all these eleventh-hour alterations, Terry Farrell (whom the producers spotted in the horror film *Hellraiser III*) became the last member of the regular *Deep Space Nine* cast to be signed on. Only one among many talented and beautiful young women trying out for the role, Farrell landed the part of Dax because she seemed to understand the concept behind the character. Some of the actresses, trying to grasp the symbiotic concept, thought that it would be a good idea to pitch their voices like a man's—not what the creators of the show had in mind. Farrell grasped the concept of an extremely old, wise mind looking at the world through the eyes of a beautiful young person—a character who would, after all, be somewhat bemused by the attentions inspired by her outward physical form after having changed bodies any number of times during the past four centuries.

Terry Farrell began shooting her first scenes for the *Deep Space Nine* pilot in full Trill makeup. Paramount Studio executives, seeing her in that makeup, reacted negatively. They didn't like the notion that this beautiful young actress had her features obscured beneath heavy makeup. Two days' worth of footage were scrapped, and makeup wizard Michael Westmore had to come up with a quick replacement design. He came up with a subtle spotting around the sides of the face that enhanced Terry Farrell's natural features rather than concealed them.

Terry Farrell was born in Cedar Rapids, Iowa, and at the age of sixteen signed with the prestigious Elite modeling agency and moved to New York City. For several years she worked as a model, appearing on the cover of such magazines as *Vogue* and *Mademoiselle*.

She got her television start in the short-lived 1984 ABC series *Paper Dolls* (with Jonathan Frakes as a costar), portraying the "smart" model Laurie Caswell. She also appeared in an episode of the new *Twilight Zone*. (In a remake of "After Hours" she plays the Anne Francis role of a mannequin that comes to life in a department store.)

Terry also had a guest appearance on *Quantum Leap* ("Leap for Lisa," in which she plays a nurse who was the love of Dean Stockwell's character when he was in the Navy. Scott Bakula's character jumps into Dean's character's body as he is accused of killing the nurse.) She's also appeared in guest star roles on *The Cosby Show* and *Family Ties*.

Her film credits include Rodney Dangerfield's *Back to School* and *Beverly Hills Madam* with Faye Dunaway. She played a victim of serial killer Ted Bundy in the film *Deliberate Stranger* with Mark Harmon, and recently costarred in *Hellraiser III: Hell on Earth* as a reporter. She is now a resident of Los Angeles where she lives with her dog, Freckles.

Farrell read for the part on the *Next Generation* set and "survived the technobabble," as she put it. Farrell was quoted in *Starlog* magazine on Jadzia's sex life by stating—"Dax would say, 'Hey! Sex is just for procreation.' Though after three hundred years, I would imagine I'm pretty good at it." She was also quoted about being thrilled to get the job as Dax, since she was such a *Star Trek* fan: "I was freaking out! I said, 'I used to watch *Star Trek* when I was a little girl.' My grandma made me a Tribble once. It was just too weird."

# SECURITY CHIEF ODO

Fifty years before the Federation came to *Deep Space Nine*, a spacecraft was found drifting not far from Bajor near the Denorios asteroid belt. Aboard it was an alien who had no memory of who he was or where he was from. He came to be called Odo. Since he was found by Bajorans, he lived among them. At first he was sort of an "elephant man," a source of curiosity and humor as he turned himself into a chair or a pencil. Raised with no knowledge of his past or who he really is, Odo the shape shifter chose to adopt a humanoid form to better relate to the races he grew up among.

Odo's true shape is that of a formless blob. He sleeps in a bucket at night, as he must return to his true form once each day. Although he has adopted a humanoid shape, he resents it. As a result, Odo performs a uniquely important role in the ensemble of main characters. He is the character who explores and comments on human values. And because he is forced to pass as one of us, his point of view usually comes with a cynical edge.

With the Cardassians in charge on Bajor and in control of the station known as *Deep Space Nine,* Odo found himself having to associate with them. The more he got to know them the less he liked what he knew. But even the Cardassians needed people to keep the order and thus Odo secured the job of chief of security on *Deep Space Nine.* In the course of his duties he got to know the Ferengi, Quark, and learned that the Cardassians could have learned things about treachery from the Ferengi.

When the Bajorans overthrew the decades of iron rule of the Cardassians, Odo was determined to maintain order and kept the station from being trashed even more than it had been. At least what remained could be repaired. Without Odo's influence the Cardassians would have doubtless destroyed the station to insure that the Bajorans couldn't use it to their advantage.

Odo finds that working with the Federation, and Commander Ben Sisko, is far more to his liking than what he endured under the Cardassians. He respects Sisko, but is not reluctant to stand up to him when he feels that his authority is being challenged. In "The Passenger," when a Federation deridium shipment was due and a security officer named Primmin was sent by the Federation, Odo demanded that he remain in charge of security for the station. Sisko agreed that Odo's authority in security matters was final, and he made it clear to Primmin not to challenge or belittle Odo's authority. After all, Odo knew the station well and had even dealt with the Cardassians long before the Federation was involved with *Deep Space Nine.* Odo had more than authority, he possessed knowledge vital to the position of responsibility he held.

With the discovery of the stable wormhole, Odo believes that the Gamma Quadrant might well be where he's from, but he has yet to pursue that possibility, as it would mean abandoning his hard-earned position on the station. Although he doesn't know anything about his species, he is certain that justice is an integral part of their being because the necessity for it runs through every fiber of his body, like a racial memory. That's why he became a lawman, and when it comes to doing his job, he doesn't always follow the letter of the law. The way he figures it, laws change but justice is justice.

## RENE AUBERJONOIS

Born in New York City in 1940, Rene was raised nearby in Rockland County. He took to the stage at age sixteen thanks to the tutelage of noted actor and family friend John Houseman. The son of a news correspondent, he moved with his family to London, where he continued training in the theater while he was still in high school. Rene returned to the United States to attend college, and received a Bachelor of Arts degree in Drama from Carnegie-Mellon University in Pennsylvania.

Following college he began his theatrical career in Washington, D.C., at the Arena Stage. After that he traveled between New York and Los Angeles while appearing in a number of stage productions. In San Francisco he helped found the American Conservatory Theater, and also the Mark Taper Forum in Los Angeles and the Brooklyn Academy of Music Repertory Company in New York City. The actor has starred in such stage productions as *Twelfth Night* and *Richard III*.

Rene's first appearance on Broadway was with Katharine Hepburn in the musical *Coco*, for which he won the prestigious Tony Award. He also received

Tony Award nominations for his performances in the Broadway productions of *The Good Doctor, Big River,* and for his role as movie mogul Buddie Fidler in the musical *City of Angels.*

The actor's film debut was in the 1970 motion picture *M*A*S*H.* His other feature film credits include *Brewster McCloud, McCabe and Mrs. Miller, Images, Pete 'n' Tillie, The Hindenburg* (with George C. Scott), the 1976 version of *King Kong,* and *Police Academy 5.* On television he appeared in such made-for-TV films as *Panache* in 1976. Rene is also a two-time Emmy Award nominee for his performance in ABC's *The Legend of Sleepy Hollow.*

He was also the voice of Peter Parker on a Spiderman record released in the late 70s. He was continuing his stage work during that period as well and appeared in a Joseph Papp production of *King Lear* with James Earl Jones.

Auberjonois won a Best Supporting Actor in a Comedy Emmy Award for his work as Clayton Endicott III in *Benson,* which starred Robert Guilluame, a series on which Rene appeared for six years. He's also known for his work on Showtime's *Faerie Tale Theater* in "The Frog Prince" with Shelley Duvall, and on that program's production of "Sleeping Beauty." He's also guest starred on many television shows, such as *L.A. Law, Civil Wars,* and *Matlock.* In 1993 he also appeared in the USA Network movie *Wild Card.* He is also widely known for his role as the voice of the cleaver-wielding chef in the Disney animated classic *The Little Mermaid.*

*Star Trek* fans will recognize him as the conspiratorial assassin Colonel West in *Star Trek VI: The Undiscovered Country.* (He saw part of his role edited from the film, then restored on the home video release.) This placed him on the *Star Trek* scene and helped lead to his being cast in the role of Odo.

"Odo is a curmudgeon of sorts," the actor states. "He is very rigid and uptight, yet there is a wonderful humor about him. Because he does not know where he comes from or who he is, there is an existential struggle going on within him."

# DOCTOR JULIAN BASHIR

**BY KAY DOTY**

Julian Bashir can't remember a time when he didn't want to be a doctor. His father was wealthy and could afford to educate his son in any profession he chose. The boy chose medicine and never wavered.

Unlike so many children whose intellect is at or near genius level, Julian was a sociable child. But he had a tendency to choose his friends from among the offspring of doctors and scientists. He loved games, but not being particularly good at them, he was usually one of the first to be eliminated from competition.

When this occurred, Julian would seek out his host's library and immerse himself in whatever medical and/or science tapes, journals, and books he might find there. Having tucked himself into a quiet corner or an isolated sofa to study his find, he was frequently an unseen listener to the conversations of his elders who might gather there.

This secret was first discovered when his friend's father and two colleagues were discussing a new technique that Julian had recently read about. His eagerness to learn more about the procedure was his undoing. Momentarily forgetting his status as an eavesdropper, he unwound himself from his hideaway in the folds of a deep chair, a series of questions tumbling from his lips.

The doctor's initial irritation at the boy's presence was soon allayed by the considerable knowledge, indicated by his questions, that he had gained on his own. His enthusiasm to learn and ability to absorb highly technical information earned him the privilege of sitting in on the doctors' informal gatherings at social functions.

"Well, I wasn't exactly invited," Julian would explain years later, "but they didn't kick me out when I joined them."

He was frequently told he could stay only if he was quiet and didn't interrupt. This was often difficult for the boy who had many questions, but he did as he was told, enjoying what were some of the happiest moments of his young life.

Julian made his first discovery of the workings of an emergency medical center by accident. He was twelve when a friend was injured in one of their ball games and he helped carry the boy to a nearby center for treatment.

Julian was enthralled from the moment he walked through the door. He instantly loved the smell of the center, the professionalism of the medical staff, and the array of equipment that was visible from his seat in the waiting room. While he waited, he helped dispel his teammates' fear about their friend. Later, when a young couple came in with a sick baby, he somewhat allayed the parents' fears by assuring them of the excellence of the staff. Their concern for their child was too great to wonder at the comfort being offered by one so young.

Julian had made a wonderful new discovery during his visit to the center. He began frequenting the facility, his eyes filled with wonder at seeing all the fantastic things he had only studied about. At first the staff considered him a nuisance and ordered him to leave, but he could no more stay away than he could go without eating.

He made himself useful by tidying the waiting room, getting drinks for people, and making calls to worried relatives of sick and injured patients. He was careful not to interfere with the staff as they went about their duties. After a time they accepted him and even asked him to do small tasks for them.

## MOMENT OF TRUTH

The highlight of his preteen life occurred when an explosion filled the medical center with an overflow of seriously injured people. When he heard a doctor call repeatedly for a nurse, and none was free, Julian offered to help.

"Get scrubbed, then get back here and assist me," the doctor barked.

Julian didn't have to be told twice, and he was back at the doctor's side in minutes. His impromptu assignment included handing instruments to the doctor, moving gurneys carrying treated patients out of the operating area to make room for the next one needing treatment, and sponging perspiration from the doctor's face. The memory of the one task that would remain with him for the balance of his life was of gently covering the face of a young girl who did not survive.

Nearly six hours passed before the last patient had been treated and removed from the emergency area. Fatigue dulled his expressive eyes and draped a gray pallor over his face as Julian and the exhausted medics collapsed in the staff lounge. The doctor who had put Julian to work studied the dark-haired youth, still clad in his green, several-sizes-too-large, blood-soaked surgery gown.

"Young man," the doctor said softly after studying the boy for several moments, "I would have lost at least two of those people if you hadn't been there to help me. You saved their lives. All of us owe you a debt of gratitude. Don't ever give up your dream to become a doctor."

"I won't, sir," the boy replied quietly, too tired to say more, but the sunshine of his smile drove the fatigue from his eyes, and the gloom from the lounge.

It wasn't until he was a teenager that Julian made the decision to practice space medicine. He had visited the Lunar recreational facilities on the moon countless times, but it wasn't until his parents took him on an extended tour of Earth's neighbors in the galaxy that Julian began his love affair with the stars.

The first stop on their odyssey into outer space was a visit to the Mars shipbuilding yard where his father had business interests. His mother's plans did not include Julian, so he went to his favorite tourist attraction—the base sick bay. He'd had the foresight to obtain a letter of introduction to the Mars chief medical officer from one of the doctors at the medical center; thus when he presented himself at the front desk, he was granted a tour of the facility.

## ALIEN SPECIALIST

Julian was so impressed that he knew in his heart space was where he wanted to practice medicine. In addition to that decision, he was so fascinated with the wide variety of aliens he encountered that he determined his studies would include as many alien-life courses as the Starfleet Medical Academy had to offer.

Being Julian, he didn't wait until he entered the Academy to begin his study of aliens. This was a whole new world of medicine that he hadn't previously considered, but by the time he walked into the Academy as a lowly first-year student, he knew more about the anatomy of many of the alien beings in the galaxy than most of his classmates would know when they graduated.

Some of Julian's favorite texts were written by such doctors and scientists as the legendary Admiral Leonard McCoy, whose career covered nearly thirty years on two of the *Enterprise* starships; Zefram Cochrane, inventor of the warp-drive formula; and such Vulcan healers as Commander Selar.

With all of his advanced knowledge, Julian could have challenged numerous courses and finished in far less than the usual eight years. Fearing he might miss vital information by skipping classes, Julian spent the allotted time in training, but his early studies helped him to complete his Academy classes in record time, thus allowing him plenty of opportunity to pursue his considerable interest in members of the opposite gender.

Nor did he want for female companionship. His dark good looks, ready smile, and charming personality assured him of that. And while he didn't exactly leave a trail of broken hearts, there were a few who deeply regretted their parting when he moved on. Julian looked on life as a great adventure, and he was not ready to dull his excitement at seeing the beckoning universe by making encumbering commitments.

Julian graduated second in his class. He missed just one question on the oral examination, or he would have been class valedictorian. He was actively sought after for a variety of positions on numerous ships, but the post he wanted wasn't on a ship. It was on a space station at the edge of Federation territory.

Through all his travels, his studies, and his knowledge of the surrounding galaxies, Julian never lost his love of adventure. When he arrived at *Deep Space Nine*, he brought with him a naïveté that often irritates his more experienced fellow officers.

The thought of encountering spies, criminals, and other disreputable characters excites him. The new doctor is sometimes inclined to be innocently arrogant. He is an excellent doctor, knows it, and sees no reason to hide his light under a barrel. The one thing that transcends his normal genial good nature is the lack of proper fixtures and supplies in his sick bay. He believes every being has a right to the best care that he can provide, and until Starfleet and the Federation send him the latest equipment, he is not certain he can always give that care.

One of the most pleasant features of his posting on *Deep Space Nine* is the beautiful science officer, Lieutenant Jadzia Dax. He knows she is a Trill and is host to a symbiont, but that just piques his interest. She does not return his ardor, making her even more desirable to him. Meanwhile his healthy libido doesn't prevent him from observing other fascinating females who frequent the station.

Dr. Julian Bashir arrived on the station with stars in his eyes, searching for adventure and ready to gallop into places where hardened space veterans know better than to go. In the meantime it did not take his fellow officers long to realize that Starfleet sent them one of the brightest doctors to come out of the Academy in a long time.

## SIDDIG EL FADIL

Siddig's parents were living in the Sudan at the time of his birth. They left Africa to return to their native England when he was less than a year old. He was educated in English public schools, including a year at University College in London.

He worked two years in a men's clothing store, then quit and enrolled in an acting school, believing that would be the best way to learn to direct. He became a student at the London Academy of Music and Dramatic Arts (LAMDA) and appeared as the lead in such productions as *Hamlet* and *Arthur*. Upon completion of the three-year program at LAMDA, he joined the Manchester Library Theatre in London, where he appeared in productions of *Brother Eichemann* and *Sinbad the Sailor*.

After being cast in several minor stage roles, he became bored and swore that he'd never act again. But never is a long time, especially for a broke, out-of-work former actor and would-be director. He finally got to try his hand at directing at the Arts Threshold Theatre, with productions of *Lotus and the Rats* and *Julius Caesar*. It was while he was working there as a director that he secured an acting role on television. He was offered a role in a six-part miniseries, *Big Battalions*, in which he played a Palestinian. He accepted the part and made his television debut in 1991.

A fine performance in the miniseries led to the role of King Faisal in *A Dangerous Man—Lawrence After Arabia*, and that led to Dr. Bashir in *Deep Space Nine*. Siddig El Fadil was cast in the role of *Deep Space Nine*'s Doctor Julian Bashir almost by a fluke. PBS stations carried the British-made film in which El Fadil played King Faisal, but it was a minor role. The made-for-TV movie didn't attract much of the viewing public, but one who did see the show was Rick Berman, co-executive producer of *Deep Space Nine*.

As King Faisal in this British television drama about T. E. Lawrence, El Fadil was made up to portray a man much older than himself, and Piller and Berman were so impressed by his performance as the king that they seriously thought about trying him out for the role of another leader, Commander Sisko. When Paramount's representatives in Great Britain tracked El Fadil down in London, they relayed some surprising information to Rick Berman: El Fadil was only in his mid-twenties, a bit younger than the actor they hoped to find for the role of Sisko! On the other hand, it would obviously have been a great mistake to pass up an opportunity to employ an actor as good as El Fadil, so they had him read for the part of the young medical officer.

Berman had been quite impressed with El Fadil's performance, stating, "He just blew me away." The people at Paramount liked what they saw and invited the young actor to come to the States for further testing. Everyone thought he was wonderful, ending their search for the space station doctor.

Berman and coproducer Michael Piller had not envisioned a doctor with a British accent, but the actor's versatility and fresh look made him their first, and only, choice. Paramount officials believe that these attributes, along with his good looks and personable demeanor, will soon make him a fan favorite.

El Fadil, who is single, says he may go back to London during hiatus, but is happily exploring as much of America as his ten- to sixteen-hour work days will allow. He lives in West Hollywood, is beginning to make friends away from the studio, and enjoys life in a way that a year ago he would have said was impossible. A wide smile lights up his face when he talks about a long run with *Deep Space Nine* and the *Star Trek* universe, but insists he is more interested in the present, and believes the future will take care of itself.

# QUARK

The Ferengi race has been a part of *Star Trek: The Next Generation* since the first season of that series. They are ugly, sexist, greedy little aliens who are interested only in profit and getting their hands on anything they happen to fancy.

All of the worst things that capitalists and businessmen have ever been accused of are considered positive traits by the Ferengi. They are taught from childhood that ethics and fairness are the province of interfering do-gooders, as represented by the people in the Federation. They also resent that they are not trusted as it makes it more difficult to cheat their clients.

Quark runs many of the entertainment concessions on *Deep Space Nine* including the bar/restaurant/gambling house and the holosuite brothel upstairs (where one's every fantasy can be played out). He spends most of his time behind the bar. If there is some scam being run in the sector, Quark is often involved. But beyond the malevolence, he is a charming host (in a Ferengi sort of way) and forges an interesting relationship with Sisko. They actually enjoy sparring, and now and then the Ferengi lends a hand to solve a problem for the commander, as long as there's something in it for him.

Quark learned well in his upbringing, and when he opened "Quark's Place" on the Promenade of *Deep Space Nine*, it was with the blessings of his Cardassian hosts. They were the power controlling Bajor then and Quark knew that travelers on their way to exploit the resources of the bedeviled planet would want to stop off to slake their thirst, do a little gambling, and indulge in the wide array of sexual delights available in Quark's holosuites. The Cardassians respected Quark's ruthlessness. When the Bajorans revolted and received official recognition from the Federation as a sovereign world, the Cardassians had no choice but to vacate the space station. Quark chose to remain behind, though, anticipating that this turn of events would make *Deep Space Nine* busier than ever. What Quark didn't anticipate was that the only stable wormhole in the galaxy would be discovered nearby, making the space station a key stopover point for commerce involved with the otherwise distant Gamma Quadrant.

While Sisko distrusts Quark and Odo openly dislikes him, the Ferengi's influence is beyond dispute so they allow him to continue his business. While they cannot expect Quark to run a completely honest establishment (for a Ferengi that would be unheard of), it has been made clear to Quark that should he be caught cheating anyone he'll be forced to make restitution. Although an annoying prospect, this has just made Quark that much more clever.

Although a craven character at heart who is not above begging for his life, Quark is willing to deal with anyone, including a serial murderer, such as was shown in the episode "The Passenger." Quark even became involved in the attempted theft of a Federation shipment by providing mercenaries for the killer, Vantaka, to use in the crime. They failed and Quark managed to escape being implicated. Quark is willing to let anyone take the rap for him. When he and a cousin cheated some aliens by selling them defective warp engines, Quark implicated his cousin, who went to prison for the crime.

Quark and Odo have a history. The security chief was on *Deep Space Nine* with Quark when the Cardassians were there, so he knows what the Ferengi is capable of. Odo is more than willing to confront Quark and accuse him of whatever he believes the Ferengi to be guilty of. Presently they have a truce, so Odo will not roust Quark unless he has a very good reason. In the episode "The Nagus," Odo actually saved Quark's life by uncovering the fact that the real Nagus was still alive, and the security chief arrived just in time to prevent Quark from being assassinated when the Ferengi was locked into an airlock and threatened with being blasted into space.

Quark's sexist attitudes make Kira an obvious adversary. He is consumed with passion for Dax but has come on to Kira as well, inviting her for a drink and once putting his hand on her waist, whereupon she threatened him. Quark's good-natured reply was, "I love a woman in uniform!"

Quark's relationship with Commander Sisko is less certain. While Sisko tends to find Quark amusing, and for the most part harmless, he has the power to shut Quark down at any time if he chooses to.

## ARMIN SHIMERMAN

Armin was born and raised in Lakewood, New

Jersey, and moved to Los Angeles when he was seventeen. By that time Shimerman had decided that he would pursue a career in the legal field. But when his mother wanted to see him make more friends in Los Angeles, she got him to join a community theater that was run by one of her relatives. He landed major roles in both high school and college stage productions when he attended the University of Southern California.

After graduating from the University of California at Los Angeles, Armin moved to New York City. In New York he appeared in several regional theater productions for the Tyrone Guthrie Theater, the American Shakespeare Festival, and the New York Shakespeare Festival. On Broadway, Armin appeared in such productions as *St. Joan*, *I Remember Mama*, and *The Threepenny Opera*.

Upon returning to Los Angeles, the actor made appearances on such television series as *L.A. Law*, *Who's the Boss*, *Married with Children*, *Alien Nation* ("Gimme, Gimme"), and *Cop Rock*. Shimerman is also widely known for his two-and-a-half-year stint in the role of Pascal on CBS's *Beauty and the Beast*. He wore makeup for this character, which to a small degree prepared him for what he'd encounter on *The Next Generation* and *Deep Space Nine*. On the non-*Star Trek* front Shimerman played Cousin Bernie on the critically acclaimed but low-rated series *Brooklyn Bridge*.

Armin Shimerman began his *Star Trek* career, in successive months, portraying the "talking wedding box" that announced Deanna's engagement in the first-season episode "Haven," and appearing as Letek (one of the first Ferengi seen) in "The Last Outpost." As Letek he was a more menacing character than Quark is. He appeared as a Ferengi again, this time as Bractor in "Peak Performance."

Being transformed into Quark requires three

hours in the makeup chair, and it takes fifty minutes to strip it off again at the end of the shooting day. Although there is a top piece, which the actor puts on his head, the face is achieved with makeup and isn't just a mask. "Michael Westmore, who is the genius behind all the makeups on *Star Trek*, doesn't believe in rubber masks," the actor explains. "He believes that they don't look real. They don't work well with the actor's face, and all of his Emmys prove that he's right." But Armin doesn't mind the three-hour stint in the makeup chair. "It makes for a lot of overtime," he quips. "It's a great job! I'm making a lot of money," he says, sounding a lot like the character he portrays. The jagged Ferengi teeth are made from an alginate and just pop on over his real teeth and are held in place by Fixodent or Poligrip. "They work!" he says enthusiastically, although it's doubtful that he'll be chosen to do an on-air product endorsement by the manufacturer.

Armin's makeup lady who does the rigorous and meticulous job of applying his Ferengi makeup is Karen Westerfield. She was part of the team that won an Emmy for the makeup on *The Next Generation* in 1992. The look of the Ferengi was originally designed by Michael Westmore, and Shimerman created much of the individual Ferengi characterization when he played the first Ferengi ever seen in the *Star Trek* universe. In describing what having the makeup applied is like, it starts with the headpiece. "It's delicately applied around the eyes. Then the mask [facial makeup] has to be joined to the ears on the helmet. The scarlet around the eyes is what I love the most because the eyes immediately pop out because of the scarlet." The costume was designed by Robert Blackman. "After about the second hour I begin to transform psychologically and mentally into Quark and I become an extrovert."

Shimerman has started making appearances at *Star Trek* conventions and he describes them as being "like news conferences. You go out and you take questions and you try to answer as best you can and sometimes you make things up."

Shimerman describes the Ferengi as being "a group of aliens who are the capitalists of the universe. We're out to make a buck and accumulate as much money as we can. I think of ourselves as the robber barons like the Carnegies, Rockefellers, and people like that." When asked whether Quark prefers money or women, Armin replies, "That's a tough decision."

In describing the concessions he has at Quark's place, he says, "I have my own ATM machines. I run the bar. I run something called the holosuites upstairs from my bar. Whatever fantasies you have, I can find a program so that you'll be satisfied upstairs in the holosuites, and I make a little profit off of that." Shimerman also says that the ears of the Ferengi are their erogenous zones.

When asked why no women Ferengis have ever been seen on any of the *Star Trek* series, Armin explains that the reason is that "Ferengi females are all nude." This is not just a glib throwaway line, as in "The Last Outpost," when Letek sees Tasha Yar, he remarks how disgusting it is that the humans make their women wear clothes. In the second season of *DS9*, however, we do finally "see" a Ferengi woman ("Rules of Acquisition"); but as she is masquerading as a male, she is fully clothed at all times.

PART

# APPENDICES

# THE NEXT GENERATION: *EPISODE GUIDE* *SEASONS 1-7*

## AST:

| | |
|---|---|
| **CAPTAIN JEAN-LUC PICARD** | Patrick Stewart |
| **COMMANDER WILLIAM RIKER** | Jonathan Frakes |
| **LIEUTENANT COMMANDER GEORDI LA FORGE** | LeVar Burton |
| **LIEUTENANT WORF** | Michael Dorn |
| **DOCTOR BEVERLY CRUSHER** | Gates McFadden |
| **COUNSELOR DEANNA TROI** | Marina Sirtis |
| **LIEUTENANT COMMANDER DATA** | Brent Spiner |
| **WESLEY CRUSHER** | Wil Wheaton |
| **LIEUTENANT TASHA YAR** | Denise Crosby |
| **ENSIGN RO LAREN** | Michelle Forbes |
| **DOCTOR KATHERINE PULASKI** | Diana Muldur |
| **CHIEF MILES O'BRIEN** | Colm Meaney |

# SEASON ONE

### PISODES ONE AND TWO:

*"ENCOUNTER AT FARPOINT"*

Written by D. C. Fontana and Gene Roddenberry
Directed by Corey Allen
Guest Cast: John deLancie, Michael Bell, DeForest Kelley, Colm Meaney, Cary Hiroyuki, Timothy Dang, David Erskine, Evelyn Guerrero, Chuck Hicks

Picard meets Q and frees an alien creature that has secretly been imprisoned and enslaved on Farpoint Station.

### EPISODE THREE:

*"THE NAKED NOW"*

Teleplay by J. Michael Bingham
Story by John D. F. Black and J. Michael Bingham
Directed by Paul Lynch
Guest Cast: Benjamin W. S. Lum, Michael Rider, David Renan, Skip Stellrecht, Kenny Koch

A sequel and largely a remake of the original *Star Trek* episode "The Naked Time."

### EPISODE FOUR:

*"CODE OF HONOR"*

Teleplay by Kathryn Powers and Michael Baron

Directed by Russ Mayberry
Guest Cast: Jessie Lawrence Ferguson, Karole Selmon, James Louis Watkins, Michael Rider

Tasha Yar is kidnapped and has to fight for her freedom.

### EPISODE FIVE:

### "THE LAST OUTPOST"

Teleplay by Herbert Wright
Story by Richard Krzemian
Directed by Richard Colla
Guest Cast: Darryl Henriques, Mike Gomez, Armin Shimerman, Jake Dengal, Tracey Walter

The *Enterprise* encounters the fearsome Ferengi at last, but they don't quite measure up.

### EPISODE SIX:

### "WHERE NO ONE HAS GONE BEFORE"

Written by Diane Duane and Michael Reaves
Directed by Rob Bowman
Guest Cast: Biff Yeager, Charles Dayton, Victoria Dillard, Stanley Kamel, Eric Menyuk, Herta Ware

The introduction of the Traveler and his relationship with Wesley Crusher which came full circle in a seventh-season episode "Journey's End."

### EPISODE ELEVEN:

### "LONELY AMONG US"

Script by D. C. Fontana
Story by Michael Halperin
Directed by Cliff Bole
Guest Cast: Colm Meaney, Kavi Raz, John Durbin

Picard is possessed by an alien entity.

### EPISODE EIGHT:

### "JUSTICE"

Teleplay by Worley Thorne
Story by Ralph Willis and Worley Thorne
Directed by James L. Conway
Guest Cast: Josh Clark, David Q. Combs, Richard Lavin, Judith Jones, Eric Matthew, Brad Zerbst, David Michael Graves

On the gardenlike planet of Rubicam II, Wesley breaks an unwritten law and is sentenced to death. Picard must violate the Prime Directive in order to save him, in the meantime dealing with an arbitrary "god" who does not approve of the ship's presence.

**EPISODE NINE:**

*"THE BATTLE"*

Teleplay by Herbert Wright
Story by Larry Forester
Directed by Rob Bowman
Guest Cast: Frank Corsentino, Doug Warhit, Robert Towers

A Ferengi plots to get revenge on Picard, and the lure is Picard's long-lost starship the *Stargazer*.

**EPISODE TEN:**

*"HIDE AND Q"*

Teleplay by C. J. Holland and Gene Roddenberry
Story by C. J. Holland
Directed by Cliff Bole
Guest Cast: John deLancie, Elaine Nalee, William A. Wallace

Q returns to bedevil the *Enterprise* and test Riker with the gift of ultimate power.

**EPISODE ELEVEN:**

*"HAVEN"*

Teleplay by Tracy Tormé
Story by Tracy Tormé and Lan Okun
Directed by Richard Compton
Guest Cast: Danzita Kingsley, Carel Struycken, Anna Katrina, Raye Birk, Michael Rider, Majel Barrett, Rob Knepper, Nan Martin, Robert Ellenstein

Deanna Troi discovers that her long-arranged marriage is about to come to pass, whether she wants it to or not.

**EPISODE TWELVE:**

*"THE BIG GOODBYE"*

Written by Tracy Tormé
Directed by Joseph L. Scanlan
Guest Cast: Mike Genovese, Dick Miller, Carolyn Alport, Rhonda Aldrich, Eric Cord, Lawrence Tierney, Harvey Jason, William Boyett, David Selburg, Gary Armagnal

On the holodeck, Picard and company discover that there is more about this device than they ever imagined. Introduction of the Dixon Hill holodeck program.

**EPISODE THIRTEEN:**

*"DATALORE"*

Teleplay by Robert Lewin and Gene Roddenberry
Story by Robert Lewin and Maurice Hurley
Directed by Rob Bowman

Guest Cast: Biff Yeager

The introduction of Data's evil twin, Lore, who fortunately didn't appear very often throughout the seven-season series.

**EPISODE FOURTEEN:**

*"ANGEL ONE"*

Teleplay by Patrick Berry
Directed by Michael Rhodes
Guest Cast: Karen Montgomery, Sam Hennings, Leonard John Crowfoot, Patricia McPherson

The *Enterprise* discovers starship crash survivors on Angel One who threaten the status quo of this matriarchal planet.

**EPISODE FIFTEEN:**

*"11001001"*

Written by Maurice Hurley and Robert Lewin
Directed by Paul Lynch
Guest Cast: Carolyn McCormack, Iva Lane, Kelli Ann McNally, Jack Sheldon, Abdul Salaam El Razzac, Ron Brown, Gene Dynarski, Katy Boyer, Alexandra Johnson

Alien bynars steal the *Enterprise* in order to try to save their own world whose computer brain has crashed. Introduction of the holodeck character Minuet.

**EPISODE SIXTEEN:**

*"TOO SHORT A SEASON"*

Teleplay by Michael Michaelian and D. C. Fontana
Story by Michael Michaelian
Directed by Rob Bowman
Guest Cast: Clayton Rohner, Marsha Hunt, Michael Pataki

Retired Federation negotiator Mark Jameson takes a forbidden youth drug in order to confront an old enemy one last time.

**EPISODE SEVENTEEN:**

*"WHEN THE BOUGH BREAKS"*

Teleplay by Hannah Louise Shearer
Directed by Kim Manners
Guest Cast: Dierk Torsek, Michele Marsh, Dan Mason, Philip N. Waller, Connie Danese, Jessica and Vanessa Bova, Jerry Hardin, Brenda Strong, Jandi Swanson, Paul Lambert, Ivy Bethune

A legendary planet allows itself to be discovered so that it can kidnap children from the *Enterprise* in order to preserve life on their world.

**EPISODE EIGHTEEN:**

*"HOME SOIL"*

Teleplay by Robert Sabaroff
Story by Karl Guers, Ralph Sanchez and Robert Sabaroff
Directed by Corey Allen
Guest Cast: Walter Gotell, Elizabeth Lidsey, Mario Roccuzzo, Carolyn Barry, Gerard Pendergast

A world being terraformed turns out to have a native life form previously undiscovered.

**EPISODE NINETEEN:**

*"COMING OF AGE"*

Written by Sandy Fries
Directed by Michael Vejar
Guest stars: Estee Chandler, Daniel Riordan, Brendan McKane, Wyatt Knight, Ward Costello, Robert Schenkkan, Robert Ito, John Putch, Stephan Gregory, Tasia Valenza

Wesley tries out for Starfleet Academy, while on the *Enterprise* Picard is grilled about some recent command decisions.

**EPISODE TWENTY:**

*"HEART OF GLORY"*

Teleplay by Maurice Hurley
Story by Maurice Hurley and Herb Wright & D. C. Fontana
Directed by Rob Bowman
Guest Cast: Vaughn Armstrong, Robert Bauer, Brad Zerbst, Dennis Madalone, Charles H. Hyman

The first Klingon episode of *TNG*, and it's a spectacular outing.

**EPISODE TWENTY-ONE:**

*"ARSENAL OF FREEDOM"*

Teleplay by Richard Manning and Hans Beimler
Story by Maurice Hurley and Robert Lewin
Directed by Les Landau
Guest Cast: Vincent Schiavelli, Marco Rodriguez, Vyto Ruginis, Julia Nickson, George De La Pena

On a desolate, uninhabited planet, a landing party discovers that automated weapons systems are still hunting for prey.

**EPISODE TWENTY-TWO:**

*"SYMBIOSIS"*

Teleplay by Robert Lewin, Richard Manning and Hans Beimler
Story by Robert Lewin

Directed by Win Phelps
Guest Cast: Merritt Butrick, Judson Scott, Kimberly Farr, Richard Lineback

The *Enterprise* encounters two societies wherein one preys on the other in a particularly parasitic fashion.

### EPISODE TWENTY-THREE:

### "SKIN OF EVIL"

Teleplay by Joseph Stephano and Hannah Louise Shearer
Story by Joseph Stephano
Directed by Joseph L. Scanlan
Guest Cast: Walker Boone, Brad Zerbst, Raymond Forchion, Mart McChesney, Ron Gans as the *voice of Armus*

The *Enterprise* encounters a being of pure evil marooned on a desolate world—a being that slays Tasha Yar.

### EPISODE TWENTY-FOUR:

### "WE'LL ALWAYS HAVE PARIS"

Teleplay by Deborah Dean Davis and Hannah Louise Shearer
Directed by Robert Becker
Guest stars: Isabel Lorca, Rod Loomis, Dan Kern, Jean-Paul Vignon, Kelly Ashmore, Lance Spellerberg, Michelle Phillips

The *Enterprise* investigates a distress call and encounters time distortions that threaten that entire region of space.

### EPISODE TWENTY-FIVE:

### "CONSPIRACY"

Teleplay by Tracy Tormé
Story by Robert Sabaroff
Directed by Cliff Bole
Guest Cast: Michael Berryman, Ursaline Bryant, Henry Darrow, Robert Schenkkan, Jonathan Farwell

A conspiracy of alien beings which can possess human hosts threatens the stability of the Federation.

### EPISODE TWENTY-SIX:

### "THE NEUTRAL ZONE"

Written by Maurice Hurley
From a story by Deborah McIntyre and Mona Clee
Directed by James L. Conway
Guest Cast: Marc Alaimo, Anthony James, Leon Rippy, Gracie Harrison

The *Enterprise* finds twentieth-century humans preserved in a lost satellite. The Romulans also make contact after a fifty-year silence.

# SEASON TWO

## PISODE TWENTY-SEVEN:

*"THE CHILD"*

Written by Jaron Summer, Jon Povil and Maurice Hurley
Directed by Rob Bowman
Guest Cast: Seymour Cassel, R. J. Williams, Dawn Arnemann, Zachary Benjamin, Dore Keller

In this script originally conceived for the never produced 1977 *Star Trek* TV series, Deanna becomes pregnant by an alien entity.

## EPISODE TWENTY-EIGHT:

*"WHERE SILENCE HAS LEASE"*

Written by Jack B. Sowards
Directed by Winrich Kolbe
Guest Cast: Earl Boen, Charles Douglas

The *Enterprise* enters a region of space where a strange alien entity tries to use the vessel as the subject in an experiment.

## EPISODE TWENTY-NINE:

*"ELEMENTARY, DEAR DATA"*

Written by Brian Alan Lane
Directed by Rob Bowman

Guest Cast: Daniel Davis, Alan Shearman, Biff Manard, Diz White, Anne Ramsay, Richard Merson

Data plays Sherlock Holmes on the holodeck, and inadvertently creates a Professor Moriarty who is more than his match as well as self-knowing.

**EPISODE THIRTY:**

*"THE OUTRAGEOUS OKONA"*

Teleplay by Burton Armus
Story by Les Menchen, Lance Dickson and Kieran Mulroney
Directed by Robert Becker
Guest Cast: William O. Campbell, Douglas Rowe, Albert Stratton, Joe Piscopo

The *Enterprise* picks up an escaped thief who is also being hunted by a young woman's outraged father. On the holodeck, Data creates a standup comic in order to learn about humor.

**EPISODE THIRTY-ONE:**

*"LOUD AS A WHISPER"*

Written by Jacqueline Zambrano
Directed by Larry Shaw
Guest Cast: Howie Seago, Marnie Mosiman, Thomas Oglesby, Leo Damian

Famed negotiator Riva has no gene for hearing, so he uses three companions—the Chorus— to express his thoughts for him, except when he wishes to express himself to Deanna Troi, who reciprocates his attraction for her.

**EPISODE THIRTY-TWO:**

*"UNNATURAL SELECTION"*

Written by John Mason and Mike Gray
Directed by Paul Lynch
Guest Cast: Patricia Smith, J. Patrick McNamara, Scott Trost

The *Enterprise* encounters a plague of old age which infects a research station and Dr. Pulaski.

**EPISODE THIRTY-THREE:**

*"A MATTER OF HONOR"*

Teleplay by Burton Armus
From a story by Wanda M. Haight, Gregory Amos and Burton Armus
Directed by Rob Bowman
Guest Cast: John Putch, Christopher Collins, Brian Thompson

Riker volunteers to be the first human to serve with the Klingons.

### EPISODE THIRTY-FOUR:

*"THE MEASURE OF A MAN"*

Written by Melinda M. Snodgrass
Directed by Robert Scheerer
Guest Cast: Amanda McBroom, Clyde Kusatsu, Brian Brophy

Data is put on trial to judge his value as an individual, and to determine whether he has human rights.

### EPISODE THIRTY-FIVE:

*"THE SCHIZOID MAN"*

Teleplay by Tracy Tormé
Story by Richard Manning and Hans Beimler
Directed by Les Landau
Guest Cast: W. Morgan Sheppard, Suzie Plakson, Barbara Alyn Woods

Data is possessed by the mind of a brilliant scientist who is determined to live on in the android body.

### EPISODE THIRTY-SIX:

*"THE DAUPHIN"*

Written by Scott Rubinstein and Leonard Mlodinow
Directed by Rob Bowman
Guest Cast: Paddi Edwards, Jamie Hubbard, Madchen Amick, Cindy Sorenson, Jennifer Barlow

Wesley falls in love with a young woman who is returning to her homeworld to be its ruler.

### EPISODE THIRTY-SEVEN:

*"CONTAGION"*

Written by Steve Gerber and Beth Woods
Directed by Joseph L. Scanlan
Guest Cast: Thalmus Rasulala, Carolyn Seymour, Dana Sparks

An ancient planet containing ancient secrets is discovered, but a computer virus could destroy the *Enterprise*, if the Romulans don't do the job first.

### EPISODE THIRTY-EIGHT:

*"THE ROYALE"*

Written by Keith Mills
Directed by Cliff Bole
Guest Cast: Sam Anderson, Jill Jacobson, Leo Garcia, Noble Willingham

The *Enterprise* discovers an Earth casino/hotel on a remote planetoid, along with the ancient astronaut it was built to amuse.

**EPISODE THIRTY-NINE:**

*"TIME SQUARED"*

Teleplay by Maurice Hurley
From a story by Kurt Michael Bensmiller
Directed by Joseph L. Scanlan

The *Enterprise* encounters a shuttlecraft containing a double of Captain Picard who came from the future in order to try to avert disaster.

**EPISODE FORTY:**

*"THE ICARUS FACTOR"*

Teleplay by David Assael and Robert L. McCullough
Story by David Assael
Directed by Robert Iscove
Guest Cast: Mitchell Ryan, Lance Spellerberg

The chance to command his own ship is soured for Riker when the offer is delivered by his father, whom he hasn't seen in fifteen years.

**EPISODE FORTY-ONE:**

*"PEN PALS"*

Teleplay by Melinda M. Snodgrass
From a story by Hannah Louise Shearer
Directed by Winrich Kolbe
Guest Cast: Nicholas Cascone, Nikki Cox, Ann H. Gillespie, Whitney Rydbeck

Data communicates with an alien child, but things get complicated when it becomes apparent that she's alone on a planet racked by seismic disturbances, and the Prime Directive forbids the *Enterprise* from getting involved.

**EPISODE FORTY-TWO:**

*"Q WHO"*

Written by Maurice Hurley
Directed by Rob Bowman
Guest Cast: John deLancie, Lycia Naff

Q returns, determined to join the crew, and demonstrates his worth by revealing the existence many light-years away of a mysterious race known as the Borg.

**EPISODE FORTY-THREE:**

*"SAMARITAN SNARE"*

Written by Robert L. McCullough
Directed by Les Landau

Guest Cast: Christopher Collins, Leslie Morris, Daniel Bemzau, Lycia Naff, Tzi Ma

The *Enterprise*, under Riker's command, proceeds with a scientific mission, only to receive a distress call from a Paklid vessel, which only has sublight capacity.

### EPISODE FORTY-FOUR:

### "UP THE LONG LADDER"

Written by Melinda M. Snodgrass
Directed by Winrich Kolbe
Guest Cast: Barrie Ingham, Jon deVries, Rosalyn Landor

The *Enterprise* reaches the source of a distress signal, a class-M planet threatened by solar flares, and evacuates the entire population of several hundred.

### EPISODE FORTY-FIVE:

### "MANHUNT"

Written by Terry Devereaux
Directed by Rob Bowman
Guest Cast: Majel Barrett, Robert Costanzo, Rod Arrants, Carel Struycken, Robert O'Reilly, Rhonda Aldrich, Mick Fleetwood

Lwaxana Troi returns when the *Enterprise* transports her to the Pacifica conference. Also features the return of Dixon Hill.

### EPISODE FORTY-SIX:

### "THE EMISSARY"

Television story and teleplay by Richard Manning and Hans Beimler
From a story by Thomas H. Calder
Directed by Cliff Bole
Guest Cast: Suzie Plakson, Lance LeGault, Georgann Johnson

K'Ehleyr, a half-Klingon, half-human woman, has a mission which involves a Klingon ship with a crew that has been in cryonic suspension for seventy-five years.

### EPISODE FORTY-SEVEN:

### "PEAK PERFORMANCE"

Written by David Kemper
Directed by Robert Scheerer
Guest Cast: Roy Brocksmith, Armin Shimerman, David L. Lander

The forthcoming threat of the Borg has been taken quite seriously by Starfleet and so wargames are scheduled, among other defensive strategies.

**EPISODE FORTY-EIGHT:**

*"SHADES OF GREY"*

Teleplay by Maurice Hurley, Richard Manning and Hans Beimler
Story by Maurice Hurley
Directed by Rob Bowman

While surveying an uncharted planet, Riker is stung by an indigenous life form and suffers flashbacks to scenes from earlier episodes.

# SEASON THREE

## EPISODE FORTY-NINE:

### "EVOLUTION"

Teleplay by Michael Piller
Story by Michael Piller and Michael Wagner
Directed by Winrich Kolbe
Guest Cast: Ken Jenkins

When the *Enterprise* arrives to view a rare stellar event, their computer goes haywire due to Wesley's nanotechnology creatures who have escaped.

## EPISODE FIFTY:

### "THE ENSIGNS OF COMMAND"

Written by Melinda M. Snodgrass
Directed by Cliff Bole
Guest Cast: Eileen Seeley, Mark L. Taylor, Richard Allen

The mysterious Sheliak finally speak to the Federation, and they want a Federation colony in their sector to clear out, or else, even though the colonists have no intention of leaving.

## EPISODE FIFTY-ONE:

### "THE SURVIVORS"

Written by Michael Wagner

Directed by Les Landau
Guest Cast: John Anderson, Anne Haney

When a Federation colony is attacked and sends out a distress call, the *Enterprise* arrives to find that all life on Rana IV has been obliterated, with the exception of a small plot of greenery occupied by a pair of elderly Earth botanists.

## EPISODE FIFTY-TWO:

### *"WHO WATCHES THE WATCHERS"*

Written by Richard Manning and Hans Beimler
Directed by Robert Weimer
Guest Cast: Kathryn Leigh Scott, Ray Wise, James Greene, Pamela Segall, John McLiam, James McIntire, Lois Hall

The arrival of an *Enterprise* Away Team coincides with a survey post's discovery by two Mentakans, who believe that gods have come to their world. As a result Picard has to try to undo the cultural contamination this has caused.

## EPISODE FIFTY-THREE:

### *"THE BONDING"*

Written by Ronald D. Moore
Directed by Winrich Kolbe
Guest Cast: Susan Powell, Gabriel Damon, Raymond D. Turner

Worf's Away Team explores ancient ruins on a planet depopulated by war millennia earlier, but an explosive device leftover from that conflict explodes, killing the ship's archaeologist, Lieutenant Marla Astor, leaving her twelve-year-old son Jeremy an orphan.

## EPISODE FIFTY-FOUR:

### *"BOOBY TRAP"*

Written by Ron Roman, Michael Piller, Richard Danus and Michael Wagner
Directed by Gabrielle Beaumont
Guest Cast: Susan Gibney, Albert Hall, Julie Warner

The *Enterprise* finds the perfectly preserved remains of a thousand-year-old Promelian battle cruiser in an asteroid field that was the site of an ancient space battle. But they also fall into the trap which lured the ancient warship there.

## EPISODE FIFTY-FIVE:

### *"THE ENEMY"*

Written by David Kemper and Michael Piller
Directed by David Carson
Guest Cast: John Snyder, Andreas Katsulas, Steve Rankin

Geordi is stranded on a world ravaged by electromagnetic storms and has to depend on a Romulan for aid.

**EPISODE FIFTY-SIX:**

*"THE PRICE"*

Written by Hannah Louise Shearer
Directed by Robert Scheerer
Guest Cast: Matt McCoy, Elizabeth Hoffman, Castulo Guerra, Scott Thomson, Dan Shor, Kevin Peter Hall

When a wormhole appears in the Barzan system, the exploitation rights are opened for negotiation, with several worlds bidding against each other. In the midst of this, Troi falls in love with one member of the negotiating team, a man who is secretly telepathic.

**EPISODE FIFTY-SEVEN:**

*"THE VENGEANCE FACTOR"*

Written by Sam Rolfe
Directed by Timothy Bond
Guest Cast: Lisa Wilcox, Joey Aresco, Nancy Parsons, Stephen Lee, Mark Lawrence

A world once torn by clan warfare, Acamar has achieved unity after many generations. But the remnants of one ancient clan have planned vengeance for a long time, and they refuse to be halted by any peace treaty.

**EPISODE FIFTY-EIGHT:**

*"THE DEFECTOR"*

Written by Ronald D. Moore
Directed by Robert Scheerer
Guest Cast: James Sloyan, Andreas Katsulas, John Hancock, S. A. Templeman

A Romulan scout ship fleeing across the border of the Neutral Zone is detected by the *Enterprise*, and onboard is an important Romulan military official who has vital information about an impending Romulan sneak attack.

**EPISODE FIFTY-NINE:**

*"THE HUNTED"*

Written by Robin Bernheim
Directed by Cliff Bole
Guest Cast: Jeff McCarthy, James Cromwell

Roga Danar is an escaped Angosian prisoner who was a super soldier, until the war ended and all of his kind were segregated from the rest of normal society, but his people have begun to fight for their rights—rights they earned in the war.

**EPISODE SIXTY:**

*"THE HIGH GROUND"*

Written by Melinda M. Snodgrass
Directed by Gabrielle Beaumont
Guest Cast: Kerrie Keene, Richard Cox, Marc Buckland, Fred. G. Smith, Christopher Pettiet

Beverly Crusher is kidnapped while helping victims of a terrorist bombing on Rutia IV. But when the terrorists believe that the Federation is helping their enemies, they target the *Enterprise* for destruction.

**EPISODE SIXTY-ONE:**

*"DEJA Q"*

Written by Richard Danus
Directed by Les Landau
Guest Cast: John deLancie, Corbin Bernsen, Richard Cansino, Betty Muramoto

Attempts to keep a planet's moon from dropping out of orbit seem futile. Then Q appears on the bridge, naked and claiming to have been stripped of his powers.

**EPISODE SIXTY-TWO:**

*"A MATTER OF PERSPECTIVE"*

Written by Ed Zuckerman
Directed by Cliff Boles
Guest Cast: Craig Richard Nelson, Gina Hecht, Mark Margolis

When the Tanuga IV orbiting research station explodes just as Riker beams back to the *Enterprise*, Commander Riker is accused of the murder of the scientist who had been in charge there.

**EPISODE SIXTY-THREE:**

*"YESTERDAY'S ENTERPRISE"*

Teleplay by Ira Steven Behr, Richard Manning, Hans Beimler and Ronald D. Moore
From a story by Trent Christopher Ganing and Eric A. Stillwell
Directed by David Carson
Guest Cast: Denise Crosby, Christopher McDonald, Tricia O'Neil

When another *Enterprise* appears out of the past through a rift in space, all of history changes and Picard finds himself fighting a losing battle against the relentless Klingon Empire—with Tasha Yar at his side once more.

### EPISODE SIXTY-FOUR:

*"THE OFFSPRING"*

Written by Rene Echevarria
Directed by Jonathan Frakes
Guest Cast: Hallie Todd, Nicolas Coster

Data becomes a father when he builds an android like himself. But then Starfleet steps in to try to take possession of Data's "daughter."

### EPISODE SIXTY-FIVE:

*"SINS OF THE FATHER"*

Teleplay by Ronald D. Moore and W. Reed Moran
From a story by Drew Deighan
Directed by Les Landau
Guest Cast: Charles Cooper, Tony Todd, Patrick Massett, Thelma Lee

A Klingon exchange officer reveals that he is Worf's brother Kurn, and he has come to Worf because their deceased father has been accused of helping the Romulans during the notorious Khitomer attack years before.

### EPISODE SIXTY-SIX:

*"ALLEGIANCE"*

Written by Richard Manning and Hans Beimler
Directed by Winrich Kolbe
Guest Cast: Steven Markle, Reiner Schone, Joycelyn O'Brien, Jerry Rector, Jeff Rector

Picard finds himself held captive in a small room with three other humanoids, while an impostor helms the *Enterprise*.

### EPISODE SIXTY-SEVEN:

*"CAPTAIN'S HOLIDAY"*

Written by Ira Steven Behr
Directed by Chip Chalmers
Guest Cast: Jennifer Hetrick, Karen Landry, Michael Champion, Max Grodenchik

Picard takes a shore leave that is anything but relaxing, and meets a greedy Ferengi, mysterious Vorgons and the beautiful archaeologist/treasure hunter named Vash, who all manage to interrupt his reading of James Joyce's *Ulysses*.

### EPISODE SIXTY-EIGHT:

*"TIN MAN"*

Written by Dennis Putman Bailey and David Bischoff
Directed by Robert Scheerer
Guest Cast: Harry Groener, Michael Cavanaugh, Peter Vogt,

Colm Meaney

The *Enterprise* picks up Betazoid Tam Elbrun, a specialist in first contact, as they need to reach a distant and possibly sentient space ship, nicknamed Tin Man, before the Romulans do.

**EPISODE SIXTY-NINE:**

*"HOLLOW PURSUITS"*

Written by Sally Caves
Directed by Cliff Bole
Guest Cast: Dwight Schultz, Charley Lang, Colm Meaney

Diagnostic Engineer Reginald Barclay's fantasies have gotten way out of hand. Upon entering the holodeck, Geordi finds Barclay battling three musketeers who resemble Geordi, Data and Picard.

**EPISODE SEVENTY:**

*"THE MOST TOYS"*

Written by Shari Goodhartz
Directed by Timothy Bond
Guest Cast: Jane Daly, Nehemiah Persoff, Saul Rubinek

Space trader Kivas Fajo fakes Data's death, kidnaps him, and adds him to his collection of unique objects, and he's willing to kill anyone who would try to deprive him of his prize.

**EPISODE SEVENTY-ONE:**

*"SAREK"*

Television story and teleplay by Peter S. Beagle
From a story by Mark Cushman and Jake Jacobs
Directed by Les Landau
Guest Cast: Mark Lenard, Joanna Miles, William Denis, Rocco Sisto

When the Legarans finally agree to meet with the Federation, there's only one diplomat for the job: Sarek. But soon the crew begins showing signs of tensions, first scattered and on a small scale, but finally culminating in a huge brawl in Ten Forward.

**EPISODE SEVENTY-TWO:**

*"MÉNAGE À TROI"*

Written by Fred Bronson and Susan Sackett
Directed by Robert Legato
Guest Cast: Majel Barrett, Frank Corsentino, Ethan Phillips, Peter Slutsker, Rudolph Willrich, Carel Struycken

Tog, the main Ferengi at a diplomatic reception, is taken with Lwaxana, and so he kidnaps her, Troi and Riker.

## EPISODE SEVENTY-THREE:

### "TRANSFIGURATIONS"

Written by Rene Echevarria
Directed by Tom Benko
Guest Cast: Mark Lamura, Charles Dennis, Julie Warner

The *Enterprise* encounters a severely damaged escape pod and rescues the humanoid being inside. The being heals from his injuries at an amazing rate, but seems to be undergoing additional mutations that are unrelated to his healing process.

## EPISODE SEVENTY-FOUR:

### "THE BEST OF BOTH WORLDS, PART 1"

Written by Michael Piller
Directed by Cliff Bole
Guest Cast: Elizabeth Dennehy, George Murdock

The *Enterprise* finds a colony and its nine hundred inhabitants missing. All indications are that the Borg are responsible, and they have arrived before the Federation is ready for what they know will be a devastating war.

# SEASON FOUR

**EPISODE SEVENTY-FIVE:**

*"THE BEST OF BOTH WORLDS, PART 2"*
Written by Michael Piller
Directed by Cliff Bole
Guest Cast: Elizabeth Dennehy, George Murdock

The Borg, having absorbed Picard into their group mind, now possess all of his knowledge and experience, and resume their course toward Earth. But the *Enterprise* is determined to stop them, at any cost.

**EPISODE SEVENTY-SIX:**

*"FAMILY"*
Written by Ronald D. Moore
Directed by Les Landau
Guest Cast: Jeremy Kemp, Samantha Eggar, Theodore Bikel, Georgia Brown, Dennis Creaghan

Following his harrowing encounter with the Borg, a shaken Jean-Luc Picard returns home to France for the first time in many years, where he goes to visit his older brother Robert, who prefers the old family ways and is openly resentful of Jean-Luc for abandoning them.

## EPISODE SEVENTY-SEVEN:

### "BROTHERS"

Written by Rick Berman
Directed by Rob Bowman
Guest Cast: Cory Danzinger, Adam Ryen, James Lashly

Data seems to undergo a sudden malfunction as he abruptly takes over the *Enterprise*—he is obviously controlled by some outside force, but no one can stop him as he takes the ship to a distant planet where he finds Dr. Noonian Soong, his creator.

## EPISODE SEVENTY-EIGHT:

### "SUDDENLY HUMAN"

Teleplay by John Whelpley and Jeri Taylor
Story by Ralph Phillips
Directed by Gabrielle Beaumont
Guest Cast: Sherman Howard, Chad Allen, Barbara Townsend

The *Enterprise* rescues the crew of a disabled Tellerian training ship, one of whom is apparently human. When a genetic scan is done of the boy, it is determined beyond question that he is Jonathan Rossa, whose parents were killed in a Tellerian border war.

## EPISODE SEVENTY-NINE:

### "REMEMBER ME"

Written by Lee Sheldon
Directed by Cliff Bole
Guest Cast: Eric Menyuk, Bill Erwin

Dr. Crusher finds that people are disappearing on the *Enterprise,* but she's the only one who realizes that they are missing or were even ever there.

## EPISODE EIGHTY:

### "LEGACY"

Written by Joe Menosky
Directed by Robert Scheerer
Guest Cast: Beth Toussaint, Don Mirault

A Federation freighter sends out a distress signal while orbiting the planet where the late Tasha Yar was born. When the *Enterprise* arrives, they find that one of the survivors is Tasha Yar's sister.

## EPISODE EIGHTY-ONE:

### "REUNION"

Teleplay by Thomas Perry and Jo Perry, Ronald D. Moore and Brannon Braga

From a story by Drew Deighan, Thomas Perry and Jo Perry
Directed by Jonathan Frakes
Guest Cast: Suzie Plakson, Robert O'Reilly, Patrick Massett, Charles Cooper, Jon Steuer, Michael Rider, April Grace, Basil Wallace, Mirron Edward Willis

Worf has another encounter with K'Ehleyr, who has some news of great interest. Their first encounter years before produced a son, Alexander, and K'Ehleyr is now willing to make the marriage vows she earlier declined.

## EPISODE EIGHTY-TWO:

### *"FUTURE IMPERFECT"*

Written by J. Larry Carroll and David Bennett Carren
Directed by Les Landau
Guest Cast: Andreas Katsulas, Chris Demetral, Carolyn McCormick, Patti Yasutake, Todd Merrill, April Grace, George O'Hanlon, Jr.

Riker regains consciousness in sick bay after a hazardous Away Team mission. Dr. Crusher addresses him as "Captain," and it seems that he was infected by a virus when he beamed down, a virus that lay dormant for sixteen years and then wiped out all of his memories dating back to the time of the original infection.

## EPISODE EIGHTY-THREE:

### *"FINAL MISSION"*

Teleplay by Kacey Arnold-Ince and Jeri Taylor
Story by Kacey Arnold-Ince
Directed by Corey Allen
Guest Cast: Nick Tate, Kim Hamilton, Mary Kohnert

When Wesley is accepted to Starfleet Academy, Picard takes him along on one final mission when he goes to negotiate a dispute on a mining colony. But when their shuttle crashlands, the mission is in danger of being final in more ways than one.

## EPISODE EIGHTY-FOUR:

### *"THE LOSS"*

Teleplay by Hilary J. Bader and Alan J. Adler and Vanessa Greene
Story by Hilary J. Bader
Directed by Chip Chalmers
Guest Cast: Kim Braden, Mary Kohnert

The *Enterprise* cannot change course and is being pulled slowly along by an unknown force. Troi realizes that she has lost her empathic powers, which for a Betazoid is like going blind, while Data attempts to analyze the strange malfunctions.

**EPISODE EIGHTY-FIVE:**

*"DATA'S DAY"*

Teleplay by Harold Apter and Ronald D. Moore
Story by Harold Apter
Directed by Robert Wiemer
Guest Cast: Rosalind Chao, Sierra Pecheur, Alan Scarfe

Data sends Commander Maddox a letter describing a typical day aboard the *Enterprise* in order to help him better understand what life for the android is like. On this particular day, Data is scheduled to stand in for the father of the bride in the wedding of Keiko to Chief O'Brien.

**EPISODE EIGHTY-SIX:**

*"THE WOUNDED"*

Teleplay by Jeri Taylor
Story by Stuart Charno, Sara Charno and Cy Chernak
Directed by Chip Chalmers
Guest Cast: Bob Gunton, Rosalind Chao, Mark Alaimo, Marco Rodriguez, Time Winters, John Hancock

Picard is informed that the peace treaty with the Cardassians has been broken by the Federation ship *Phoenix*, commanded by Ben Maxwell. The Federation orders Picard to investigate, and to take a Cardassian team aboard as observers.

**EPISODE EIGHTY-SEVEN:**

*"DEVIL'S DUE"*

Teleplay by Philip Lazebnik
Story by Philip Lazebnik and William Douglas Lansford
Directed by Tom Benko
Guest Cast: Marta DuBois, Paul Lambert, Marcelo Tubert, William Glover, Thad Lamey, Tom Magee

The people of Ventax II believe that an impending apocalypse is about to occur. They are experiencing earthquakes and other signs, as predicted in the Legend of Ardra, a thousand-year-old document which seems to be a contract which promised a thousand years of peace in exchange for the ownership of the planet and its people.

**EPISODE EIGHTY-EIGHT:**

*"CLUES"*

Teleplay by Bruce D. Arthurs and Joe Menosky
Story by Bruce D. Arthurs
Directed by Les Landau

Guest Cast: Pamela Winslow, Rhonda Aldrich, Patti Yasutake, Thomas Knickerbocker

The *Enterprise* detects a class-M planet with a wormhole-like energy fluctuation nearby. Just as the ship enters the wormhole, everyone onboard but Data falls to the floor unconscious. The crew regains consciousness and find that the wormhole has apparently taken them one day's distance from their previous location in a matter of seconds.

### EPISODE EIGHTY-NINE:

#### "FIRST CONTACT"

Teleplay by Dennis Russell Bailey, David Bischoff, Joe Menosky, Ronald D. Moore and Michael Piller
From a story by Marc Scott Zicree
Directed by Cliff Bole
Guest Cast: George Coe, Carolyn Seymour, George Hearn, Michael Ensign, Steven Anderson, Sachi Parker, Bebe Neuwirth

Riker has been surgically altered to resemble a Malkorian and sent down to the planet to secretly study them. But when Riker is injured in a freak accident, he's taken to a hospital where the physicians discover that he's an alien. Although this is kept a secret from the public, it sends shockwaves through the government which had been unaware that there is life on other worlds.

### EPISODE NINETY:

#### "GALAXY'S CHILD"

Teleplay by Maurice Hurley
Story by Thomas Kartozian
Directed by Winrich Kolbe
Guest Cast: Susan Gibney, Lanei Chapman, Jana Marie Hupp, April Grace

La Forge is happy to learn that they are taking on an important passenger: Dr. Leah Brahms, whom La Forge "met" as a holographic projection in "Booby Trap."

### EPISODE NINETY-ONE:

#### "NIGHT TERRORS"

Teleplay by Pamela Douglas and Jeri Taylor
Story by Shari Goodhartz
Directed by Les Landau
Guest Cast: Rosalind Chao, John Vickery, Duke Moosekian, Craig Hurley, Brian Tochi, Lanei Chapman, Deborah Taylor

Troi has strange dreams in which she drifts in a dark cloudy vortex. The lights shine in the distance, and the phrase "eyes in the dark" is repeated. The rest of the crew also begins to have odd experiences.

### EPISODE NINETY-TWO:

*"IDENTITY CRISIS"*
Teleplay by Brannon Braga
Story by Timothy De Haas
Directed by Winrich Kolbe
Guest Cast: Maryann Plunkett, Patti Yasutake, Amick Byram, Dennis Madalone, Mona Grudt

Geordi investigates the disappearance of a science team. Tattered Starfleet uniforms and strange alien footprints are the only clues to be found. What Geordi doesn't realize is that this mystery will soon reach out to victimize him as well.

### EPISODE NINETY-THREE:

*"THE NTH DEGREE"*
Written by Joe Menosky
Directed by Robert Legato
Guest Cast: Dwight Schultz, Jim Norton, Kay E. Kuter, Saxon Trainor, Page Leong, David Coburn

La Forge takes Barclay along in a shuttlecraft to investigate a mysterious probe, which enhances Barclay's IQ to between 1200 and 1450, making him the smartest human who ever lived.

### EPISODE NINETY-FOUR:

*"QPID"*
Teleplay by Ira Steven Behr
Story by Randee Russell and Ira Steven Behr
Directed by Cliff Bole
Guest Cast: Jennifer Hetrick, Clive Revill, John deLancie, Joi Staton

In orbit around Tagus III, the *Enterprise* is the site of an archeology symposium, which is disrupted when Q appears and creates a Robin Hood scenario, whether they want it or not.

### EPISODE NINETY-FIVE:

*"THE DRUMHEAD"*
Written by Jeri Taylor
Directed by Jonathan Frakes
Guest Cast: Jean Simmons, Bruce French, Spence Garrett, Henry Woronicz, Earl Billings, Anne Shea

J'Dan, a Klingon exchange officer, is caught accessing security codes. When the Romulans obtain secret information concerning the dilithium chambers, J'Dan is believed to be the spy who gave the Romulans the information, and Starfleet launches an immediate investigation.

### EPISODE NINETY-SIX:

### "HALF A LIFE"

Teleplay by Peter Allen Fields
Story by Ted Roberts and Peter Allen Fields
Directed by Les Landau
Guest Cast: David Ogden Stiers, Majel Barrett, Michelle Forbes, Terrence M. McNally, Carel Struycken

Lwaxana Troi tags along when Picard goes to greet Dr. Timicin, a scientist from Kaelon II. Timicin reveals that, on his planet, sixty is the age of the Resolution, a ceremony celebrating the life of a person— and culminating in his or her ritual suicide—and his time is fast approaching.

### EPISODE NINETY-SEVEN:

### "THE HOST"

Written by Michel Horvat
Directed by Marvin V. Rush
Guest Cast: Franc Luz as Odan, Barbara Tarbuck, Nicole Orth-Pallavicini, William Newman, Patti Yasutake, Robert Harper

Odan is an emissary on his way to negotiate a dispute between two moon colonies. Beverly Crusher falls in love with him, unaware that he is actually a Trill.

### EPISODE NINETY-EIGHT:

### "THE MIND'S EYE"

Teleplay by Rene Echevarria
Story by Ken Schafer and Rene Echevarria
Directed by David Livingston
Guest Cast: Larry Dobkin, John Fleck, Edward Wiley, Denise Crosby (Majel Barrett receives screen credit as the voice of the computer for the first time in the history of the series)

The *Enterprise* takes a Klingon ambassador to K'Reos, a Klingon colony where a fight for independence is under way. What they don't know is that Geordi has been kidnapped by Romulans and programmed to be an assassin in order to shatter the Federation/Klingon alliance.

### EPISODE NINETY-NINE:

### "IN THEORY"

Written by Joe Menosky and Ronald D. Moore
Directed by Patrick Stewart

Guest Cast: Michele Scarabelli, Rosalind Chao, Pamela Winslow

Data's study of human behavior leads him to a romance with another officer, Jenna.

**EPISODE ONE HUNDRED:**

*"REDEMPTION I"*

Written by Ronald D. Moore

Directed by Cliff Bole

Guest Cast: Robert O'Reilly, Tony Todd, Barbara March, Gwynyth Walsh, Ben Slack, Nicholas Kepros, J. D. Cullum, Denise Crosby

Gowron's ship appears and the Klingon confers with Picard: he needs help to avert a Klingon civil war, in exchange for fighting for him.

# SEASON FIVE

## EPISODE ONE HUNDRED ONE:

### "REDEMPTION II"

Written by Ronald D. Moore
Directed by David Carson
Guest Cast: Denise Crosby, Tony Todd, Barbara March, Gwynyth Walsh, J. D. Cullum, Robert O'Reilly, Michael G. Hagerty, Fran Bennett, Nicholas Kepros, Colm Meaney, Timothy Carhart

As the Klingon crisis continues, Worf and Kurn narrowly escape their enemies, and Picard argues that the Federation must cut the supply line between the Romulans and the Klingons.

## EPISODE ONE HUNDRED TWO:

### "DARMOK"

Teleplay by Joe Menosky
Story by Philip Lazebnik and Joe Menosky
Guest Cast: Paul Winfield, Richard Allen, Colm Meaney, Ashley Judd

The *Enterprise* has been assigned the delicate task of negotiating with a race with whom successful negotiations have never before been made. While the Federation has encountered the Children of Tama before, they could never manage to communicate with them.

## EPISODE ONE HUNDRED THREE:

### "ENSIGN RO"

Teleplay by Michael Piller
Story by Rick Berman and Michael Piller
Directed by Les Landau
Guest Cast: Michelle Forbes, Scott Marlowe, Frank Collison, Jeffrey Hayenga, Harley Venton, Ken Thorley, Cliff Potts

Admiral Kennelly wants Picard to find Orta, a Bajoran terrorist leader, and get him to halt his attacks. To accomplish this, Kennelly has Ensign Ro Laren, a Bajoran, transferred to the *Enterprise*. She is a former Starfleet officer who was courtmartialed and sent to prison for an incident on Garon II.

## EPISODE ONE HUNDRED FOUR:

### "SILICON AVATAR"

Teleplay by Jeri Taylor
Story by Lawrence V. Conley
Directed by Cliff Bole
Guest Cast: Ellen Geer, Susan Dion

The Crystalline Entity, last seen in "Datalore," suddenly threatens a Federation colony. Dr. Kila Marr, an expert on the entity, has been studying the scenes of its attacks for years—ever since her young son fell victim to it.

## EPISODE ONE HUNDRED FIVE:

### "DISASTER"

Teleplay by Ronald D. Moore
Story by Ron Jarvis and Philip A. Scorza
Directed by Gabrielle Beaumont
Guest Cast: Rosalind Chao, Colm Meaney, Michelle Forbes, Erika Flores, John Christian Graas, Max Supera, Cameron Arnett, Dana Hupp

The *Enterprise* has hit a quantum filament and the various decks on the ship are cut off from each other as emergency procedures go into effect.

## EPISODE ONE HUNDRED SIX:

### "THE GAME"

Teleplay by Brannon Braga
Story by Susan Sackett, Fred Bronson and Brannon Braga
Directed by Corey Allen
Guest Cast: Ashley Judd, Katherine Moffat, Colm Meaney, Patti Yasutake, Wil Wheaton

Riker returns from Risa and brings a game back with him

which is both addictive and dangerous. When Wesley Crusher figures out what's going on, he finds everyone else on the *Enterprise* is against him.

## EPISODE ONE HUNDRED SEVEN:

### "UNIFICATION I"

Teleplay by Jeri Taylor
Story by Rick Berman and Michael Piller
Directed by Les Landau
Guest Cast: Joanna Miles, Stephen Root, Graham Jarvis, Malachi Throne, Norman Large, Daniel Roebuck, Erick Avari, Karen Hensel, Mark Lenard, Leonard Nimoy

Picard journeys to Vulcan to learn why Spock has gone to Romulus without authorization. When Picard arrives at Sarek's residence, he learns that Sarek is dying.

## EPISODE ONE HUNDRED EIGHT:

### "UNIFICATION II"

Teleplay by Michael Piller
Story by Rick Berman and Michael Piller
Directed by Cliff Bole
Guest Cast (Additional): Denise Crosby, Vidal Peterson, Harriet Leider

On Romulus, Spock tells Picard that his mission is no concern of Starfleet as he is on a personal peace mission. But it is all a plot by the Romulans to invade Vulcan before anyone can stop them and thereby achieve unification on their terms.

## EPISODE ONE HUNDRED NINE:

### "A MATTER OF TIME"

Written by Rick Berman
Directed by Paul Lynch
Guest Cast: Matt Frewer, Stefan Gierasch, Sheila Franklin, Ghay Garner

The *Enterprise* encounters a time traveler who claims to be from the future and has come back to see events destined to occur on that particular day, but he refuses to reveal what they are.

## EPISODE ONE HUNDRED TEN:

### "NEW GROUND"

Teleplay by Grant Rosenberg
Story by Sara Charno and Stuart Charno
Directed by Robert Scheerer

Guest Cast: Brian Bonsall

The *Enterprise* arrives at Lemma II and Dr. Ja'Dar briefs them on the Soliton Wave discovery. The wave will be generated on the planet's surface to propel an unmanned test ship waiting in its path. But when the experiment goes wrong, the colony on Lemma II is threatened with destruction.

## EPISODE ONE HUNDRED ELEVEN:

### *"HERO WORSHIP"*

Teleplay by Joe Menosky
Story by Hilary J. Bader
Directed by Patrick Stewart
Guest Cast: Joshua Harris, Harley Venton

When an Away Team beams over to the *Vico*, a disabled exploratory vessel, they find everyone dead except a young boy, who believes that he is responsible for the death of his parents and the rest of the *Vico*'s crew.

## EPISODE ONE HUNDRED TWELVE:

### *"VIOLATIONS"*

Teleplay by Pamela Gray and Jeri Taylor
Story by Shari Goodhartz, T. Michael and Pamela Gray
Directed by Robert Wiemer
Guest Cast: David Sage, Eve Brenner, Rosalind Chao, Ben Lemon, Rick Fitts, Doug Wert, Craig Benton

A delegation of Ullians—telepathic humanoids—is being transported by the *Enterprise*. But soon after their arrival, certain crewmembers begin to fall into deathlike comas.

## EPISODE ONE HUNDRED THIRTEEN:

### *"MASTERPIECE SOCIETY"*

Teleplay by Adam Belanoff and Michael Piller
Story by James Kahn and Adam Belanoff
Directed by Winrich Kolbe
Guest Cast: Ron Canada, Dey Young, John Snyder, Sheila Franklin

A previously unknown colony is a sealed off, balanced and all-too-perfect society. Their main problem now, though, is that a stellar core fragment is headed toward their homeworld of Moab IV.

## EPISODE ONE HUNDRED FOURTEEN:

### *"CONUNDRUM"*

Teleplay by Barry Schkolnick
Story by Paul Schiffer

Directed by Les Landau
Guest Cast: Erich Anderson, Michelle Forbes, Liz Vassey, Erick Weiss

The *Enterprise* is investigating subspace signals and encounters a small vessel that begins scanning them. The computers go down and a wave of light sweeps through the inside of the ship. When it passes, no one can remember who they are or what they're doing there, but the computers tell them that they are at war.

## EPISODE ONE HUNDRED FIFTEEN:

### "POWER PLAY"

Teleplay by Rene Balcer, Herbert J. Wright and Brannon Braga
Story by Paul Ruben and Maurice Hurley
Directed by David Livingston
Guest Cast: Rosalind Chao, Colm Meaney, Michelle Forbes, Ryan Reid

Troi, Data and O'Brien are taken over by hostile alien entities after they beam down to a planet while investigating a distress signal. Troi claims to be Bryce Shumar of the starship *Essex*, and all she wants is to get her crew's remains from the planet where their consciousnesses have been trapped for two hundred years.

## EPISODE ONE HUNDRED SIXTEEN:

### "ETHICS"

Teleplay by Ronald D. Moore
Story by Sara Charno and Stuart Charno
Directed by Chip Chalmers
Guest Cast: Caroline Kava, Brian Bonsall, Patti Yasutake

When Worf's spine is broken, questions arise. Dr. Crusher wants to use existing technology to help him regain most of his motor functions. Dr. Toby Russell, a neuro-geneticist, wants to try an experimental new technique of cloning a new spine and transplanting it—an untested procedure.

## EPISODE ONE HUNDRED SEVENTEEN:

### "THE OUTCAST"

Written by Jeri Taylor
Directed by Robert Scheerer
Guest Cast: Melinda Culea, Callan White, Megan Cole

The *Enterprise* has been contacted by the J'Naii, an androgynous race, who need assistance in locating a missing shuttle. When Riker falls in love with one of the J'Naii, they discover that in a genderless society, gender tendencies are considered offensive—and illegal.

## EPISODE ONE HUNDRED EIGHTEEN:

### "CAUSE AND EFFECT"

Written by Brannon Braga
Directed by Jonathan Frakes
Guest Cast: Michelle Forbes, Patti Yasutake, Kelsey Grammer

The story begins on Stardate 45652.1, as the *Enterprise* enters the uncharted Typhon Expanse. When the *Enterprise* collides with a mysterious starship, destruction results and a time loop begins the journey all over again, with no one aware of their impending destruction.

## EPISODE ONE HUNDRED NINETEEN:

### "THE FIRST DUTY"

Written by Ronald D. Moore and Naren Shankar
Directed by Paul Lynch
Guest Cast: Ray Walston, Robert Duncan McNeill, Ed Lauter, Richard Fancy, Jacqueline Brookes, Wil Wheaton

Starfleet Academy contacts Picard to tell him that there's been an accident. Wesley was hurt, but not seriously, although another cadet was killed and an investigation (and a coverup) are underway.

## EPISODE ONE HUNDRED TWENTY:

### "COST OF LIVING"

Written by Peter Allan Fields
Directed by Winrich Kolbe
Guest Cast: Majel Barrett, Brian Bonsall, Tony Jay, Carel Struycken, David Oliver, Albie Selznick, Patrick Cronin, Tracy D'Arcy, George Ede, Christopher Halsted

Worf and Alexander's relationship continues to show some strains, and Lwaxana tells Troi that she's getting married again and that she wants the ceremony performed in Ten Forward.

## EPISODE ONE HUNDRED TWENTY-ONE:

### "THE PERFECT MATE"

Teleplay by Gary Perconte and Michael Piller
Story by Rene Echevarria and Gary Perconte
Directed by Cliff Bole
Guest Cast: Famke Janssen, Tim O'Connor, Max Grodenchik, Mickey Cottrell, Michael Snyder, David Paul Needles, Roger Rignack, Charles Gunning, April Grace

Two warring planets have agreed to a ceremony of reconciliation to end their decades-long conflict. An item in the cargo bay is vital to this peace ceremony. It is a woman who is in stasis, and two Ferengi are bent on stealing her.

**EPISODE ONE HUNDRED TWENTY-TWO:**

*"IMAGINARY FRIEND"*

Teleplay by Edithe Swensen and Brannon Braga
Story by Jean Louise Matthias, Ronald Wilkerson and Richard Fligel
Directed by Gabrielle Beaumont
Guest Cast: Noley Thornton, Shay Astar, Jeff Allin, Brian Bonsall, Patti Yasutake, Sheila Franklin

Troi talks to Clara Sutter, a little girl who tells her about Isabella, her imaginary friend. But when the *Enterprise* enters a strange nebula, Isabella becomes real, and potentially dangerous.

**EPISODE ONE HUNDRED TWENTY-THREE:**

*"I, BORG"*

Written by Rene Echevarria
Directed by Robert Lederman
Guest Cast: Jonathan Del Arco

When a young Borg is found alive at a crash site, Picard is stunned by the news. He orders the Away Team back to the ship, but Crusher argues against leaving the young Borg to die.

**EPISODE ONE HUNDRED TWENTY-FOUR:**

*"THE NEXT PHASE"*

Written by Ronald D. Moore
Directed by David Carson
Guest Cast: Michelle Forbes, Thomas Kopache, Susanna Thompson, Shelby Leverington, Brian Cousins, Kenneth Meseroll

Geordi and Ro are declared dead after an apparent transporter accident, but they are just intangible and invisible to normal sight. When Geordi and Ro overhear the Romulans planning to sabotage the *Enterprise* in order to keep their interphase generator from being discovered, they search for a way to save their ship.

**EPISODE ONE HUNDRED TWENTY-FIVE:**

*"THE INNER LIGHT"*

Teleplay by Morgan Gendel and Peter Allan Fields
Story by Morgan Gendel
Directed by Peter Lauritson
Guest Cast: Margot Rose, Richard Riehle, Scott Jaeck, Jennifer Nash, Patti Yasutake, Daniel Stewart

An ancient alien probe renders Picard unconscious. He awakens and finds himself on a strange planet, tended by a woman, Helene, who calls him Kamen and says that he's had a fever for three days.

**EPISODE ONE HUNDRED TWENTY-SIX:**

*"TIME'S ARROW, PART 1"*

Teleplay by Joe Menosky and Michael Piller
Story by Joe Menosky
Directed by Les Landau
Guest Cast: Jerry Hardin, Michael Aron, Barry Kivel, Ken Thorley, Sheldon Peters Wolfchild, Jack Murdock, Marc Alaimo, Milt Tarver, Michael Hungerford

Excavations beneath San Francisco reveal evidence of alien visitors on Earth in the late nineteenth century—along with Data's severed head!

# SEASON SIX

## EPISODE ONE HUNDRED TWENTY-SEVEN:

*"TIME'S ARROW, PART 2"*

Written by Jeri Taylor
From a story by Joe Menosky
Directed by Les Landau
Guest Cast: Jerry Hardin, Michael Aron, Barry Kivel, Ken Thorley, Sheldon Peters Wolfchild, Jack Murdock, Marc Alaimo, Milt Tarver, Michael Hungerford

In San Francisco in the nineteenth century, Samuel Clemens has decided that he must do something to expose the aliens he has discovered in the city. Those aliens are Data and Guinan. Meanwhile, Captain Picard, Lieutenant Riker, Dr. Crusher and Geordi have arrived in San Francisco after passing through the Devidian time portal.

## EPISODE ONE-HUNDRED TWENTY-EIGHT:

*"REALM OF FEAR"*

Written by Brannon Braga
Directed by Cliff Bole
Guest Cast: Dwight Schultz

When the USS *Yosemite* is reported lost, the *Enterprise* is dispatched to the Igo sector to search for it. Reginald

Barclay is assigned to the Away Team, but when he uses the transporter he actually sees something coming toward him in the transport stream.

### EPISODE ONE-HUNDRED TWENTY-NINE:

"MAN OF THE PEOPLE"

Written by Frank Abatemarco
Directed by Winrich Kolbe
Guest Cast: Chip Lucia, Stephanie Erb

The *Enterprise* responds to a ship in distress under attack near the planet Rekag-Seronia. Rekag-Seronia is a planet divided by political conflicts that threaten Federation trading routes. One of the passengers, Ves Alkar, is a Lumerian ambassador and is there to try to find a way to end the conflict. But the ambassador has a deadly secret.

### EPISODE ONE HUNDRED THIRTY:

"RELICS"

Written by Ronald D. Moore
Directed by Alexander Singer
Guest Cast: James Doohan

The *Enterprise*-D discovers something long theorized but never before encountered: a Dyson sphere. Upon arrival at the impossibly huge artifact, they discover a small spacecraft, the *Jenolan*, that appears to have been wrecked on the outer surface of the Dyson sphere some seventy-five years earlier.

### EPISODE ONE-HUNDRED THIRTY-ONE:

"SCHISMS"

Written by Brannon Braga
From a story by Ronald Wilkerson and Jean Matthias
Directed by Robert Wiemer

The *Enterprise* has arrived at the globular cluster known as the Amargosa Diaspora. But soon crewmen begin experiencing strange problems, including unexplained disappearances off the ship when they're asleep.

### EPISODE ONE HUNDRED THIRTY-TWO:

"TRUE Q"

Written by Rene Echevarria
Directed by Robert Scherrer
Guest Cast: Olivia D'Abo, John deLancie

A new crewmember, eighteen-year-old Amanda Rogers, joins the *Enterprise* crew while the vessel is en route to the Argolis Cluster. Amanda's parents, who died when she was an infant, were Q who had taken human form and chosen to live on Earth, and Q has arrived to determine her future.

### EPISODE ONE HUNDRED THIRTY-THREE:

"RASCALS"

Teleplay by Allison Hock
From a story by Ward Botsford, Diana Dru Botsford and Michael Piller
Directed by Adam Nimoy
Guest Cast: David Tristan Birkin, Brian Bonsall, Michael Snyder

Captain Picard, Guinan, Ensign Ro and Keiko O'Brien are returning to the *Enterprise* from shore leave aboard one of the shuttles. O'Brien locks onto the four and beams them out of the shuttle, but when they materialize on the transporter pads they all appear to be preadolescent children rather than the mature adults they really are.

### EPISODE ONE HUNDRED THIRTY-FOUR:

"A FISTFUL OF DATAS"

Written by Robert Hewitt Wolfe and Brannon Braga
From a story by Robert Hewitt Wolfe
Directed by Patrick Stewart
Guest Cast: Brian Bonsall

Worf agrees to go with his son, Alexander, to the holodeck for a nineteenth-century Western program in Deadwood, South Dakota. Meanwhile, Geordi has linked Data to the computer net, and on the holodeck all of the images suddenly have the face of Data, and things start going very wrong.

### EPISODE ONE HUNDRED THIRTY-FIVE:

"THE QUALITY OF LIFE"

Written by Naren Shankar
Directed by Jonathan Frakes
Guest Cast: Ellen Bry

The *Enterprise* has been assigned to visit a space station to monitor work on a massive project, the Tyan particle fountain. There they find small robots, called exocomps, which Data determines are self-aware. He refuses to allow them to come to harm, no matter what.

### EPISODE ONE-HUNDRED THIRTY-SIX:

"CHAIN OF COMMAND, PART 1"

Written by Ronald D. Moore

From a story by Frank Abatemarco
Directed by Robert Scheerer
Guest Cast: Ronny Cox, David Warner

Vice-Admiral Nechayev needs Picard to resign his command in order to undertake a secret mission. The Federation believes that the Cardassians are preparing to invade another disputed system, but which one? Dr. Crusher and Worf will accompany Picard, but no one else aboard the *Enterprise* will know the purpose of their absence.

**EPISODE ONE HUNDRED THIRTY-SEVEN:**

*"CHAIN OF COMMAND, PART 2"*

Written by Frank Abatemarco
Directed by Les Landau
Guest Cast: David Warner, Ronny Cox

A prisoner of the Cardassians, Picard is drugged and tortured to get information on his mission, which the Cardassians know all about anyway as they tricked the Federation into sending Picard on it to begin with.

**EPISODE ONE HUNDRED THIRTY-EIGHT:**

*"SHIP IN A BOTTLE"*

Written by Rene Echevarria
Directed by Alexander Singer
Guest Cast: Daniel Davis, Dwight Schultz, Stephanie Beacham

On the holodeck, Data is acting as Sherlock Holmes in the 221B Baker Street simulation. When Barclay runs a diagnostic on the holodeck, he encounters a protected memory file and Professor Moriarty appears, and no one can deactivate him.

**EPISODE ONE HUNDRED THIRTY-NINE:**

*"AQUIEL"*

Written by Brannon Braga and Ronald D. Moore
From a story by Jeri Taylor
Directed by Cliff Bole
Guest Cast: Renee Jones

When the *Enterprise* makes a routine stop at a space station near the border with the Klingon Empire, the station is found to be deserted. Two officers who were stationed aboard the station seem to have disappeared. What they do find is a live dog, and a glob of cellular residue which Dr. Crusher reports to be the remains of one of the missing lieutenants.

## EPISODE ONE-HUNDRED FORTY:

### "FACE OF THE ENEMY"

Written by Naren Shankar
From a story by Rene Echevarria
Directed by Gabrielle Beaumont
Guest Cast: Carolyn Seymour, Scott MacDonald

Counselor Troi awakens and is shocked to see her reflection—a reflection of a Romulan woman in full uniform. She is soon visited by a Romulan, Subcommander N'Vek, who reveals that she is on a Romulan warship, the *Khazara*.

## EPISODE ONE HUNDRED FORTY-ONE:

### "TAPESTRY"

Written by Ronald D. Moore
Directed by Les Landau
Guest Cast: John deLancie, Ned Vaughn

Captain Picard is brought unconscious into sick bay following a sneak attack on the Away Team he was leading to a peace conference. Picard, still unconscious, finds himself in a place filled with a bright light from which Q slowly emerges wearing long white robes, and states, "Welcome to the afterlife, Jean-Luc. You're dead."

## EPISODE ONE HUNDRED FORTY-TWO:

### "BIRTHRIGHT, PART 1"

Written by Brannon Braga
Directed by Winrich Kolbe
Guest Cast: Siddig El Fadil, James Cromwell

Shortly after the Federation takes charge of space station *Deep Space Nine* orbiting Bajor, the *Enterprise* arrives to assist the Bajorans on the surface who are in need of technical assistance following the destructive evacuation of the Cardassians. On the station, Worf encounters a man who claims to know where Worf's supposedly long-dead father is being held prisoner—by the Romulans.

## EPISODE ONE HUNDRED FORTY-THREE:

### "BIRTHRIGHT, PART 2"

Written by Rene Echevarria
Directed by Dan Curry
Guest Cast: Alan Scarfe, Richard Herd, Christine Rose, Sterling Macer, Jr., Jennifer Gatti

The Klingons in the Romulan prison camp do not want to be rescued because they believe they "died" at Khitomer and to return to the homeworld now would be to return in disgrace. But Worf is determined to teach the Klingon children in the camp the truth about their heritage.

### EPISODE ONE HUNDRED FORTY-FOUR:

*"STARSHIP MINE"*
Written by Morgan Gendel
Directed by Cliff Bole
Guest Cast: David Spielberg

The *Enterprise* docks at the Remmler Array where it is scheduled to be cleared of baryon particles. When Picard momentarily returns to his cabin, he discovers intruders on the *Enterprise* and he has to battle them alone while the rest of the crew is held hostage on the planet below.

### EPISODE ONE HUNDRED FORTY-FIVE:

*"LESSONS"*
Written by Ronald Wilkerson and Jean Louise Matthias
Directed by Robert Weimer
Guest Cast: Wendy Hughes

While on night watch, Picard encounters Lieutenant Commander Nella Daren, the new chief of the Stellar Sciences department. Picard keeps encountering her and finding her more interesting at each meeting.

### EPISODE ONE HUNDRED FORTY-SIX:

*"THE CHASE"*
Written by Joe Menosky
From a story by Ronald Moore and Joe Menosky
Directed by Jonathan Frakes
Guest Cast: Norman Lloyd, Linda Thorson, John Cothran Jr., Maurice Roeves, Salome Jens

Picard's old archeology teacher, Professor Galen, pays a visit to the *Enterprise*. Galen is there to offer to share his latest discoveries with him, as long as Picard agrees to accompany the professor on his newest exploration.

### EPISODE ONE HUNDRED FORTY-SEVEN:

*"FRAME OF MIND"*
Written by Brannon Braga
Directed by Jim Conway
Guest Cast: Andrew Prine, Gary Werntz, David Selburg, Susanna Thompson

Riker is in an asylum for the insane, patiently trying to explain to his doctor that he's all better now. When Riker becomes more and more angry, we see that he's onstage in the theatrical auditorium aboard the *Enterprise*, or is he?

## EPISODE ONE HUNDRED FORTY-EIGHT:

### "SUSPICIONS"

Written by Joe Menosky and Naren Shankar
Directed by Cliff Bole
Guest Cast: Peter Slutsker, James Horan, Joan Stuart Morris, Tricia O'Neil

When Guinan comes to see Dr. Crusher, Beverly is packing to return to Earth for a formal hearing on the charges of violating medical ethics, disobeying a direct order, and causing an interstellar incident.

## EPISODE ONE HUNDRED FORTY-NINE:

### "RIGHTFUL HEIR"

Written by Ronald D. Moore
From a story by James E. Brooks
Directed by Winrich Kolbe
Guest Cast: Kevin Conway, Robert O'Reilly

Picard grants Worf a leave of absence so that he can visit the planet Boreth, where a temple has been built to honor the legendary Klingon warrior Kahless, who lived hundreds of years before. Kahless had long ago united the Klingon people and promised to one day return and lead them again.

## EPISODE ONE HUNDRED FIFTY:

### "SECOND CHANCES"

Written by Rene Echevarria
From a story by Michael A. Medlock
Directed by LeVar Burton
Guest Cast: Mae Jemison

The *Enterprise* approaches Nervala-IV, a planet surrounded by a distortion field which makes transporting to and from the surface of that world difficult. They beam down and encounter someone living there—Will Riker's double!

## EPISODE ONE HUNDRED FIFTY-ONE:

### "TIMESCAPE"

Written by Brannon Braga
Directed by Adam Nimoy

The *Enterprise* and a Romulan ship become frozen in time and only Picard, Data, Geordi and Troi know how to rescue them.

## EPISODE ONE HUNDRED FIFTY-TWO:

### *"DESCENT, PART 1"*

Written by Ronald D. Moore
From a story by Jeri Taylor
Guest Cast: Jim Norton, Stephen Hawking

When the *Enterprise* reaches the Federation outpost on Ohniaka III, the Away Team finds that all 274 members of the outpost have been murdered by the Borg, who then ambush them.

# SEASON SEVEN

## EPISODE ONE HUNDRED FIFTY-THREE:

*"DESCENT, PART 2"*
Written by Rene Eschevarria
Directed by Alexander Singer
Guest Cast: Jim Norton, Stephen Hawking

Lore has brought Data under his control and is leading the Borg against the Federation, but a splinter group led by "Hugh" is determined to shatter Lore's plans.

## EPISODE ONE HUNDRED FIFTY-FOUR:

*"LIAISONS"*
Written by Jeanne Carrigan-Fauci and Lisa Rich
Story by Roger Eschbacher and Jaq Greenspan
Directed by Cliff Bole
Guest Cast: Barbara Williams

Picard's shuttle crash-lands on a planetoid where a woman living there turns out to be more than she seems, and she seems to be dangerous.

## EPISODE ONE HUNDRED FIFTY-FIVE:

*"INTERFACE"*
Written by Joe Menosky

Directed by Robert Wiemer
Guest Cast: Madge Sinclair, Ben Vereen

While using a virtual reality probe on a disabled vessel, Geordi encounters an entity that claims to be his mother.

### EPISODE ONE HUNDRED FIFTY-SIX:

*"GAMBIT I"*

Written by Naren Shankar
Story by Christopher Hatton and Naren Shankar
Directed by Alexander Singer
Guest Cast: Robin Curtis, Richard Lynch

Riker goes undercover to search for Captain Picard who has disappeared, but all evidence leads to the conclusion that Jean-Luc is dead.

### EPISODE ONE HUNDRED FIFTY-SEVEN:

*"GAMBIT II"*

Written by Naren Shankar
Story by Christopher Hatton and Naren Shankar
Directed by Alexander Singer
Guest Cast: Robin Curtis, Richard Lynch

Jean-Luc has taken the name Galen and joined a team of pirates who are plundering ancient archeological sites in search of certain artifacts, but only their Romulan commander knows the truth behind the search.

### EPISODE ONE HUNDRED FIFTY-EIGHT:

*"PHANTASMS"*

Written by Brannon Braga
Directed by Patrick Stewart

Data has been having strange dreams which are actually clues to a menace which is affecting the *Enterprise*, even the dream where Troi is a cake they cut up and eat.

### EPISODE ONE HUNDRED FIFTY-NINE:

*"DARK PAGE"*

Written by Hilary J. Bader
Directed by Les Landau
Guest Cast: Majel Barrett

When Lwaxana goes into a coma, Deanna must enter the woman's mind and learns a terrible truth that her mother had hidden from her.

### EPISODE ONE HUNDRED SIXTY:

*"ATTACHED"*

Written by Naren Shankar
Story by Nicholas Sagan
Directed by Jonathan Frakes

Picard and Crusher are kidnapped by one of the warring factions on a planet where neither side will trust the other, or anyone else.

## EPISODE ONE HUNDRED SIXTY-ONE:

### *"FORCE OF NATURE"*

Written by Naren Shankar
Directed by Robert Lederman

A team of alien scientists insists that the Federation's warp drive engines present a danger to their corridor in space.

## EPISODE ONE HUNDRED SIXTY-TWO:

### *"INHERITANCE"*

Written by Dan Koeppel and Rene Echevarria
Story by Dan Koeppel
Directed by Robert Scheerer

Data meets a woman who actually assisted Dr. Noonian Soong in the creation of the android, but it turns out that she is more than she seems.

## EPISODE ONE HUNDRED SIXTY-THREE:

### *"PARALLELS"*

Written by Brannon Braga
Directed by Robert Wiemer

When Worf returns to the *Enterprise* from a Klingon tournament, he finds things changed, and they keep on changing, particularly when he meets his wife—Deanna Troi.

## EPISODE ONE HUNDRED SIXTY-FOUR:

### *"THE PEGASUS"*

Written by Ronald D. Moore
Directed by LeVar Burton
Guest Cast: Terry O'Quinn

When Admiral Pressman arrives onboard the *Enterprise*, it becomes clear that Riker's old commander and he no longer see eye to eye, particularly about a dangerous secret they share.

## EPISODE ONE HUNDRED SIXTY-FIVE:

### *"HOMEWARD"*

Written by Naren Shankar
Story by Spike Steingasser

Directed by Alexander Singer
Guest Cast: Paul Sorvino

Worf's stepbrother refuses to stand by and do nothing when Picard invokes the Prime Directive and refuses to save the remnants of a people doomed by their dying world.

### EPISODE ONE HUNDRED SIXTY-SIX:

*"SUB ROSA"*

Written by Brannon Braga
Story by Jeri Taylor
Directed by Jonathan Frakes

When Dr. Crusher buries her grandmother on the Caldos Colony, she encounters a family ghost.

### EPISODE ONE HUNDRED SIXTY-SEVEN:

*"LOWER DECKS"*

Written by Rene Echevarria
Story by Ronald Wilkerson and Jean Louise Matthias
Directed by Gabrielle Beaumont
Guest Cast: Shannon Fill

A group of junior officers find themselves tested in more ways than one during a secret mission near the Cardassian demilitarized zone.

### EPISODE ONE HUNDRED SIXTY-EIGHT:

*"THINE OWN SELF"*

Written by Ronald D. Moore
Story by Christopher Hatton
Directed by Winrich Kolbe

Data, suffering from amnesia, tries to pass himself off as a human when he enters a village on a primitive world where a substance the people found is slowly poisoning them with radioactivity.

### EPISODE ONE HUNDRED SIXTY-NINE:

*"MASKS"*

Written by Joe Menosky
Directed by Robert Wiemer

The *Enterprise* encounters a strange alien archive which is drawn into the ship and starts to transform it into an ancient artifact, including Data.

### EPISODE ONE HUNDRED SEVENTY:

*"EYE OF THE BEHOLDER"*

Written by Rene Echevarria

Story by Brannon Braga
Directed by Cliff Bole

The suicide of a crew member leads to the unraveling of a mystery that dates back to the original construction of the *Enterprise*.

**EPISODE ONE HUNDRED SEVENTY-ONE:**

"GENESIS"

Written by Brannon Braga
Directed by Gates McFadden

The crew of the *Enterprise* is infected by a cellular virus which causes it to transform and deevolve into a variety of bizarre manifestations.

**EPISODE ONE HUNDRED SEVENTY-TWO:**

"JOURNEY'S END"

Written by Ronald D. Moore
Directed by Corey Allen
Guest Cast: Wil Wheaton

Wesley Crusher has graduated from Starfleet Academy, but upon returning to the *Enterprise* he discovers that he no longer wants to remain in Starfleet and even opposes their plan to relocate a settlement of Native Americans from the Cardassian neutral zone.

**EPISODE ONE HUNDRED SEVENTY-THREE:**

"FIRSTBORN"

Written by Rene Echevarria
Story by Mark Kalbfeld
Directed by Jonathan West
Guest Cast: Brian Bonsall

At a Klingon outpost, Worf and Alexander meet a mysterious stranger who has an important impact on both their lives.

**EPISODE ONE HUNDRED SEVENTY-FOUR:**

"BLOODLINES"

Written by Nicholas Sagan
Directed by Les Landau
Guest Cast: Lee Arenberg, Ken Olandt

Picard's old Ferengi enemy, Bok (see "The Battle," first season) is back and has discovered that Jean-Luc has a long-lost son whose life he threatens.

## EPISODE ONE HUNDRED SEVENTY-FIVE:

*"EMERGENCE"*

Written by Joe Menosky
Story by Brannon Braga
Directed by Cliff Bole

The *Enterprise* is acting strangely and doing things on its own which are completely inexplicable in normal terms.

## EPISODE ONE HUNDRED SEVENTY-SIX:

*"PREEMPTIVE STRIKE"*

Written by Rene Echevarria
Story by Naren Shankar
Directed by Patrick Stewart
Guest Cast: Michelle Forbes

Ensign Ro returns to the *Enterprise* after special training and is sent on an undercover mission to infiltrate the Maquis, the anti-Cardassian terrorist group operating in the Demilitarized Zone.

## EPISODE ONE HUNDRED SEVENTY-SEVEN AND ONE HUNDRED SEVENTY-EIGHT:

*"ALL GOOD THINGS" (two-hour episode)*

Written by Ronand D. Moore and Brannon Braga
Directed by Winrich Kolbe

Jean-Luc encounters Q once more and also finds that he has become unstuck in time as he moves back and forth through three time periods which are all related and connected by the same menace which must be conquered in each time and place simultaneously.

# DEEP SPACE NINE:

## *EPISODE GUIDE*
## SEASONS 1-2

**AST:**

| | |
|---|---|
| **COMMANDER BENJAMIN SISKO** | Avery Brooks |
| **SECURITY CHIEF ODO** | Rene Auberjonois |
| **DOCTOR JULIAN BASHIR** | Siddig El Fadil |
| **LIEUTENANT JADZIA DAX** | Terry Farrell |
| **JAKE SISKO** | Cirroc Lofton |
| **CHIEF OF OPERATIONS MILES O'BRIEN** | Colm Meaney |
| **QUARK** | Armin Shimerman |
| **MAJOR KIRA NERYS** | Nana Visitor |

# SEASON ONE

**PISODE ONE:**

*"EMISSARY"*

Teleplay by Michael Piller
Story by Rick Berman and Michael Piller
Directed by David Carson
Guest Cast: Patrick Stewart as *Jean-Luc Picard*
Aron Eisenberg: *Nog*
Max Grodenchik: *Ferengi Pit Boss*
Majel Barrett: *Computer Voice*

Commander Sisko arrives on *Deep Space Nine* along with his son and a grudge against Captain Picard of the USS *Enterprise*.

**EPISODE TWO:**

*"PAST PROLOGUE"*

Written by Kathryn Powell
Directed by Winrich Kolbe
Guest Cast: Jeffrey Nordling, Andrew Robinson, Gwynyth Walsh, Barbara March, Susan Bay, Vaughn Armstrong

A man who seeks refuge on *Deep Space Nine* is a former Bajoran terrorist who has now set his sights on driving the Federation off Bajor.

### EPISODE THREE:

*"A MAN ALONE"*

Teleplay: Michael Piller
Story by Gerald Sanford and Michael Piller
Guest Cast: Rosalind Chao, Edward Lawrence Albert, Max Grodenchik, Peter Vogt, Aron Eisenberg

When an old enemy of Odo's turns up dead, he's blamed for the crime because no one else could have gotten into the locked room and past the sensors.

### EPISODE FOUR:

*"BABEL"*

Teleplay by Michael McGreevey and Naren Shankar
Story by Sally Caves and Ira Steven Behr
Guest Cast: Jack Kehler, Matthew Faison, Ann Gillespie, Geraldine Farrell

A mysterious virus afflicts nearly everyone on the space station with a case of aphasia, which causes them to speak in gibberish.

### EPISODE FIVE:

*"CAPTIVE PURSUIT"*

Teleplay by Jill Sherman Donner and Michael Piller
Story by Jill Sherman Donner
Directed by Corey Allen
Guest Cast: Gerrit Graham, Scott MacDonald, Kelly Curtis

A vessel arrives at the space station with a being who is pursued by aliens, only he was born and bred to be hunted, and that's the way he likes it, in spite of O'Brien's attempts to help him.

### EPISODE SIX:

*"Q LESS"*

Teleplay by Robert Hewitt Wolfe
Story by Hannah Louise Shearer
Directed by Paul Lynch
Guest Cast: John deLancie, Jennifer Hetrick

When Vash arrives on the space station after spending two years in the Gamma Quadrant, Q shows up trying to convince her to go back with him.

### EPISODE SEVEN:

*"DAX"*

Teleplay by D. C. Fontana and Peter Allan Fields
Story by Peter Allan Fields

Guest Cast: Gregory Itzin, Anne Haney, Richard Lineback, Fionnula

When a team arrives on *Deep Space Nine* and attempts to kidnap Dax, a story of treachery involving Curzon Dax arises, and Odo has to find the truth because Dax won't discuss the past.

**EPISODE EIGHT:**

*"THE PASSENGER"*

Teleplay by Morgan Gende, Robert Hewitt Wolfe, and Michael Piller
Story by Morgan Gendel
Directed by Paul Lynch
Guest Cast: Caitlin Brown, James Lashly, Christopher Collins, James Harper

When a serial killer dies on the space station, his mind hitchhikes aboard another body until he's ready to kill again.

**EPISODE NINE:**

*"MOVE ALONG HOME"*

Teleplay by Frederick Rappaport and Lisa Rich & Jeanne Carrigan-Fauci
Story by Michael Piller
Directed by David Carson
Guest Cast: Clara Bryant, Joel Brooks, James Lashly

When aliens from the Gamma Quadrant arrive on the space station, rather than meet with Sisko all they want to do is go to Quark's place and play games, especially one they brought with them.

**EPISODE TEN:**

*"THE NAGUS"*

Teleplay by Ira Steven Behr
Story by David Livingston
Directed by David Livingston
Guest Cast: Wallace Shawn, Max Grodenchik, Lou Wagner, Tiny Ron, Barry Gordon, Lee Arenberg, Aron Eisenberg

When the Ferengi leader, the Nagus, arrives on the space station, he calls a meeting and chooses Quark to be his successor, whereupon the assassination attempts on Quark's life begin.

**EPISODE ELEVEN:**

*"VORTEX"*

Written by Sam Rolfe

Directed by Winrich Kolbe
Guest star: Cliff DeYoung

A wanted man is captured on the space station, but when Odo is assigned to take the man back to his homeworld, the outlaw taunts Odo with an artifact that hints at a place that might contain clues to Odo's mysterious origins.

**EPISODE TWELVE:**

## "BATTLE LINES"

Written by Richard Danus and Evan Carlos Somers
Story by Hilary Bader
Directed by Paul Lynch
Guest Cast: Jonathan Banks, Camille Saviola

When Kai Opaka requests to be taken on a visit to the Gamma Quadrant, no one expects to find themselves on a planetoid where men have been imprisoned to fight among themselves and die, only to be resurrected over and over again.

**EPISODE THIRTEEN:**

## "THE STORYTELLER"

Written by Kurt Michael Bensmiller and Ira Steven Behr
Story by Kurt Michael Bensmiller
Directed by David Livingston
Guest Cast: Gina Philips, Jim Jansen, Kay E. Kuter, Frances Praksti

Julian and O'Brien are called on to help a Bajoran village deal with an annual menace which can only be fought by uniting everyone in the village.

**EPISODE FOURTEEN:**

## "PROGRESS"

Written by Peter Allan Fields
Directed by Les Landau
Guest Cast: Brian Keith as *Mullibok*

Commander Sisko is slated to supervise an operation involving the tapping of the molten core of the fifth Bajoran moon of Jeraddo for the purposes of a large-scale energy transfer. But the planet must be devoid of life for this to be accomplished so that no one is hurt, and when unauthorized personnel are discovered to be living there, Major Kira goes to investigate.

**EPISODE FIFTEEN:**

*"IF WISHES WERE HORSES"*

Written by Nell McCue Crawford, William Crawford and Michael Piller
Based on a story by Nell McCue Crawford and William Crawford
Directed by Rob Legato
Guest Cast: Michael John Anderson, Hana Hatae, Keone Young

Strange things happen when people's fantasies start taking on solid form aboard the station, including a double for Dax who loves Julian. But on the dark side a gigantic vortex threatens to engulf the space station.

**EPISODE SIXTEEN:**

*"THE FORSAKEN"*

Written by Don Carlos Dunaway and Michael Piller
Based on a story by Jim Trombetta
Directed by Les Landau
Guest Cast: Majel Barrett as *Lwaxana Troi*

When a group of diplomats arrives on *Deep Space Nine* on a fact-finding mission to the wormhole, Commander Sisko recognizes it as a pointless extravagance and assigns Dr. Bashir to be the host for the delegation, much to Julian's dismay. Complicating this is the fact that Lwaxana Troi is among them, and she's taken a shine to Odo.

**EPISODE SEVENTEEN:**

*"DRAMATIS PERSONAE"*

Written by Joe Menosky
Directed by Cliff Bole

The senior staff on *Deep Space Nine* start adopting strange new personas after a Klingon ship returns from the Gamma Quadrant and blows up nearby.

**EPISODE EIGHTEEN:**

*"DUET"*

Written by Peter Allan Fields
Story by Lisa Rich and Jeanne Carrigan-Fauci
Directed by James L. Conway
Guest Cast: Harris Yulin as *Aamin Marritza*

A Cardassian who arrives on the space station may be the legendary butcher of Gallitepp who was responsible for thousands of Bajoran deaths.

**EPISODE NINETEEN:**

*"IN THE HANDS OF THE PROPHETS"*

Written by Robert Hewitt Wolfe
Directed by David Livingston
Guest Cast: Philip Anglim, Louise Fletcher, Rosalind Chao, Robin Christopher, Michael Eugene Fairman

Vedek Winn complains that Keiko is teaching Bajoran children scientific ideas that conflict with their religious beliefs, which creates a dangerous controversy on the station.

# SECOND SEASON

## PISODE TWENTY:

*"THE HOMECOMING"*

Written by Ira Steven Behr
Story by Jeri Taylor and Ira Steven Behr
Directed by Winrich Kolbe
Guest Cast: Richard Beymer, Frank Langella, Max Grodenchik, Marc Alaimo

A legendary hero of the Bajoran war against the Cardassians is discovered to be still alive in a secret prison camp, and Kira goes to rescue him. [Part one of three.]

## EPISODE TWENTY-ONE:

*"THE CIRCLE"*

Written by Peter Allan Fields
Directed by Corey Allen
Guest Cast: Louise Fletcher, Philip Anglim, Frank Langella, Richard Beymer, Mike Genovese, Eric Server, Anthony Guidera, Stephen Macht, Bruce Gray

A group of Bajorans known as the Circle is opposed to the Federation presence on Bajor and wants them to leave. But then how will Bajor defend itself against a possible Cardassian reoccupation? [Part two of three.]

### EPISODE TWENTY-TWO:

*"THE SIEGE"*

Written by Michael Piller
Directed by Winrich Kolbe
Guest Cast: Louise Fletcher, Philip Anglim, Frank Langella, Richard Beymer, Rosalind Chao, Max Grodenchik, Katrina Carlson, Hana Hatae, Steven Weber, Stephen Macht, Aron Eisenberg

Kira is kidnapped by the Circle and Quark discovers who is really supplying the Circle with secret assistance. [Part three of three.]

### EPISODE TWENTY-THREE:

*"INVASIVE PROCEDURES"*

Written by John Whelpley and Robert Hewitt Wolfe
Story by John Whelpley
Directed by Les Landau
Guest Cast: John Glover, Megan Gallagher, Tim Ross, Steve Rankin

A man who had been rejected for being a Trill host kidnaps Dax and forces Dr. Bashir to place her Trill inside of him.

### EPISODE TWENTY-FOUR:

*"CARDASSIANS"*

Written by James Crocker
Story by Gene Wolande and John Wright
Directed by Cliff Bole
Guest Cast: Rosalind Chao, Marc Alaimo, Andrew Robinson, Robert Mandan, Vidal Peterson, Dion Anderson, Terrance Evans

The fact that Bajorans are raising Cardassian war orphans leads to a controversy that could topple an important Cardassian political leader, and Gul Dukat is the instigator.

### EPISODE TWENTY-FIVE:

*"MELORA"*

Written by Evan Carlos Somers, Steven Baum, Michael Piller and James Crocker
Directed by Winrich Kolbe
Guest Cast: Daphne Ashbrook, Peter Crombie, Don Stark, Ron Taylor

When a woman from a low-gravity world arrives on *Deep Space Nine*, Dr. Bashir at first clashes with her, then finds his feelings softening.

### EPISODE TWENTY-SIX:

*"RULES OF ACQUISITION"*

Written by Ira Steven Behr

Directed by David Livingston
Guest Cast: Wallace Shawn, Helene Udy, Brian Thompson, Max Grodenchik, Emilia Crow, Tiny Ron

The Nagus has Quark undertake a mission to the Gamma Quadrant to attempt to make contact with the Dominion in order to begin trade negotiations. Assisting Quark is Pel, a Ferengi who harbors a shocking secret.

### EPISODE TWENTY-SEVEN:

*"NECESSARY EVIL"*

Written by Peter Allan Fields
Directed by James L. Conway
Guest Cast: Max Grodenchik, Marc Alaimo, Robert Mackenzie, Katherine Moffat

A five-year-old unsolved murder involves Kira, and leads to Odo recalling how he first came to be appointed head of security by the Cardassians.

### EPISODE TWENTY-EIGHT:

*"SECOND SIGHT"*

Written by Mark-Gehred-O'Connell, Ira Steven Behr and Robert Hewitt Wolfe
Story by Mark Gehred-O'Connell
Directed by Alexander Singer
Guest Cast: Richard Kiley, Salli Elise Richardson, Mark Erickson

Ben Sisko meets a mysterious woman on the space station who turns out to have a very strange origin, one which threatens their relationship.

### EPISODE TWENTY-NINE:

*"SANCTUARY"*

Written by Frederick Rappaport
Story by Gabe Essoe and Kelley Miles
Directed by Les Landau
Guest Cast: William Schallert, Andrew Koenig, Aron Eisenberg, Michael Durrell, Betty McGuire, Robert Curtis-Brown, Kitty Swink, Deborah May, Leland Orser, Nicholas Shaffer

A small vessel finds its way through the wormhole, and it turns out to be the first of three million refugees who are searching for a new home—Bajor makes it clear that their world won't be that place.

### EPISODE THIRTY:

*"RIVALS"*

Written by Joe Menosky

Story by Jim Trombetta and Michael Piller
Directed by David Livingston
Guest Cast: Chris Sarandon, Barbara Bosson, Rosalind Chao, Max Grodenchik, Albert Henderson

Miles and Julian get involved in a racquetball match that has everyone on the station betting on the outcome.

**EPISODE THIRTY-ONE:**

*"THE ALTERNATE"*

Written by Bill Dial
Directed by David Carson
Guest Cast: James Sloyan, Matt McKenzie

When Odo and his old mentor visit a world in the Gamma Quadrant searching for clues to the shape shifter's origin, strange events occur after they return to the space station.

**EPISODE THIRTY-TWO:**

*"ARMAGEDDON GAME"*

Written by Morgan Gendel
Directed by Winrich Kolbe
Guest Cast: Darleen Carr, Rosalind Chao

When Miles O'Brien and Dr. Bashir help dispose of the last of a deadly plague virus known as "harvesters," the aliens whom the plague once threatened decide that anyone who knows the secret of the "harvesters" must be eliminated.

**EPISODE THIRTY-THREE:**

*"WHISPERS"*

Written by Paul Robert Coyl
Directed by Les Landau
Guest Cast: Rosalind Chao

When O'Brien returns to *Deep Space Nine* after a mission, he finds that everyone is acting strangely, and Commander Sisko seems to be giving O'Brien assignments to keep him out of the way when a diplomatic mission is slated to arrive.

**EPISODE THIRTY-FOUR:**

*"PARADISE"*

Written by Jeff King, Richard Manning and Hans Beimler
Story by Jim Trombette and James Crocker
Directed by Corey Allen
Guest Cast: Gail Strickland, Steve Vinovich

When Commander Sisko and Chief O'Brien discover life forms on an M-Class planet during a colonization survey, they find the crew of a Federation craft that had crashed on the planet a decade earlier, and the leader of the survivors doesn't want to be rescued.

### EPISODE THIRTY-FIVE:

*"SHADOWPLAY"*

Written by Robert Hewitt Wolfe
Directed by Robert Scheerer
Guest Cast: Philip Anglim, Kenneth Mars, Kenneth Toby, Noley Thornton

Odo and Dax find a colony on an uncharted planet where people keep disappearing, but they soon find that things are more than they seem.

### EPISODE THIRTY-SIX:

*"PLAYING GOD"*

Written by Jim Trombetta and Michael Piller
Story by Jim Trombetta
Directed by David Livingston
Guest Cast: Geoffrey Blake, Ron Taylor, Richard Poe, Chris Nelson Norris

Jadzia plays hostess to Argen, a Trill host candidate who is there to learn from her what it is like to be a Trill.

### EPISODE THIRTY-SEVEN:

*"PROFIT AND LOSS"*

Written by Flip Kobler and Cindy Marcus
Directed by Robert Wiemer
Guest Cast: Mary Crosby, Andrew Robinson, Michael Reilly Burke, Heidi Swedberg, Edward Wiley

Quark's old lover turns on *Deep Space Nine* and she's on the run from the Cardassians because of her work with the anti-government underground.

### EPISODE THIRTY-EIGHT:

*"BLOOD OATH"*

Written by Peter Allan Fields
Directed by Winrich Kolbe
Guest Cast: John Colicos, Michael Ansara, William Campbell, Bill Bolender, Christopher Collins

When three Klingons arrive on the space station, they are there looking for Curzon Dax to aid them in fulfilling an eighty-year-old oath to kill the assassin of their children.

**EPISODE THIRTY-NINE:**

*"THE MAQUIS—PART I"*

Written by James Crocker
Story by Rick Berman, Michael Piller, Jeri Taylor and James Crocker
Directed by David Livingston
Guest Cast: Marc Alaimo, Bernie Casey, Michael Rose, Steven John Evans

Problems in the demilitarized zone lead Sisko to accept assistance from Gul Dukat in learning the truth about a revolutionary group called the Maquis.

**EPISODE FORTY:**

*"THE MAQUIS—PART II"*

Written by Ira Steven Behr
Story by Rick Berman, Michael Piller, Jeri Taylor and Ira Steven Behr
Directed by Corey Allen
Guest Cast: Marc Alaimo, Bernie Casey, Michael Rose, John Schuck, Tony Plana, Bertila Damas, Michael Bell, Amanda Carlin

Things heat up as we learn more about the Maquis and their grievances against the Cardassians, and how much the Cardassians are truly to blame.

**EPISODE FORTY-ONE:**

*"THE WIRE"*

Written by Robert Hewitt Wolfe
Directed by Kim Friedman
Guest Cast: Andrew Robinson, Paul Dooley, Jimmie F. Skaggs, Ann Gillespie

Dr. Bashir discovers a secret that Garak has kept for years—a secret that could cost the Cardassian outcast his life.

**EPISODE FORTY-TWO:**

*"CROSSOVER"*

Written by Peter Allan Fields and Michael Piller
Story by Peter Allan Fields
Directed by David Livingston
Guest Cast: Andrew Robinson, Stephen Gevedon, Jack R. Orend, Dennis Madalone, John Cothran, Jr.

A malfunction in their shuttle causes Kira and Julian to cross over into a parallel universe where life on *Deep Space Nine* is very different from what they knew.

## EPISODE FORTY-THREE:

*"THE COLLABORATOR"*

Written by Gary Holland, Ira Steven Behr and Robert Hewitt Wolfe
Story by Gary Holland
Directed by Cliff Bole
Guest Cast: Philip Anglim, Louise Fletcher, Bert Remsen, Camille Saviola

With the election of the new Kai coming up, Kira finds herself having to investigate whether Vedek Bareil collaborated with the Cardassians during the occupation.

## EPISODE FORTY-FOUR:

*"TRIBUNAL"*

Written by Bill Dial
Directed by Avery Brooks
Guest Cast: Rosalind Chao, Fritz Weaver, John Beck, Richard Poe, Julian Christopher

Miles O'Brien is captured by Cardassians and put on trial for collaborating with the Maquis.

## EPISODE FORTY-FIVE:

*"THE JEM'HADAR"*

Written by Ira Steven Behr
Directed by Kim Friedman
Guest Cast: Aron Eisenberg, Molly Hagan, Alan Oppenheimer, Cress Williams

On a trip into the Gamma Quadrant, Ben Sisko and Quark are captured by the Jem'Hadar, the shock troops of the mysterious Dominion, who demand that the Federation cease using the wormhole.

*Brent Spiner has appeared at a number of STAR TREK conventions over the years. The following article is based on two such appearances, his first convention appearance, on November 24 and 25, 1989, and a later one on November 24, 1991.*

# BRENT SPINER—IN PERSON

## BY DIANA COLLINS AND JAMES VAN HISE

Microphone in hand, Spiner glided across the stage, sporting the same hairstyle and round gold-framed glasses he'd worn during his Oscar-night *Tonight Show* appearance with Jay Leno. He was dressed in a tailored suit accented by a black turtleneck and black suede shoes. His first words to the audience were, "Once again I'm feeling like Elvis." He began crooning, "Are you lonesome tonight?" his tenor voice achieving a decent fake-Elvis vocal quality; the audience applauded. Then he asked, "Can you imagine thousands of Brent Spiner imitations years from now? And how do you know that I'm not one now?"

Brent Spiner's "lounge act" was on a roll as he quickly changed accents with the routine. Repeating his line, "Good evening ladies and germs!" from his comedic *TNG* episode with Joe Piscopo, Spiner next faked a British accent used in his cameo appearance in *What's Alan Watching?*, introducing imaginary Beatles onstage behind him.

Warmed up, Spiner exclaimed, "It's great to be back in New York and onstage again! I miss being on the stage and would like to think that I have at least one play in me . . . perhaps even a musical. Did anyone see any of my musicals?"

Fans yelled names—*Sunday in the Park With George, Big River, The Three Musketeers*, and finally *What's Alan Watching?* Spiner quipped, "That's not a musical!" amid audience snickers.

"I shopped before the con for an overcoat in Barney's men's store in Manhattan, for obvious reasons. I had never needed one in L.A.

"A clerk approached to wait on me.

"Clerk: 'You look familiar but I can't seem to place you.'

"Spiner: 'Okay, I'll give you a hint. I'm an actor.' The clerk scratched his head. 'I'll give you a second hint, I'm on television.' The clerk pondered further without success. 'Okay, this will definitely give it away. On television you'd probably notice that I have a green hue.'

"He suddenly burst out, 'Oh, you're Lou Ferrigno!'

Sly expression and eyebrows arched. "'Yes I am. How'd you guess?!'" To which the audience howled.

## THE AUDITION

But how did Brent Spiner, struggling actor, become Data, one of the most popular characters on television?

"From being in several Broadway plays in New York I came to Los Angeles to do *Little Shop of Horrors*. It was a tremendous play," he recalled. "After that I did mostly villain of the week guest appearances in *Hill Street Blues, Cheers, Night Court* and other TV shows. I feel very fortunate to be doing something with this long a run and feel very proud of it. Unlike so many other actors who do shows that aren't meaningful, *Star Trek* is a show about the positive aspect of humanity which contains a morality play and an entertaining plot that holds to Gene Roddenberry's vision and values."

And as to how Brent actually landed that now-popular role, he explained, "The producers interviewed many actors for the part. It came down to two of us. Fortunately Tom Cruise didn't want to commit himself for that long," which amused the audience. "Actually Eric Menyuk, who played the Traveler in two Wesley episodes, was the other candidate for the part of Data. Very fortunately for me, I got the part."

## LIFE BEFORE *STAR TREK*

When someone wondered if he could change anything in his professional or personal life, such as his appearance in the film *Rent Control*, Brent chuckled and said, "*Rent Control* was really a bad movie. I was glad I made it. It's an amazing credit to the producer, actually, because the movie was made on a budget of only $100,000 and looks like it must have cost more than $200,000. To answer your question, perhaps I wouldn't have done those couple episodes of *Mama's Family*. I knew the director of *Night Court* and agreed to do *Mama's* in exchange for being on *Night Court*. Generally I felt I have been exactly where I wanted to be. I learned from the beginning of my career that I knew I had to suffer to be an actor. So I was prepared."

Regarding his experience on *Night Court*, Spiner recalled that, "It was great and easier to do than a *Star Trek* episode because it was only a half-hour show. It would be rehearsed during the week, then filmed in front of a live audience on Fridays. I would love to do another one. In fact there has been a script waiting for two and a half years for me to do. I had gotten Paramount's permission to do it, too. I've never had the time to get around to it."

One of the other shows Spiner appeared in prior to *The Next Generation* is *The Twilight Zone*, and while discussing the episode he was in he stated, "I consider *The Twilight Zone* to be one of the greatest shows on TV. I was thrilled just to be a part of it."

## THE DIFFICULTIES OF BEING DATA

But what is it really like playing Data and what's the most difficult part of playing the role?

"I'd have to say that learning the lines is the hardest part. When you're a young actor in a school play, your family and friends always ask, 'How do you learn all those lines?' Well, in my role it's not just that I have to learn so many of them, but most of them are words I've never said before in my life! Mike Okuda and Rick Sternbach invent all of these wonderful futuristic technical-scientific things and make up words that don't exist to fit their ideas. Getting those words from my head to my mouth is the difficult part. I have a personal rule that I don't go to bed at night until I can get the next day's script words from my head to my mouth. So I spend many sleepless nights working on it till I can get it out of my mouth."

And what does he think about the way that the insides of Data's body have been exposed in certain episodes?

"At this time I think they have opened up every part of my body that's possible! Michael Westmore and his son, who are the makeup and electronic prosthetic geniuses, have done a fabulous job of making all of it appear so realistic."

One of the difficulties of playing Data involves

the extensive makeup he must wear, which smears easily.

"I had to train myself over the years of production not to touch myself. Can you imagine just five years ago I didn't know how to do that? Actually it is very difficult not to smudge makeup all over everything. Particularly the face of the comm station that my fingers are frequently typing on will get pretty disgusting. Now and then the director or camera man will notice it looks awful, stop the camera and have someone clean off the Plexiglas."

## DATA AND SPOCK

And then there's the matter of what it's like playing the character of Data himself—or is it "itself"?

"Every acting role has its set of problems to work out. I'm fortunate to be playing an android. Since nobody knows what it's like to be an android or what one is supposed to act like, I can play it any way I like. No one can be too critical about my style." And the contact lenses? "They're yellow on the iris part with a clear center which is a prescription contact. So fortunately I don't see everything in yellow."

Because he plays an android, he was asked whether the other actors try to make him laugh during scenes.

"Each episode is shot from five different angles. We have five to seven rehearsals before the final filming. I usually laugh during that time. The first time we say our lines, it's funny. By the second or third time it's no longer funny. By the tenth time it becomes funny again."

In "Reunification," Spock met the cast of the *Next Generation* for the first time, which couldn't help but make people wonder what it was like working with Leonard Nimoy.

"It was good to work with Leonard Nimoy," he explained. "He's very professional. It was like working with a visiting dignitary. At first we were all pretty nervous and on our best behavior. After awhile we realized that Leonard was a fun person on the set, too. So we went back to our usual antics after a few days and he seemed to enjoy our bad lounge act routines."

## FAVORITE TREKS

Because Spiner wears makeup to alter his facial color and texture, as well as the contact lenses, it is not as easy to recognize him in public as one might think.

"Sometimes people will see me in a restaurant and I can always tell because they get this puzzled look on their faces, so I try to help them out by . . . [he twitches his head with the jerky movements of an android]. Then they recognize me as the RCA dog."

There have been many novels written with additional adventures of *Next Generation* characters, but Spiner has not had the time to read any of them. "I'm lucky to read one book per year. The filming schedule makes my day so long [12-16 hours on the set] that my main hobby is sleeping. I'm getting real good at it, too."

Asked what his favorite episodes of the old *Star Trek* and *The Next Generation* are, someone shouted out "The Naked Now" before he could even reply. Brent responded, "So you liked that one, too, huh? I really enjoyed my interactions with Tasha. Completely arrogantly I like the episodes that I had major roles in, such as 'Measure of a Man,' which had something to say about the state of humanity. Also I liked 'Offspring' a lot due to the directing of Jonathan Frakes and working with the actress who did an outstanding job playing my daughter, Lal."

As to his favorite of the original *Star Treks*, he zeroed in on one of the motion pictures. "I'd have to say the movie *Wrath of Khan* because Ricardo Montalban was brilliant in it. Critics and I especially liked the scene where Kirk is yelling, 'Kaaaaaaahhhhhhhhhhhnnnnnnnnn!'" The audience cheered at Brent's Shatner/Kirk impression.

## BRENT'S COSTARS

Brent was asked about his fellow actors on *The Next Generation*. "Everybody in the cast is great and wonderful to work with," Spiner stated, "and it must be a nightmare for actors on other shows who don't get along because we all have to work twelve to fifteen hours per day together."

Asked about the specific actors, Brent began, "It's an honor and pleasure to work with Patrick Stewart. He's the finest Shakespearean actor alive today. And Patrick tells us—" as he slips into an imitation of Stewart "—he's witty, intelligent, a real sex symbol, sophisticated, etc."

Regarding Marina Sirtis, Brent stated that she's "the best Greek/British actress on television or theater." In describing LeVar Burton, he said, "A real prince of Africa, who when President of the U.S. will unite the nations of the world. Mr. Metaphysical!"

Gates McFadden, who had been forced out at the end of the first season, had just recently returned; the third season had gotten underway a couple of months before Spiner's convention appearance. "I'm really glad that she's back," Brent said enthusiastically. "She's gorgeous and it's wonderful to work with her again."

Then there's Michael Dorn. "All men on *Star Trek* see themselves as sex symbols. Well, Michael *really* is one and certainly does have a way with women.

In comparison, the first woman I had a serious love relationship with looked more like Vic Tayback."

The newest cast member at the time was also the best known: Whoopi Goldberg. "A great comedian," said Brent, "and terrific woman in every way."

Then there was the youngest cast member, Wil Wheaton. "We call him 'Cool Breeze' now. I used to be a 'Cool Breeze' once, when I was more his age. Now I'm just 'hot air.'"

And, of course, Jonathan Frakes, "A tremendous person and he gets bigger, nicer, and more tremendous every year. Jonathan will be directing this year and we are really looking forward to it because we aren't allowed to give the directors a hard time, normally."

## THE MAN BEHIND PICARD

Regarding what personalities Brent likes to imitate, he zeroed in on a certain British cast member. "The person I most often like to imitate says this: *Pontiac!* Patrick Stewart says he does that commercial in his American accent."

The actor stated that he and Stewart might be doing Shakespeare together sometime in the future.

"Patrick Stewart and I have talked about doing *The Merchant of Venice*, where I'll play Shylock one night and he'll play that character the next night."

And what is it like working with Patrick Stewart?

"Patrick is one of the best actors I know. In the beginning of *Star Trek:—The Next Generation*'s filming, he took everything *very* seriously. One day the director of an early episode complained to the producers that he didn't think he could stand to finish filming because we were too loud, boisterous, and wild. Patrick was stricken by the comment and we were all hanging our heads in shame. Then the next day, as we're walking onto the rolling green hills in the Tasha holodeck good-bye scene, Patrick breaks into song: 'The hills are alive, with the sound of music!' Then we were sure that we'd loosened him up."

Does Brent plan to do any writing, directing or producing on *Star Trek: The Next Generation*?

"I haven't had the time to prepare to direct. I had thought of directing for awhile in the beginning. But after I saw how much extra time that Jonathan and Patrick had to spend learning the intricacies of directing, I changed my mind."

## WORKING WITH WHOOPI

Regarding what it's like to work with Whoopi Goldberg, Brent enthusiastically replied, "Whoopi is sensational! It's a thrill to be working with her. She brought her well-deserved Oscar on the set the next day after receiving it. She let everyone hold it, too! She's the most available person I've ever met. Whoopi knows everybody and everybody seems to know her. We hang out together sometimes because we like the thirties, forties and fifties music and movies. We recently went to the American Cinema Awards together. It's a benefit for the Old Actor's Home. We were sitting at a table with Dean Stockwell, Rutger Hauer, and all kinds of famous stars. I got to meet the Bowery Boys, Clayton Moore, and many other retired actors as well.

"When it was time for us to go home, Whoopi had Shelley Winters in tow and asked if I could drive her home as well. I'm thinking, she's asking me if I want to drive Shelley Winters home? No problem! Shelley told us a story on the way about how she's been living in the same house since 1952. When I let her out, I offered to walk her to the door. She said, 'Don't be silly, I'm fine.' To make sure she was all right, Whoopi and I wanted to wait there in the car until she went in. She went up to the door, stopped, looked around, and walked back a few paces and seemed confused. I called out to her and asked if there was something we could do to help. Once she realized we were still there, Shelley walked back to my car and said that wasn't her house. So we had to drive around to find her house. Can you imagine she'd been living there since 1952 and couldn't find her house?"

## NAKED TIMES

On the subject of "The Naked Now," someone asked why he put his elbow out and took a fall at the end of the scene. "That wasn't in the script at all. It was just something that I had ad-libbed for fun, fully expecting it to be cut from the film. When they went to do the final editing, it had to be saved because they didn't have any other good takes and there wasn't enough time to do the scene over again. I was happy it made it into an episode because I liked how it turned out." And as to whether it was hard to do the drunk scene in that episode, the actor stated, "Acting drunk is the most difficult thing to play, especially if you don't drink. And *of course* I don't drink," he said, smirking and then looking innocent.

The episode "The Naked Now" includes the now-famous sequence in which Tasha Yar seduces Data. When asked about this, he said, "Well, I certainly think Data and Tasha had something going! And I think that Tasha was more than a crush. I remember it vividly. After all, Data kept that holograph picture of her, didn't he? It's even in my hotel room tonight!"

Spiner revealed an interesting piece of information regarding the episode featuring Tasha Yar's funeral and her final message, which was played on the holodeck. There was a personal message for

Data that said: "Data, it *did* happen." Regarding why the line was cut, he explained, "The producers decided to cut it from the episode because they didn't feel it was the right thing for Tasha to say. I don't know all their reasons for it, but I would have liked to have kept that part in the script."

Jonathan Frakes had revealed at another convention that he'd always wanted to play a trombone and finally got that opportunity in an episode of *TNG*, so when Brent Spiner was asked what he'd like to play if he got the chance, someone in the audience piped up with "Tasha Yar." Brent laughed and said, "Yes, Tasha Yar—definitely! *Seriously*, I've wanted to do about two or three thousand things on the show. But nothing in particular that I can think of at the moment. Perhaps the trombone as well, but I don't really know how to play it."

## PERFORMING ART

On the subject of whether he actually plays any of the musical instruments Data is supposed to be able to master, he stated, "I play only a very bad guitar. Once I auditioned for a film about Horton Foote. During the audition the director requested that I play the guitar and sing. So I think I decided to play the Randy Newman song 'Marie.' He was listening and asked what the song was. After that I think Randy Newman got the part instead of me."

Regarding another type of performance art, he discussed the episode in which Dr. Crusher taught Data to dance.

"I do know some things about dance. I took tap dancing when I was sixteen years old. The dancing for the episode took a week to rehearse. Gates did all of the choreography work to create the dance routine. Gates has tremendous experience in dance. For instance, she was the lead choreographer in a couple of Muppet movies and has done several things along those lines."

But what was actually the most physically difficult episode to perform in? "Brothers" is the episode he cited as the one he felt was almost technically impossible to do.

"There were many tiny sequences that had to be positioned right. I used a video feedback and split screen to do all three parts. Even then, it took many takes to get each sequence in sync. For example, when I was playing Dr. Soong's part, I would take a pencil and wave it in front of Data to make him follow its movement. Then as I switched roles to play Data, I had to remember exactly where my eyes should be focused to follow a pencil that wasn't there. The timing was too difficult to use a stand-in to copy Dr. Soong's motions. All I could do was relate to the sequence of dialogue words to where each pencil movement should be. The most difficult thing to accomplish was when Dr. Soong held Data's face in his hands and patted it. That was something a stand-in had to do, since it would be impossible for me to hold my face with my own hands. It took a long time to get it technically correct on film, but very satisfying to have accomplished."

## INSIDE DATA

One of the questions people wondered about during the early seasons of *The Next Generation* was whether Data would ever become human, which for a time seemed to be the android's goal. But Spiner stated that this would never happen. "No, Data is Pinocchio, just like Gene Roddenberry has envisioned him. I think Data will continue, but never quite make it, to become more and more human as time goes on. And like any other character on the show he should grow and develop, too. This year he has not really reversed that development. It's time for the third-season stories to develop other characters and ideas besides Data right now."

In explaining Data and exactly how childlike the character is supposed to be, Spiner quipped, "I'd like to think that Data's character is the adult and Brent Spiner is the child."

Another popular episode which strongly features the character of the android is "Elementary, Dear Data," and one fan wondered whether Brent was a fan of Sherlock Holmes and if he had any input on that particular episode.

"I have always loved Sherlock Holmes, especially Basil Rathbone, Chris Plumber, Frank Langella, and yes, [Jeremy] Brett, too, very much. And I was a big fan of the Chandler novels as a youth, too. So I was very excited to be playing a Sherlock Holmes character. But I had nothing to do with it being thought up or produced in an episode." As to whether the actors have any influence on the characters or storyline in a script, Brent explained, "Not a whole lot. Actors are just taking the initial direction that they want to go with the character. Directors aren't interested in our input. They are trying to look at the strengths of the actors and match that with the casting to come up with a finished product."

At another convention, Jonathan Frakes had remarked that Brent Spiner liked to play practical jokes, and when asked about this Brent replied, "When Jonathan doesn't know what to say, he lies. Actually there's not enough time [in the day's filming schedule] to set up any real practical jokes. However, it is a wild set full of comedians and everyone is *on* all the time.

Spiner was asked about whether Data is subject to the three laws of robotics created by Isaac Asimov, and Brent responded that the android wasn't; Data is controlled by Gene Roddenberry.

## OUTSIDE DATA

Then a fan bluntly asked Brent if he wore a wig. "No, it's my very own hair. They dye it to darken it every day and slick it back. When Gene Roddenberry originally cast me as Data, he asked me if I would mind altering my appearance in some way. I told him, I can do that! Later Gene asked me if I'd be willing to shave my head. I told him, well, I guess I wouldn't be doing the part. So Gene had me go through something like thirty-six makeup tests, the colors ranging from battleship gray to bubblegum pink, including orange eyes. My makeup they finally selected is really bright gold, but the camera lighting cancels it out in some way."

This is also what he regards as the one drawback to playing the character. "The makeup is a drag to wear. It takes an hour and a quarter to put it on and twenty minutes to get it off. I can only get it off with kerosene. I've swallowed a lot of kerosene since I've begun this role. I asked Gene why a brilliant scientist like Noonian Soong, with the advanced technology of the time, couldn't have made Data with normal-looking skin. Gene has a way of asking questions to make you see his way of thinking. GR asked, 'What makes you think that Data's skin isn't better?' Michael Westmore puts on the gold makeup personally for me every morning. Once when Michael didn't come in because he was home sick, another person did my makeup that morning. But when they began shooting, it didn't look right in the camera. So they called Michael in anyway to do it himself."

Someone wondered whether Spiner realized when he got the role that Data would become a character as popular as Spock was on the original series. At this he revealed, "When my agent got me the audition for *Star Trek: The Next Generation*, I was given all the character scripts to read. Having read the script for Data, I told them I was definitely interested in Data and auditioned for the part seven or eight times. I didn't anticipate that it would be the most popular character [he thanked the questioner for the comment], but I certainly thought it would be a nice character to play."

## COMEDY TREK

Early in the series Joe Piscopo appeared in a holodeck sequence, and while Brent enjoyed working with him, he wasn't their original choice for that role.

"It was my idea to work with Jerry Lewis. Unfortunately Jerry was busy that week. We went through a lot of names of comedians before we were able to get one to perform on the show." These days that probably would not be as big a problem. As to whether Brent ever thought about doing stand-up comedy himself, he replied, "No, it's very dangerous work. When you're standing onstage doing comedy, it's not a character in wardrobe and makeup. It means they hate *you* if they don't clap, not your character."

A strangely worded question was asked: If Data lives forever, what did Brent like best about the character?

"I feel silly talking about him being immortal," Brent stated, and then added, "He's a character with no potential for cruelty. He's an outsider and yet he's incredibly capable, despite being an outsider. I think those qualities are his best ones."

## DATA'S LAUGH

On the subject of laughter, Brent was asked whether he could perform the same laugh Data used when Q gave him that brief ability in the "Hide and Q" episode.

"Sorry, I can't do that laugh on cue after so long a period. When I saw that the script called for Data's first laugh, I was very nervous about getting it just right. Originally that scene was supposed to be filmed at the end of the day on Friday. Thankfully production delays caused them to be unable to get to that scene until after the weekend. So I practiced and practiced all weekend until I felt it was right.

"Monday morning when I did the laugh for the camera, I got it right the first time! When the director said 'Cut!,' Patrick Stewart dared me to be able to do it again. As it turned out, I did it again three more times to capture it on film with different angles, and I was successful each time, fortunately."

A fan from Texas asked Brent where he went to high school. "I went to Bel Air High School in Houston. It was a great school to go to if you wanted to be an actor. Harlan G. Andrews was the principal. He was the brother of the late actor Dana Andrews and looked just like him. You may have heard of Cecil Pickett, my acting teacher. I went to high school with Randy and Dennis Quaid, Cindy Pickett from *St. Elsewhere* and Robert Wuhl from *Batman*. I went to probably fourteen different colleges in all, foremost in my mind is the University of Houston and Trinity College in Dublin, Ireland. I even attended the famous Strasberg Institute of New York. I haven't seen anyone I knew there getting any good acting work. But many people I went to high school with are doing plenty of acting, directing, and producing for movies and TV."

## A VARIETY OF ROLES

As to what he looks for in a role, Spiner explained, "In the old days I took a part for the work and money. These days I only accept the parts whose characters are fun and humorous to me." Regarding any famous roles he might like to play he stated, "Yes, some Shakespearean roles. I once played Shylock in college, which is, oddly enough, one of Patrick Stewart's most famous Shakespearean roles. As a matter of fact, there's even a twisted bit of Shylock's dialogue from *The Merchant of Venice* in 'The Naked Now.' ['If you prick me, do I not. . . leak?'] But I had nothing to do with it being in the script."

On the subject of why he finally decided to make a convention appearance, he gave the following as his reason. "A year of facing the demons in my life and things that scare me, and I finally decided to do it. You see there is no way to prepare for this. You have to be yourself. I guess it took me awhile to try it and I still wasn't prepared for this experience."

When it comes to acting, Spiner was asked if he preferred playing roles with dark humor in them such as he'd done on *Night Court* as well as in the movies *Miss Firecracker* and *Rent Control*. "I played in *Miss Firecracker* because my best friend from high school, Tommy Schlamme, was the director. Trey Wilson from my high school is in it. I do like that style of humor."

Since Brent Spiner is an odd name, someone asked whether that was his real name. "Yes," he replied, "it's the name I was born with. I was named by my mother after the actor, George Brent, who in later years I discovered was really a very boring actor. When I mentioned it to my mother, she told me I was also a very boring child."

## INSIDE STAR TREK

At the time of this convention, the character of Lore had only appeared in "Datalore," but fans were wondering whether Data's evil twin would be returning. "Marina said I am closer in character to

Lore than to Data. I'd like to see Lore come back. After all, he was just beamed out into space with a phaser weapon in his hand. He's probably wreaking havoc all over space by now." And of course Lore did return in season four's "Brothers."

Spiner cited the episode "Loud As a Whisper" as being very special because they worked with Howie Seago, a deaf actor. "That was a very educational experience for us all. The sound stage tends to get very loud at times and it can be distracting to all of the actors. But Howie couldn't hear any of that, so his focus was intense and concentrated at all times. His interpreter taught me sign, which was in ASL [American Sign Language], and Howie wanted it to be correct. But he was incredibly sensitive about every aspect of how it was done, including wanting the audience to see Data struggle with the translations so television viewers wouldn't assume that signing was extremely easy to learn or master. And he didn't want to discourage deaf viewers who might be struggling with ASL themselves."

## ACTING TECHNIQUES

Acting and learning lines isn't an easy thing to do, as Spiner readily admitted. "If I really think about it, I don't know how I manage to do it. Sometimes on Sunday night I look at the next week's script and as I run down the page I see what we've come to call 'Data Babble' and shake my head. But by rehearsal time, it just happens. I can't explain how or why."

This also had much to do with how Brent prepared himself emotionally for the scene in "Measure of a Man," when Riker tears off Data's arm. "Physically, well, we had Dr. Crusher standing by with a surgical team just in case. . . . Emotionally, hmmm, I can't really put it into words."

Brent revealed that even before his involvement

with *TNG* he was interested in science fiction. "Yes, I read Asimov, Heinlein, and particularly watched a lot of science fiction films."

At the time of this interview, which was two years into the series, Spiner was asked if there was one scene in the series he would want to be remembered for if the show suddenly disappeared. He thought about it for a moment, and then said, "Naaah."

Does it bother him that he'll be remembered by audiences as Data for the rest of his life?

"I don't mind at all. If Art Carney doesn't mind being remembered as Norton on *The Honeymooners*, I certainly don't mind being Data."

# HONORS FOR GENE RODDENBERRY

## A STAR ON THE WALK OF FAME AND A TRIBUTE

### THE WALK OF FAME

The stars came out early on September 4, 1985, to honor the man who created *Star Trek*, and who, two years later, would repeat that notable success by creating *Star Trek: The Next Generation*.

Nearly all the luminaries from the original series were on hand that day to honor Gene Roddenberry for his years of accomplishment: Leonard Nimoy, DeForest Kelley, James Doohan, Walter Koenig, Nichelle Nichols, George Takei and, of course, Majel Barrett (and their son, Rod). Also on hand were Roger C. Carmel, Susan Oliver, Fred Phillips, and Grace Lee Whitney. William Shatner was unable to attend due to work commitments, even though he was only just over the hill, five miles away.

The unveiling of this star on the Hollywood Walk of Fame was the culmination of over a year of lobbying efforts by fans, spearheaded by Susan Sackett, Gene Roddenberry's assistant. Donations were required to pay the $3,000 fee that covers the cost of the star and the ceremony involved (the fee has since gone up). It was a touch-and-go situation for a while because many names are nominated each year, but only a few are chosen. Roddenberry's choice is particularly distinguished—he was the first screenwriter to be so honored. This caused a minor furor among Hollywood insiders, but more on that later.

## HOORAY FOR HOLLYWOOD

It was overcast before the ceremony began at 12:30 P.M., but as the Los Angeles Police Pipe Band broke into a rousing bagpipe melody before the festivities, the clouds parted, the sun broke through, and spirits brightened accordingly.

As usual, Johnny Grant, the "Honorary Mayor of Hollywood" and chairman of the Walk of Fame committee, served as master of ceremonies for the event. With a recording of "Hooray for Hollywood" playing over the loudspeakers, the festivities began.

Grant kicked everything off by saying, "Hello, everybody, and welcome to another Walk of Fame ceremony. Today we honor the creator and producer of the original *Star Trek* television series, Gene Roddenberry!" Cheers greeted the mention of the honored guest's name.

Grant then read some telegrams that had been received from friends and supporters who had not been able to attend the ceremony, but who had wanted to convey their feelings publicly.

"Congratulations Big Bird—to the creator and prime spirit, it will be a pleasure to walk on you. The Vulcans send their love—Mark Lenard."

Then he read, "Dear Gene, everywhere I go, I hear your name on the lips of people saying how incredible is the talent of Roddenberry for having written the *Martian Chronicles*. At the same time, everywhere you go, do you not hear the magic name Ray Bradbury, who created *Star Trek*? No matter how you play it, isn't it wonderful? Love to you on this special, fine day—Ray Bradbury!"

## LIST OF ACCOMPLISHMENTS

Grant then introduced Gene by giving a brief rundown of his accomplishments.

Gene Roddenberry led a life as exciting as nearly any high adventure fiction. A native Texan who spent his youth in Los Angeles, he later studied aeronautical engineering at UCLA. During World War II he served as a pilot and flew eighty-nine sorties. He was decorated with the Distinguished Flying Cross and the Air Medal. It was during this time that he began to write, selling stories to flying magazines and later poetry to such publications as the *New York Times*. After the war, he continued to fly for Pan American World Airways—until he saw television for the first time. Correctly estimating television's future, he left his flying career behind and moved to Hollywood. While establishing himself as a writer, he joined the Los Angeles Police Department. Soon, he was selling scripts to such shows as *Good Year Theatre, Dragnet, Naked City* and many others. Established as a writer, he turned in his badge and became a freelancer. Later he was head writer for the highly popular television series, *Have Gun, Will Travel*. *Star Trek* followed in 1966, and we all know the rest is history.

*Star Trek* later went on to win science fiction's coveted Hugo Award and was the first television series to have an episode preserved in the Smithsonian

Institute. In 1979, Roddenberry produced *Star Trek: The Motion Picture,* which led to the sequels *Star Trek II: The Wrath of Khan* and *Star Trek III: The Search for Spock.* He was the executive consultant for all *Star Trek* films. Gene was in steady demand as a lecturer and a keynote speaker for such organizations as NASA, the Smithsonian Institute, the Library of Congress, and top universities. He served as a member of the Writer's Guild Executive Council, was a former governor of the Television Academy of Arts and Sciences, and was a member of the board of the directors of the National Space Institute. The father of three, Gene lives in Los Angeles with his lovely wife Majel."

## A TRIBUTE FROM LEONARD NIMOY

Then Johnny Grant completed his introduction by asking the crowd of family, friends, and Trekkers from around the world to help him and the Hollywood Chamber of Commerce give a warm welcome to Roddenberry as they dedicated a star on the Hollywood Walk of Fame to him. "Scotty, beam him aboard!" was Grant's final line.

Bill Welsh gave Roddenberry a special Walk of Fame jacket emblazoned with Gene's name. Maria Hernendez from City Councilman Michael Woo's office then stated, "The mayor has proclaimed today Gene Roddenberry Day and the council has said: 'Now therefore be it resolved that the City Council of the city of Los Angeles congratulates Mr. Roddenberry on his many accomplishments and wishes him continued success.'" This is done whenever someone is given a star on the Walk of Fame or a similar honor. Once there was even a Freddy Krueger day (*Nightmare on Elm Street*), but they tend not to talk about that.

Then some guests were introduced to the assembled multitude.

Leonard Nimoy stated, "This is a wonderful day for Gene, obviously, and for all of us connected with *Star Trek*. I'll tell you just one brief story. When we were preparing the series, I wasn't sure that the ears were going to work out right, and I thought if these ears don't work, I'm going to be Dumbo of the year. So I went to Gene and said, 'I'm really nervous about it, Gene.' Before we started shooting I said maybe we should just drop the ears because they don't look right, and he said, 'I'll tell you what. You wear them for thirteen weeks and if it doesn't work out, we'll get you an ear job.'

"Gene, I'm glad you talked me into it. Congratulations today. I think it's wonderful for you, wonderful for *Star Trek*, and we're really happy to be here with you to celebrate."

## ON WITH THE SPEECHES

When Walter Koenig was introduced, he stated, "Not only is Mr. Roddenberry an extraordinary man and a gentleman we all admire, but he is also the very first writer to be honored on the Hollywood Walk of Fame."

Johnny Grant quickly jumped in to add, "Just to keep the record straight, he has several colleagues who are already here. There has been much controversy over this. He is being honored today for everything he did in television." A mini-controversy had indeed grown up over Roddenberry's receiving the star, because he was the first writer who wasn't also an actor or director to be granted one. This tended to make the Writer's Guild look bad, since they had nothing to do with nominating him, nor had they ever nominated any other writers in their membership for the honor during the guild's more than forty-year history. That Roddenberry is also a producer helped blur that he was being honored as a writer.

On with the speeches.

Nichelle Nichols: "Gene Roddenberry, I'm so proud of you, as I've always been. I'm so grateful to you for thinking of Uhura, and my hailing frequencies are always open for you!"

Harve Bennett, the producer of *Star Trek II, III* and the then-upcoming *IV* had these kind words: "I have only one word for a man who makes what has followed his genius so easy, and that is *mazel tov*!"

## RODDENBERRY REMEMBERS

When Roddenberry was finally able to speak for himself, after all the glowing praise from his friends and colleagues, he was able to voice his thoughts about this very special moment in his life.

He noted that as a Los Angeles policeman, he had walked the boulevard on foot patrol. The star was a double pleasure. When he had been a policeman, his scripts were beginning to sell and his producers didn't know he was a policeman. Gene was afraid if they found out they might not buy them, so his time here on Hollywood Boulevard was spent mostly jumping from one dark doorway to another."

Gene then introduced his mother and his son, Gene Jr., as well as his brother Bob, Gene's two daughters, and his sister, whom he described as, "A much better writer than I am."

Clearly nervous, surrounded as he was by people who were there to pay him tribute, Roddenberry thanked a group of other people, too. When he went places, people often asked him, "What are Trekkies? What are *Star Trek* fans?" Some of them got an idea that they are people who dress in funny clothes and go around making signs and so on. He agreed that some of them do that and have fun doing that, but he pointed out that *Star Trek*'s Trekkies range the entire audience and include astronauts, physicians, and physicists, as well as twelve- and fourteen-year-old kids. In the twenty years he had been associated with *Star Trek*, he never had a bad experience with a *Star Trek* fan. "They're incredible people and I want you to applaud them! They are people who believe in humanity and believe they are going to make it."

He also concurred with the crowd on Hollywood Boulevard. "This city, Los Angeles, is the twenty-first-century city in the making. It is becoming a Third World city; I think that's marvelous. The mixture of races and colors and religions here says that democracy, damnit, does work and it's a great thing and you haven't seen anything yet. The Los Angeles that's ahead of us, if we can keep peace and order on our streets, we can become anything we want and do anything we want to do in Los Angeles. And I think we will."

## SPACE THE FINAL . . .

When asked to do the introduction from the *Trek* television series, Roddenberry drew a blank, and even with coaxing wasn't able to recall it at all. Finally, he laughed and said, "I just write these things. I'm not a performer. I believe them all and I believe in humanity. I'm not done writing about humanity. We are an incredible species. You've seen Los Angeles, you've just seen humanity. We're still just a child-creature, we're still being nasty to each other around the world and all the children go through those phases, but we are growing up and moving into adolescence, now. When we grow up, man, we are going to be something and we're going to do it, too! Thank you all so very much. Thank all of you that came out and bless you all."

Roddenberry's speech clearly reflected how he viewed the future and in some ways indicated the type of future he'd portray in his new version of *Star Trek* just two years later.

When Roddenberry finally saw the star unveiled, he was surrounded by his friends as Johnny Grant concluded by saying, "Ladies and gentlemen, we welcome to the Walk of Fame, Gene Roddenberry!" The crowd cheered and applauded. The moment had arrived. *Star Trek* had really made a star out of its creator. The 1,810th star on the Hollywood Walk of Fame, located at 6683 Hollywood Boulevard, is a lasting tribute to the imagination behind the spirit that endures—the spirit of *Star Trek.*

## HONORS FOR RODDENBERRY AND *STAR TREK*

Three years later, on March 30, 1988, *Star Trek: The Next Generation* was nearing the end of its first year and Gene Roddenberry was honored with a special program under the heading of the Museum of Broadcasting. Every spring the Museum of Broadcasting in Los Angeles spotlights individuals and television programs that excel in some manner. Gene was the focus of such a tribute, not just for *Star Trek,* but for his entire career in television as both writer and producer. When Gene came out on stage that night in 1988, he was greeted with thunderous applause. After the auditorium finally quieted, the writer-producer smiled in appreciation and began reading the speech he had prepared.

He mused that perhaps he should have started with a confession, sometimes he got the feeling he seemed to be saying *Star Trek* was an inspired vision of the human future, which he did not mean and honestly did not believe. I made *Star Trek* for a twentieth-century audience using twentieth-century people and morals and situations. Were he to present the twenty-third or twenty-fourth century as he really believed they would be, the audiences would hate him. I'd probably be arrested. My view is that there is no way that you're going to have an *Enterprise* flying up there and going from star to star in the next fifty years, or the next hundred years, or the next three hundred years. The next big move humans are going to make is to fly out there and visit this new world that's coming closer and closer."

## THE DISTANT FUTURE

Roddenberry continued with great feeling. "We can now get to the shores of some of these worlds out there with no more trouble than our ancestors had bringing rowboats out of ships over to these shores. In my opinion, we will no doubt spend the next thousand years, probably, conquering our solar system about the same way we conquered this new world. It's well worthwhile conquering this solar system because at the center of this solar system of ours is a nuclear-powered furnace that has all the energy we'll need for a thousand years to take the incredible raw materials that are out there on these nine worlds and bend it into things we need.

"Most people don't realize how incredibly far away the stars are. We've got all we can do to travel around this solar system, which is fine with me because I don't want these people out here going to stars where there are other life forms and screwing them up! After we've conquered our solar system, and presumably grown into an adult species, then we can be trusted to go to the stars and to contact other life forms. It's a system I like very much."

## THE ARTHUR C. CLARKE CONNECTION

Roddenberry credited science fiction author Arthur C. Clarke as being the reason he was on the stage being honored that night.

He recalled the summer of 1969, ten weeks after the first *Star Trek* [TV series] had finished shooting and had been canceled for consistently low ratings. Being unemployed, he was able to attend a conference in Arizona where Clarke was the principal speaker and Roddenberry admired him as the author of things from *Childhood's End* to *2001: A Space Odyssey* and as an equally brilliant scientist and futurist.

Imagine Gene's surprise when he heard Clarke praising the success of *Star Trek*. He could hardly believe his ears when he heard Clarke congratulating him on what he had managed to accomplish in three years of this utter failure—particularly since it had been labeled by the American television industry as a childish and expensive flop. Gene told Clarke that no advertising company had the slightest interest in even the first rerun of this monstrosity. He remembered Clarke smiling and pointing out that during the end of the television series, man had landed on the moon. Man—human—had walked on another world, and he said that in his opinion Gene should relax and that in time it would no longer be considered a foolish fantasy.

"Well, it's a pleasure to be here," Gene said with great warmth and pride.

## LOOKING BACK

Moving on to his other work in television, Gene discussed the first series he was head writer for—*Have Gun, Will Travel*. He remarked that, "It's been twenty-five years since I wrote that series, but I realize now that I was writing science fiction then, too." Gene had kind words for the star of that show. "Richard Boone, unlike many in our business, really treasured writers and directors and was a very nice man to work with, and I wish he was still here."

The program that night involved showing clips from shows Gene had worked on, from *Have Gun, Will Travel* to *The Lieutenant*, which he produced and wrote right before he did *Star Trek*. Upon viewing these segments from shows he hadn't seen in twenty-five years or more, Gene stated, "It's fascinating to me to watch these things because I realize that I've been writing and studying the same type of thing, and gravitated toward the same type of writing, all my life."

Clips were then shown from other shows, including the *Star Trek* first-season episode "The Devil in the Dark," which Gene commented on afterward. "You'll notice how crude the first *Star Trek* appeared. Like in the cavern, the floors were all level. Believe it or not, we didn't have the money to ramp them. We made those *Star Trek*s for $184,000. It was the first time in a science fiction show that anyone had a monster and decided to make it a mother. This had never been done, and when I suggested it, everyone was looking around saying, 'Are you sure we can do that?' That was one of the first shows we did, and we were still learning to do *Star Trek*. For me it was a very heartwarming thing to watch that one and see where we were at and where we've come today."

## THE HOLLYWOOD WAY

Roddenberry talked about what it was and is like to be a writer in Hollywood. Speaking from his then-current position as producer of *The Next Generation,* he stated in no uncertain terms that any producer would stand in the driving rain for two days to get a show that is somewhat shootable. "You don't have to know anyone. You have to be good. You have to practice your trade. You have to do as I did and as all the writers I knew in those days did—watch television with the sound turned off so you can see how picture goes to picture. Then listen to just the sound without the picture. Learn your art and you'll sell. Write, write, write. You may get by easier, but you'll never really be good unless you do these things."

Then someone in the audience, who was apparently ignorant of much which was already known about the behind-the-scenes problems on the first season of *The Next Generation,* asked Gene if he was going to get writers like Harlan Ellison or David Gerrold to work on the series. "Most of those I wouldn't want in the same room with me," Gene promptly replied. Inexplicably, many in the audience thought this was funny, and some even applauded. "I've given all of them a chance," he continued.

Gene then went on to add that, "David Gerrold has been condemning the show constantly. I had him on staff for many, many months; he never wrote an episode we could shoot! So beware these people that are loud voiced. Give your attention to people who quietly do good work." As detailed in other books, Gerrold, Fontana, and Ellison have related very different recounting of these conflicts. Now, with Gene's death, it is too late to repair these rifts and perhaps they are best left forgotten. Many conflicts of ego arise in a creative and highly paid industry such as television.

## THE KLINGON QUESTION

On a lighter note, Gene was asked how he would explain the difference in appearance between the Klingons in the old series and the Klingons in the new series. "Easiest thing in the world," he replied. "In the old series we had no money! The cheapest thing we could do was to stick mustaches on them. In the new series we had some money and we said, 'Hey, c'mon, not everybody looks like central casting.'"

When someone inquired whether it was a conscious effort that *The Next Generation* did not employ as much violence as the old *Star Trek*, Gene explained that, "I think we tried to stay away from violence in the old, but don't forget, we started the old series in the time of cowboys, and all of us became more and more civilized as the years went by. The third year of *Star Trek*, and the second, were more civilized than the first. In *Star Trek: The Next Generation* we're very much changed people. We grow and our characters grow with us. Those of you who really want to be in the creative elements of television or film or whatever, you're on to a great thing."

Roddenberry read a great deal throughout his life, but he tended to make somewhat exaggerated claims as to what his accomplishments in this area of home study amounted to. "I have had, on *Star Trek*, in the reading and studying and so on that I've done, the equivalent of several doctorates. You grow. You learn. You study astronomy and science. You study politics. All the things that are worthwhile. I wake up, and have for thirty-five years now, at five o'clock in the morning. I get at least two hours of good reading in before my family is up at seven, and I've been doing that for thirty-five years. I invite you to the wonder of that, and you can realize, too, on whatever shows you write, science fiction or otherwise."

## DRAMATIC IDEALS

Roddenberry felt very strongly about the importance of drama and what it could accomplish in reaching people. In being honored for his work in television, he felt this was a perfect forum to explain just why television drama was important. "You learn. You test humans. Drama is an incredible school in life, and many scientists today are beginning to say that science and art are sort of the twin faces of the same kind of thing facing different ways. I've found, over these years, that the great profit I've made on *Star Trek* is the circle of acquaintances I have. I can go to M.I.T. and lecture there. NASA invites me there every year or two. The Smithsonian Institute; I participated in helping design some of the Air and Space Museum."

A common question regards the crossover possibilities since "Encounter at Farpoint" featured a guest appearance from Dr. McCoy. In 1988, Gene was trying to downplay the overlap between the two series. "We've got a new show which has to be different, or I don't have the enthusiasm of the writers and the technicians unless they have their show that they can do," Gene said. "So very purposely, I've kept the old characters out. I hate to! Those are my children, too. I love them. I have a new family and I must be true to the new family. The easiest way to fall on your ass is to be nice to everybody and never take a firm stand one way or the other.

For those of you who do produce, or who are going to, have the courage of your convictions. You may make a lot of mistakes, and I have, but at least if I go down to defeat, it'll be on the basis of my mistakes, not on others."

Gene was sixty-six in 1988 and producing a major television series. When asked if he was going to use directors who worked on the original *Star Trek*, he said they were too old. "We did that show twenty-three years ago," he said. "Many directors that we used then were people in their maturity at that time. Styles of directing change and so on. I love our old directors! Some of them got very busy and very rich. I choose what I think is best for the show, and I know sometimes people think that I'm a little hard-hearted. Thank God I'm behind the camera because I find my actors getting a bit old on that [earlier] show. I don't [get old]." Unfortunately, Gene perpetuated the Hollywood system that deems most talent over forty as "too old," even though he himself by and large escaped the consequences of ageism in Hollywood.

## OUT WITH THE OLD . . .

Gene seemed more open to the idea of perhaps using some of the old writers from the original series, but he revealed his concerns about that quite openly. "I like those writers. I like [Robert] Bloch. I haven't seen anything he's done recently, but certainly I would listen very carefully to anything he had to say if he wanted to come by and suggest some ideas. I'm also looking for young new writers. Some of them [the old writers] I feel might be set kind of in the mold of science fiction of those [earlier] days, and I'd be glad to find out I'm wrong. We have not had much luck calling in the old writers. A lot of time has gone by. They have become set in their ways. They have become successes in their own ways. I'd love to use them," he concluded, but clearly he wasn't going to go out of his way to give the older writers a real chance again.

Gene almost revealed the behind-the-scenes disputes he was having with the Writer's Guild of America when someone asked him how he felt about the Hollywood writers' strike that was then going on. "I'm a charter member of the guild," he said. "I've supported them in strike after strike, and I wish them good luck this time. I have some quarrels with the guild now because there're some things that have come up where the guild hasn't been representing me.

"When you're a success, you're no longer represented because they want to represent the freelance writers. I feel that I should be represented as well as any writer who's sold two or three scripts. The hyphenate [writer-producer] quarrel has always been out there and I don't think it's been resolved by the guild. I'm passionately a guild member and I think there're good things they've done."

When asked whether he's suffered studio interference with *The Next Generation* as he had in the sixties on the original *Star Trek*, Gene stated he's had none. "It's been so successful that everything I've asked for on the show I've gotten. I'm not asking for unreasonable things and they certainly have been supportive. I have gone, on a couple of the shows, a hundred eighty, a hundred ninety thousand dollars over budget, and that's serious money, but I explained why it was necessary. They listened and nodded and said, 'Okay, watch what you're doing, but we're not going to fire a guy who created this thing a second time.' I'm going to try not to take advantage of them. The new Paramount has a new level of executive that I haven't seen before in television, where they honestly care about what you do and care about the writing and the tools you need. I think we writers should encourage studios like that."

The highlight of the evening arrived when Gene announced that "The Big Goodbye" episode of *Star Trek: The Next Generation* had won the coveted Peabody Award for television excellence. Clearly Gene felt his efforts to bring back *Star Trek* had been recognized. He had rewritten the first dozen episodes, including "The Big Goodbye." Even though the series subsequently offered superior stories, it was not so honored again. The evening still proved a fitting tribute to three decades in the industry. None then imagined Gene would die just three and a half years later.

*Star Trek* goes on, undiminished in popularity, spawning more spin-offs. They are all tribute to the imagination of Gene Roddenberry.